In the American Grain

By William Carlos Williams

† *City Lights Books*

IN THE AMERICAN GRAIN

ESSAYS BY
WILLIAM CARLOS WILLIAMS

Introduction by Horace Gregory

A NEW DIRECTIONS BOOK

Library of Congress Catalog Card Number: 56–13360
(ISBN: 0-8112-0230-5)

First published in 1956 as New Directions Paperbook No. 53.

Manufactured in the United States of America

Published in Canada by George J. McLeod, Ltd., Toronto
New Directions Books are published for James Laughlin
by New Directions Publishing Corporation,
80 Eighth Avenue, New York 10011.

TWELFTH PRINTING

In these studies I have sought to re-name the things seen, now lost in chaos of borrowed titles, many of them inappropriate, under which the true character lies hid. In letters, in journals, reports of happenings I have recognized new contours suggested by old words so that new names were constituted. Thus, where I have found noteworthy stuff, bits of writing have been copied into the book for the taste of it. Everywhere I have tried to separate out from the original records some flavor of an actual peculiarity the character denoting shape which the unique force has given. Now it will be the configuration of a man like Washington, and now a report of the witchcraft trials verbatim, a story of a battle at sea—for the odd note there is in it, a letter by Franklin to prospective emigrants; it has been my wish to draw from every source one thing, the strange phosphorus of the life, nameless under an old misappellation.

WILLIAM CARLOS WILLIAMS

Contents

Contents

Introduction

"History, history!" says Dr. William Carlos Williams, and then with brilliant asperity continues, "We fools, what do we know or care?"

The quantum of irony in Dr. Williams' remark, though clear enough, should be carefully considered, and in the way I read it, it might well be taken as a warning. History is a humiliating subject for any man to think of knowing: and however much, however little we know of it, we always care, and that is where the trouble is likely to begin. The desire to know history is a near relative of the desire to know truth, and that is where, for most of us, a pit lies waiting. It is a deep pit, overlaid with an innocent branch or two, cut down from a nearby tree, and among a scattering of wilted leaves, there are easily plucked twigs and tamed, resistant grasses. At its sides and at an attractive distance, one also finds rare specimens of jungle flora. It is a pretty place and only a very few of the so-called professional historians come back from it alive. For the moment I can remember the names of only three who came back whole: Herodotus, Edward Gibbon and Henry Adams, and of these, Herodotus, being the eldest and most respectable, is best known as "the father of lies."

Perhaps there has always been a great number of different kinds of people who were eager to think of themselves as historians. Perhaps this was always so, but during the last few years, there seems to have been an increase of their published work; they seem to have become more vocal, more insistent that the field of history is theirs to have and to hold, and is in itself a proof of their authority to speak aloud. There it is, that deep pit, growing more inviting every day: and to it come engineers and social-workers, members of the D.A.R. and psychiatrists, economists and students of anthropology, newspaper men and politicians by the hundreds, research workers in the sciences, and, no doubt, an aviator or two. Executives of all kinds have come to it, from insurance company offices, from the stock exchange, from banks to overawe club banquets or trustee meetings or to deliver commencement-day addresses at schools and colleges. And in addition to all these, there are those many talkative members of a generation (of whom some write novels) who have a strong memory of what their grandfathers told them about the Civil War. The clearing in the jungle shines before them and they walk into it.

Of course we have always known that history, like poetry, is an ancient trap laid for the credulous and literal-minded. This common knowledge has been abroad so long that we are apt to forget the obvious hint that only those who have imagination survive their fall from unhappy innocence. Many, and I would say, far, far too many, are still victims of that fall: good, earnest people who are maimed and battered, who are forced to carry on a half-existence, distrusted by their fellows and of continual embarrassment to their friends.

Nor is it enough to have convictions and a powerful will to interpret them. Here history most resembles truth, and however violent its events have been and however lively they still appear, its exterior seems almost passive, and certainly tempting, if not altogether calm. Here, it seems to be waiting for the strong man to claim it, to do whatever he pleases with it and to make it his own forever. To use history for their purposes alone is the common ambition of the politician and the political journalist, and some have done so, and have made that great pit yield great profits for them. But even here imagination has been translated into action, and when that happens politicians become statesmen and mere corporals become heroes—and here it is not what they do to history that matters, but what history does to them.

There must be imagination at work to discern the fabulae of history, to know their mutable faces, to know their language. Those who ignore them are sure to be lost at the deepest level of the pit. Their shrewdness is then known for the true stupidity it is and always has been. They are the lost, the very lost, who are forgotten with remarkable ease and are unearthed only by industrious persons in libraries for whom the discovery of an unknown name may score a one-hundredth of a point toward a Ph.D.

It is in this relationship between what is sometimes called fabulae and what is sometimes called fact that the "historical imagination" plays its part. And here there has been a long established kinship between the historical imagination and poetry. The serious historian of the ancient world is careful never to forget his Homer. He may discriminate among the fabulae that Homer has set before him, and in the course of his researches, he may reject a number of them. But there they are and they happen to remain in a better state of preservation than the buried cities unearthed by archeologists. There is a particular kind of reality alive within them that will permit neither neglect nor violation: and in the reading and interpretation of history everything falls dead unless that reality is perceived. The truth of events as a cautious historian may come to know it, and the meaning of that same truth to a people who have converted it into a common heritage demand a living, active synthesis. This is as true today as it always was, and the fabulae of American history, youthful and knowingly familiar as they may seem to some of us, are no exceptions to the rule.

One might almost say that the active fabulae of a human culture are the means through which it lives and grows. They enter deeply into the very idiom of national speech; their meanings shift as the spoken language changes. On this continent, they are "in the American grain" and it is human-ly impossible to adopt an impartial or what was once called a scientific attitude toward them. Science, as we have come to know it, is none too quiet in making its own discrimina-tions, and shall we say it has its own signs, its own language by which its own truths are tested and modified? Shall we say that the imagination of a Willard Gibbs, whose language is abstract only to those who do not understand it, has its own nucleus of fabulae—or shall we call them the mathe-matical symbols of reality?

Our nationality which answers to the name of American is neither at the center of a huge continent nor is it floating loosely around its East, West and Tropical coast lines and harbors. It is a language, and it requires a particularly active and discerning imagination to keep pace with it and to speak it truly. Without knowing that language as well as the signs or symbols it employs, the would-be historian is almost help-less. Lacking that particular insight, the professional his-torian is in the same unfortunate position as that of the non-professionals who cross his field He may contribute a formula or a theory toward a revaluation of history in gen-eral, but he will need some one at his side to translate it, some one to make it intelligible to Americans.

It is at this point that Dr. Williams' discovery of an Amer-ican heritage becomes important. His manner is almost aggressively non-professional and rightly so, for he is not here to record American history nor to give us a new se-quence of events. He is here to present its signs and signa-tures, its backward glances and, by implication, its warn-ings for the future.

If I have misled some readers into thinking that *In the American Grain* is an historical text-book, or a book of essays in history or a series of historical narratives, I wish to correct that impression before I go one word further. It is none of these. It is a source book of highly individual and radical discoveries, a book of sources, as one might say that a river is a source of health to the fields and orchards through which it runs. And like that river in its uneven course, now quick in sunlight and now flowing to hidden roots of trees and flowers, the book has subterranean depths and turnings. I think it is not too much to say that this analogy also resembles its early reputation.

In the American Grain was first published in 1925 and before that date an early chapter appeared in *Broom*. I have no way of knowing how many people saw a few of its chapters in magazines or read the book, but I do know that as it fell slowly out of print, its reputation grew. I suspect that several other writers came upon it and kept the memory of its insights and the quality of its prose within the hidden chambers of their own knowledge and imagination. My immediate example is Hart Crane's *The Bridge*, which was published five years later and which carried within it traces of the impression left upon those who first read *In the American Grain*. These traces are to be found throughout the poem: a fragment of Dr. Williams' quotation from Thomas Morton's *The New English Canaan* is reproduced on the half-title page of "Powhatan's Daughter" and like selections of material may be quickly recognized in the concluding pages of Dr. Williams' chapter on Columbus and in the closing stanzas of "Ave Maria." Even the quotation from Edgar Poe's "The City in the Sea" (whose original title was significantly written as "The Doomed City"), "Death looked gigantically down," smolders in a half-line of "The Tunnel" and also appears in Dr. Williams' book, placed over "a morose dead world, peopled by shadows and silence, and despair . . ." These similarities should not of course be read as plagiarisms, nor should we exaggerate their obvious claims to a relationship that exists between them and the publication of *In the American Grain*. The point is that Dr. Williams' book exerted an influence that rose from the subsoil of the time in which it was written, and like all work of highly original temper and spirit and clarity it survives the moment of its conception. In this respect the book has something of the same force to generate the work of others, the same brilliance, the same power to shed light in darkened places that we have learned to respect in Miss Marianne Moore's poetry and in Miss Gertrude Stein's *Three Lives*.

Another association that *In the American Grain* brings forcefully to mind is the period of critical impressionism in America, that hour in the 1920's when Mr. Sherwood Anderson published his note books and D. H. Lawrence's *Studies in Classic American Literature* were read. *In the American Grain*, though not resembling either, is of the same moment that lies behind a barrier of critical controversy in American letters dividing this moment from an hour when certain strength was derived from highly individual insights and convictions. A reaction against mere self-expression, mere sensitivity and feeling, came in with the disciples of what was then called Humanism. And against this truly reactionary movement came those who sought to clarify the direction that Parrington had already taken. At this distance the quarrel which now seems older than its years now also seems to have been one in which its two opposing factors united against a common enemy. The enemy was impressionistic thinking and activity, and in the heat of the moment, all work of personal identity and imagination became suspect. Without entering into the merits and abuses of the controversy, it should now be possible to look behind the dust raised in that hour. During the time of the rising quarrel everything that had a personal exterior aroused fears and distrust of heresy and was therefore publicly ignored or attacked as the true heresy it was supposed to signify. Through these brief years *In the American Grain* shared something of the public obscurity that was intended to cover the remains of personal heresy and choice. Meanwhile the book was kept intact for the discerning reader and as it may be read today, it retains its original coloring and a great measure of its purity.

What I have just said is another way of saying that certain recent beliefs and attitudes in criticism have begun to reverse themselves: although the mannerisms of impressionistic criticism have been properly discredited and should not be revived, it is now admitted that the writer cannot shift the very foundations of his beliefs without endangering the verbal truth of what he has to say. It has also been discovered that the raptures and ardors of sudden conversion to any cause, however valid the cause itself may be, seldom, if ever, revive the dying powers of imaginative insight and creation. Human growth is far too slow to admit violent denials of its immediate past, and writers, quite like all other human beings, become inept and voiceless should they attempt to deny the continuity of their heritage.

Anyone who has read all of Dr. Williams' prose and verse becomes aware of their great ability to grow at their own pace. And if anyone is looking for the secret of their good health and the freedom they exert within an individual speech and manner, it may be found in their determination to "stay at home," to accept the roots of their being and to grow slowly to their full maturity. This radical willingness to accept the limitations of normal growth has given Dr. Williams' work a quality that resembles an aspect of life itself; it is a kind of reality that absorbs its own mistakes and shortcomings and should be cited as an example of true well being.

The difficult question of sincerity in art, which is too often confused with gossip or speculation concerning the personal or public behavior of the man who happens to be a writer, should be referred to the continuity of his imagination and the speech that gives it meaning. We cannot expect to answer so large a question to the satisfaction of everyone and M. Paul Valéry has devoted no small degree of his fine intelligence to warn us of the dangers of considering it with any seriousness at all. Yet I believe that the more important difficulties of the question may arrive at a fruitful, if partial solution, by observing the triple unities of speech and imagination and emotion and their relationship to each other within a book.

One of the peculiarities of this moral question is its seeming lack of relevance to classical literatures: that is, it seems absurd to question the sincerity of Homer, of Sophocles, or of Aeschylus or the authors of The Palatine Anthology. In these cases the impertinence of the question seems all too clear and certainly naive. What we have learned to respect in the remains of an ancient literature—and these however dimly they may be interpreted and translated—are its elements of unity. In instances where the authorship is obscure, we can at least distinguish between the language of one period and that of another until at last we enter the world of the Middle Ages by way of Rome. The unities of time and of place in poetic drama tended to strengthen the unities of speech and of tradition—and a discernible continuity of ritual and moral attitude answers the question of sincerity before it rises to the surface of the reader's mind.

As we approach the writing of our own time, the question re-emerges in many forms and however we try to dismiss or slide beyond it, it remains to stir our sense of guilt and to evaluate the writer's integrity. One hears the word "sincerity" used as a term of polite abuse as well as dubious praise: and to us its implications may mean no more than that the writer is a good fellow of admirable intentions—give the poor dog the merits of sincerity and let his work be damned. It is sometimes futile to reply that the unintelligent, the insensible, the undiscerning, the unimaginative (if they are writers) are incapable of sincerity in what they write; their relationship to what they say is already compromised before they start; at best they are merely writing with half a voice and half an ear and their beliefs rest upon such shallow ground that they are meaningless almost before we discover what they are. I suspect that the clear evidence of sincerity in Dr. Williams' work is no mere illusion created by his literary personality, nor do I believe that the verbal continuity of In the American Grain is a fortunate accident. One cannot divorce its theme from the voice that speaks it; and even its lengthy quotations from *Poor Richard* and John Paul Jones derive their pertinence from Dr. Williams' entire scheme of presentation.

I also believe that Dr. Williams' theme, though for a separate reason, is no less dangerous than the desire to know history or a definition of sincerity which seems so necessary in describing the nature of his work. The old theme of America as a new world to be rediscovered at every turn has rather more than it full share of contradictions. The impulse to make all things new, to build new cities in a clearing of the forest, to abandon projects with the scaffolding in air, to move onward to another El Dorado is a familiar complex of the American tradition. It contains within it the sources of our wealth and poverty, our despair and hopefulness, and it is something that Herman Melville saw before him as he wrote:

> The Ancient of Days forever is young,
>   Forever the scheme of Nature thrives;
> I know a wind in purpose strong—
>   It spins *against* the way it drives.
> What if the gulfs their slimed foundations bare?
>   So deep must stones be hurled
> Whereon the throes of ages rear
>   The final empire and the happier world.

It is the "happier world" that seems so often to elude us and that Dr. Williams frequently discovers on earth and not in heaven. To make these discoveries seem alive and new also implies the cheerful will to outface the dangers of a theme that grows too large for habitation, and too many writers have already lost themselves in that blue vault in which the images of rebirth and the sensations of becoming are reiterated with alarming regularity. One might almost say that our long-continued faith in the American renaissance is an habitual response to living on this continent, as though we waked each morning to find a new world still-born at our door. The faith contains so many apparitions of a dead new world that one is now tempted to respond to them with the same gesture as John Webster's Duke of Calabria looking down at his dead sister:

> Cover her face; mine eyes dazzle: she died young.

But Dr. Williams makes this discovery of his tradition with the insight of a man who walks into a brightly lighted room and there, for the first time, actually sees the things he has lived with all his life. He then makes his selection of what truly belongs to him and discards others; he repairs some pieces that have become chipped or broken, some he adapts to his immediate needs and some he leaves untouched —but all are endowed from this moment onward with the same qualities of suspense and animation that seem to enter an old house as it waits for the arrival of an heir or a new master.

As Dr. Williams wrote in his note on poetry which appeared in *The Oxford Anthology of American Literature:*

> In my own work it has always sufficed that the object of my attention be presented without further comment. This in general might be termed the objective method . . . since the senses do not exist without an object for their employment all art is necessarily objective. It doesn't declaim or explain; it presents. . . . Times change and forms and their meanings alter. . . . Their forms must be discovered in the spoken, the living language of their day.

Therefore the earlier chapters of *In the American Grain* are rich in selection from original documents and the continuity of their naked statements is preserved by Dr. Williams' quickened adjustment of his own prose to their cadence and imagery.

Within this pattern of selection and commentary I find but one example that seems to betray the moment of time in which the book was written. During the 1920's the general feeling against Puritanism slipped into high gear and ran beyond control. The reasons for it are so well known that they deserve no further defense or contradiction. It is true that one whole side of Puritan culture represents a destructive element in the American tradition and something of its bourgeois decadence was felt and recognized in Eugene O'Neill's *The Great God Brown*. In itself it contains the ambiguity of Melville's wind that "spins against the way it drives" and like the image of that wind it seems to stir hatreds and admirations that are both too vague and too large for hasty discrimination. I would say that Dr. Williams' choice of quotation from Cotton Mather echoes the usual cry against the Puritan without revealing the full character of Mather's genius. It contains too little hint of Mather's wit and administrative abilities, and scarcely anything at all of the imagination that created political parables with such memorable skill. Dr. Williams is on firmer ground when he writes of the Puritan "spirit" and its meaning:

> And so they stressed the "spirit"—for what else could they do?—and this spirit *is* an earthly pride which they, prideless, referred to heaven and the next world. And for *this* we praise them, instead of for the one thing in them that was valuable: their tough littleness and the weight of many to carry through the cold; not their brokenness but their projection of the great flower of which they were the seed.

So with an eye that is aware of the reality existing in the fabulae of history, even to the recording of Washington's famous "reputation for truthtelling," and with a fine perception of the hidden values of sincerity, that kind of truth that is best described in the qualities he attributes to Aaron Burr, Dr. Williams creates an atmosphere that many Americans should recognize as home.

I leave the discovery of Dr. Williams' prose to his readers yet I cannot resist the temptation to quote the two closing paragraphs of his chapter on Sir Walter Raleigh, for there are few examples in twentieth century writing to equal its lyricism:

> Sing, O Muse and say, there is a spirit that is seeking through America for Raleigh: in the earth, the air, the waters, up and down, for Raleigh, that lost man: seer who failed, planter who never planted, poet whose works are questioned, leader without command, favorite deposed— but one who yet gave title for his Queen, his England, to a coast he never saw but grazed alone with genius.
>
> Question him in hell, O Muse, where he has gone, and when there is an answer, sing and make clear the reasons that he gave for that last blow. Why did he send his son into that tropic jungle and not go himself, upon so danger- ous an errand? And when the boy had died why not die too? Why England again and force the new King to keep his promise and behead him?

And there is no writer who has perceived the complex figure of Lincoln—whose very name seems always to evoke the worst of heroic rhetoric and the hackneyed gesture— with greater boldness:

> It is Lincoln pardoning the fellow who slept on sentry duty. It is the grace of the Bixby letter. The least private would find a woman to caress him, a woman in an old shawl —with a great bearded face and a towering black hat above it, to give unearthly reality.

Since the writing of Walt Whitman's elegy "When Lilacs Last in the Dooryard Bloom'd" Dr. Williams is, I think, the first American to give the huge, unwieldy myth of Lincoln a new and vivid semblance of reality. A literal reading of Dr. Williams' image is, of course, the false one, and the pit of history waits for those unhappy creatures who attempt it.

If, as I believe, *In the American Grain* contained the proofs of a living heritage in American prose some fifteen years ago, it should be said again that it seems even more alive today. And unless I am very much mistaken, that qual- ity of freshness which few poems and fewer works of prose possess will endure within it for many years to come.

HORACE GREGORY

Red Eric

RATHER THE ICE than their way: to take what is mine by single strength, theirs by the crookedness of their law. But they have marked me—even to myself. Because I am not like them, I am evil. I cannot get my hands on it: I, murderer, outlaw, outcast even from Iceland. Because their way is the just way and my way—the way of the kings and my father—crosses them: weaklings holding together to appear strong. But I am alone, though in Greenland.

The worst is that weak, still, somehow, they are strong: they in effect have the power, by hook or by crook. And because I am not like them—not that I am evil, but more in accord with our own blood than they, eager to lead—this very part of me, by their trickery must not appear, unless in their jacket. Eric was Greenland: I call it Greenland, that men will go there to colonize it.

I, then, must open a way for them into the ice that they follow me even here—their servant, in spite of myself. Yet they must follow.

It was so from the beginning. They drove me from Jaederen, my father and me. Who was this Christ, that he should come to bother me in my own country? His bishops that lie and falsify the records, make me out to be what I am not—for their own ends—because we killed a man.

Was he the first man that was ever killed, that they must sour over it? That he was important to their schemes, that he meant much to them—granted: one of their own color, we who altered him must be driven from Norway. Their courts and soft ways. Not that we killed him. One or the

1

other of us had to die, under the natural circumstance. He or we. But that if we had been killed, would he then have been driven from his country? They would have made him Archbishop.

To Iceland, then. Forget Norway. What there? My father dead. Land to the north cleared. A poor homestead. Manslaughter had driven me there. Then I married Thorhild, removed from the north and cleared land at Haukadal. Must I be meek because of that? If my slaves cause a landslide on Valthioff's farm and Valthioff's kinsman slays them, shall I not kill him? Is it proper for me to stand and to be made small before my slaves? I am not a man to shake and sweat like a thief when the time comes.

Rather say I killed two men instead of the one. They tried me among themselves and drove me out once more. To the north, then. Iceland wilderness.

There Thorgest comes to me and asks if I will lend him my outer dais-boards: ready to take me at a loss. Why else? For Eric the Red is a marked man, beyond the law, so it would seem: from that man one steals at will—being many in the act against his one. Thorgest keeps the decorated woodpieces. I go to his house and remove my property. He gives chase and two of his sons are killed in the encounter.

This time they have done the thing. They search for us among the islands—me and my people.

This is the way of it, Thorhall, this has always been the way with me from the first. Eric loves his friends, loves bed, loves food, loves the hunt, loves his sons. He is a man that can throw a spear, take a girl, steer a ship, till the soil, plant, care for the cattle, skin a fox, sing, dance, run, wrestle, climb, swim like a seal. A man to plan an expedition and pay for it, kill an enemy, take his way through a fog, a snowstorm, read a reckoning by the stars, live in a stench, drink foul water, withstand the fierce cold, the black of winter and come to a new country with a hundred men and found them there. But they have branded me. They have separated murder into two parts and fastened the worse on me. It rides in the air around me. What is it to be killed? They have had their fling at me. Is it worse, so much worse, than to be hunted about the islands, chased from Norway to Iceland, from south to north, from Iceland to Greenland, because—I am I, and remain so.

Outlaws have no friends. Murderers are run down like rabbits among the stones. Yet my ship was built, fitted, manned, given safe conduct beyond the reefs. To Thorbiorn I owe much. And so to Greenland—after bitter days fighting the ice and rough seas. Pestilence struck us. The cattle sickened. Weeks passed. The summer nearly ended before we struck land. This is my portion. I do not call it not to my liking. Hardship lives in me. What I suffer is myself that outraces the water or the wind. But that it only should be mine, cuts deep. It is the half only. And it takes it out of my taste that the choice is theirs. I have the rough of it not because I will it, but because it is all that is left, a remnant from their coatcloth. This is the gall on the meat. Let the hail beat me. It is a kind of joy I feel in such things.

Greenland then. So be it. Start over again. It turns out always the one way. A wife, her two sons and a daughter. So my life was split up. The logic of it also. This is my proof. We lived at our homestead, well rid of the world. Traders visited us. Then Lief, Eric's son, sails to Norway, a thousand miles, in one carry. But on his return, Lief the Lucky, he is driven westward upon a new country, news of which he brings to Brattahlid. At the same stroke he brings me back pride and joy-in-his-deed, my deed, Eric moving up, and poison: an edict from Olaf—from my son's mouth—solid as an axe to cut me, half healed, into pieces again.

Not that it was new. Only that here in Greenland I had begun to feel that I had left the curse behind. Here through the winters, far to the west, I had begun to look toward summer when I should be whole again. My people at work, my wife beside me, the boys free from my smear, growing in strength and knowledge of the sea. Here was an answer to them all: Thorstein and Lief Erickson, sons of Red Eric, murderer! Myself in the teeth of the world.

So they chopped me up. The Pope wins Olaf. Lief at court—Olaf commissions him to carry the thing back to Greenland. It grows like fire. Why not? Promise the weak strength and have the strength of a thousand weak at your bidding. Thorhild bars me, godless, from her bed. Both sons she wins to it. Lief and Thorstein both Christians. And this is what they say: Eric, son of evil, come and be forgiven.—Let her build a church and sleep in it.

* * *

With the years there began to be much talk at Brattahlid of Vinland the Good that Lief had first seen, that it should be explored. And so Karlsefni and Snorri fitted out a ship. Eric, too old to go with them, watches the ship depart. But Eric is in the ship, with the men, Eric the bedless, the sonless. Fate has pulled him out at the holes of his eyes and flung him again to sea as the ship steers southward. Now the glass darkens as the sea takes them to the New World.

They found wild rice, they built booths and palisades. First they traded with the Skrellings, whose cheekbones were high, whose eyes wide, then fought them. Whereas Karlsefni and his men had shown white shields before, now they took red shields and displayed them. The Skrellings sprang from their canoes and they fought together. Karlsefni and Snorri were beaten. They fell back. Then it was that Freydis, Eric's natural daughter, came out from her cabin. Seeing that the men were fleeing, she cried: Why do you flee from these wretches, when ye should slaughter them like cattle? Had I a weapon I would fight better than any of you.

Lagging behind the rest as they ran, because of her belly, she being with child, she found a dead man in front of her. It was Snorri's son, with his head cleft by a stone, his naked sword beside him. This she took up and prepared to defend herself. The Skrellings then approached her, whereupon she stripped down her shirt and slapped her breast with her bare sword. At this the Skrellings were terrified and ran down to their boats.

So, thinning out, more and more dark, it ran: Eric in Freydis' bones: Freydis now, mistress of her own ship, persuades two brothers, Helgi and Finnbogi, to sail with her again to Vinland: all to share equally the good things that might there be obtained. Lief to lend her his house there. Two ships, each to have thirty able-bodied men besides the women, but at the start Freydis violated the compact by concealing five men more. Karlsefni feared her.

Now they put out to sea, the brothers in one ship and Freydis and Karlsefni in the other, having agreed that they would sail in company. But although they were not far apart from each other the brothers arrived somewhat in advance and carried their belongings up to Lief's house. Freydis comes and does the same. The brothers withdraw and build a new house nearby. Within a month, the two houses are at odds and winter comes on.

Spring. Freydis, one night, after long thinking, arose early from her bed and dressed herself, but did not put on shoes and stockings. A heavy dew had fallen. She took up her husband's cloak, wrapped it about her and walked in the dark to the brothers' house and up to the door, which had been only partly closed by one of the men, who had gone out only a short time earlier. She pushed open the door and stood silently in the doorway for a moment. Finnbogi was awake and said: What dost thou wish here, Freydis? She answered: I wish thee to arise and go with me for I would speak with thee. They walked to a tree which lay close by the wall of the house and seated themselves upon it. How art thou pleased here, she said. He answered that he was well pleased with the place, except for the quarrel which had come up between them. They talked.

It was the brothers' boat—it seemed—she wanted, larger than her own. Finnbogi slow, thickheaded, or asleep, consents to let her have it. Freydis, split with anger or bad blood, returns home and Finnbogi to his bed.

The woman climbed into bed and awakened her husband with her cold feet. Why so cold and wet? I have been to the brothers to buy their ship, but they refused and beat me!

Thorvard roused his men. They went to the brothers' house, took them and all their people, and slaughtered them one by one as they were brought from within. Only the women were left. These no man would kill. What? said Freydis. Hand me an axe! This done, she fell upon the five women and left them dead.

In Greenland, Lief, now head of the family, has no heart to punish his sister as she deserves: But this I predict of them, that there is little prosperity in store for their offspring. Hence it came to pass that no one from that time forward thought them worthy of aught but evil. Eric in his grave.

The Discovery of the Indies

THE NEW WORLD, existing in those times beyond the sphere of all things known to history, lay in the fifteenth century as the middle of the desert or the sea lies now and must lie forever, marked with its own dark life which goes on to an immaculate fulfillment in which we have no part. But now, with the maritime successes of that period, the western land could not guard its seclusion longer; a predestined and bitter fruit existing, perversely, before the white flower of its birth, it was laid bare by the miraculous first voyage. For it is as the achievement of a flower, pure, white, waxlike and fragrant, that Columbus' infatuated course must be depicted, especially when compared with the acrid and poisonous apple which was later by him to be proved.

No more had Columbus landed, the flower once ravished, than it seemed as if heaven itself had turned upon this man for disturbing its repose. But the initiative taken, the course broached, the story must go on. He left a handful of colonists in the islands while he, himself, returned to Spain with the news and for aid.

As the outward journey had been pleasant "like April in Andalucia"—still seas, clear, fine weather and steady winds, so now the return was difficult. Through tempest, assault, trickery among the Portuguese Azores, capture and despair, he fought his way. But as he neared the home coast at last his trials grew worst of all. Everything hung on the point of being lost:

* * *

... daylight until sunset, great trouble with the wind, high and tempestuous seas. Lightning three times to the N.N.E. —sign of a great storm coming from that quarter or its opposite. We lay to most of the night, afterwards showing a little sail. In the day the wind moderated a little, but soon increased again and during the night the waves were terrible, rising against each other and so shaking and straining the *Niña* that she was in danger of being stove in. We carried the mainsail very closely reefed, so as just to give her steerway.

Meanwhile the sea and wind increased, and we began to run before it, there being nothing else to do. The caravel *Pinta* began to run before it at the same time, and Martin Alonzo ran her out of sight, although he kept showing lanterns all night and they answered us.

Sunrise the wind blew still harder, and the cross seas were terrific. Continued to show the closely reefed mainsail to enable her to rise between the waves, or she would otherwise have been swamped. Now I feared that we should perish. I should have borne this misfortune with less distress had my life alone been in peril, but what caused me boundless grief and trouble was the thought that just now when our gainsayers were to be convinced and the discovery of a New World victoriously to be announced, that just now the Divine Will should wish to block it with my destruction.

Of this mind I resolved, that even if I should die, the ship be lost, to find a means of not losing a victory already won. I wrote on a parchment, with that brevity which the time demanded, how I had discovered the lands I had promised to find, describing the route I had followed and how your Highness had possession of all that had been found by me. This folded and sealed, I had a cask brought, and having wrapped the writing in waxed cloth surrounded by a large cake of wax, I enclosed all in a barrel stoutly hooped, which I threw into the sea. All believed it some act of devotion.

Later amid showers and squalls, the wind veered to the

west and we sailed before it, in a very confused sea, for five hours. We had taken in the reefed mainsail, for fear that the wind would carry all away. That night at the time of re-peating the *Salve*, some of the men saw a light to leeward. During the night a terrible storm, expecting to be over-whelmed by the cross seas, while the wind seemed to raise the caravel into the air. In these straits, not knowing whether there was any port for shelter, I set the mainsail. . . .

* * *

Forced by the storm into Lisbon harbor, the turn of his destiny quickly multiplied his misfortunes. In Spain, when he finally arrived there, they immediately accused him of playing traitor to Castile, of having tried to bargain with the Portuguese sovereign.

But that passed; there was too much still for him to en-dure for catastrophe to have overtaken him so early; some savage power had him in its care, preserving him for its later pleasure. Now his triumph was acclaimed, his captives were paraded in Madrid, his gold was witnessed, his birds, monkeys and native implements were admired. This over, immediately the urge was on him once more. He must re-turn at once to the New World. Never content would he be for the balance of his whole life, following his fortune, whose flower, unknown to him, was past.

But now he saw before him the illusive bright future of a great empire founded, coupled with a fabulous conquest of heathendom by the only true church. Much had been prom-ised him. He had succeeded in the sternest hazard, the great first step; should not the rest prove easy and natural? It rose before him like a great gilded mountain. Again and again he calls before his mind their agreements:

* * *

. . . that henceforth I should be called Don, and should be Chief Admiral of the Ocean Sea, perpetual Viceroy and Governor of all the islands and continents that I should discover and gain in the Ocean Sea, and that my eldest son should succeed, and so from generation to generation forever.

> . . . .

Item: that of all and every kind of merchandise, whether pearls, precious stones, gold, silver, spices, etc., of whatever kind, name and sort which may be bought, bartered, discovered within the said Admiralty, your Highnesses grant from henceforth to the said Don Cristóbal, the tenth part of the whole . . . granted, in the town of Santa Fe de la Granada on the 17th day of April, in the year of our Lord Jesus Christ, 1492. I, the King. I, the Queen.

* * *

Unhappy talk. What power had such ridiculous little promises to stay a man against that terrific downpour on the brink of which they were all floating? How could a king fulfill them? Yet this man, this straw in the play of the elemental giants, must go blindly on. More and more he threw everything he had into the contest, his sons, his brothers, in the hope that his fortunes would be retrieved in the end. How could he have realized that against which he was opposed? His instinctive enemies, however, were not so backward on their part. With malicious accuracy, finding him more and more alone, they sensed everything and turned it to their own advantage, being closer to that curious self-interest of natural things than he.

Heroically, but pitifully, he strove to fasten to himself that enormous world, that presently crushed him among its multiple small disguises.

With its archaic smile, America found Columbus its first victim. This was well, even merciful. As for the others, who shall say?—when riding a gigantic Nature and when through her heat they could arrogate to themselves a pin's worth of that massive strength, to turn it against another of their own kind to his undoing,—even they are natural and as much a part of the scheme as any other.

There is no need to argue Columbus' special worth. As much as many another more successful, everything that is holy, brave or of whatever worth there is in a man was contained in that body. Let it have been as genius that he made his first great voyage, possessed of that streamlike human purity of purpose called by that name—it was still as a man that he would bite the bitter fruit that Nature would offer him. He was poisoned and his fellows turned against him like wild beasts.

Bewildered, he continued, voyage after voyage, four times, out of his growing despair; it seemed that finally by sheer physical effort a way must be found—till the realization of it all at last grew firmly upon him:

* * *

Seven years passed in discussion and nine in execution, the Indies discovered, wealth and renown for Spain and great increase to God and to his Church. And I have arrived at and am in such condition that there is no one so vile but thinks he may insult me.

What have I not endured? Three voyages undertaken and brought to success against all who would gainsay me; islands and a mainland to the south discovered; pearls, gold, and, in spite of all, after a thousand struggles with the world and having withstood them all, neither arms nor counsels availed, it cruelly kept me under water.

If I were to steal the Indies or the land which lies beyond them from the altar of St. Peter and give them to the Moors, they could not have greater enmity toward me in Spain.

When on my last voyage, having turned homeward, I had left Paria (Brazil) and come again to Española (Porto Rico), I found half the people in revolt; and the Indians on the other side grievously harassed me. It was at this time that Bobadilla came to Santo Domingo. I was at La Vega. He took up his abode in my house and, just as he found it, so he appropriated everything to himself. Well and good; perhaps he was in want of it. On the second day after his arrival he created himself Governor.

I thought the affair would end like that of Hojeda and the others, but I restrained myself when I learned for certain from the friars that your Highnesses had sent him. I wrote to him that his arrival was welcome, that I was prepared to hand it over to him as smooth as my palm. But he gave me no answer. On the contrary, he put himself in a warlike attitude and compelled all who were there to take an oath to him as Governor. Together with them, he ordered inquisitions concerning me, the like whereof were never known in hell. I was made prisoner and returned to Spain in the condition of which you know.

I should have freed myself forever from this affair and undertaken that holy pilgrimage which has long been in my heart had it been honorable to my Queen to do so. But the support of Our Lord and Her Highness made me persevere. I undertook a fresh voyage to the new Heaven and Earth. And if this, the most honorable and profitable of all, is held in small esteem in Spain, it is because it has been looked upon as my work.

Up to the period of reaching these shores, I experienced most excellent weather, but the night of my arrival came on with a dreadful tempest, and the same bad weather has continued ever since. On reaching the island of Española, I despatched a packet of letters, by which I begged as a favor that a ship be supplied me at my own cost in lieu of one of those that I had brought with me, which had become unseaworthy, and could no longer carry sail. The letters were taken, and your Highnesses will know if a reply has been given them. For my part I was forbidden to go on shore.

The tempest was terrible throughout the night, all the ships were separated, and each one driven to the last extremity without hope of anything but death; each of them also looked upon the loss of the rest as a matter of certainty. What man was ever born, not even excepting Job, who would not have been ready to die of despair at finding himself as I then was, in anxious fear for my own safety, and that of my son, my brother and my friends, and yet refused permission either to land or to put into harbor on the shores which by God's mercy I had gained for Spain sweating blood?

And this is the thing which calls most loudly for redress and remains inexplicable to this moment. The lands in this part of the world, which are now under your Highnesses' sway, are richer and more extensive than those of any other Christian power, and yet, after that I had, by the Divine Will, placed them under your high and royal sovereignty, and was on the point of bringing your Majesties into receipt of a very great and unexpected revenue; and while I was waiting for ships to convey me to safety, and with a heart full of joy, to your royal presence, victoriously to announce the news of the gold that I had discovered, I was arrested and thrown with my two brothers, loaded with irons, into a ship, stripped, and very ill treated without being allowed any appeal to justice.

Who could believe that a poor foreigner would have risen against your Highnesses, in such a place without any motive or argument on his side; without even the assistance of any other Prince upon whom to rely; but on the contrary amongst your own vassals and natural subjects, and with my sons staying at the royal court? I was twenty-eight years old when I came into your Highnesses' service, and now I have not a hair upon me that is not gray; my body is infirm, and all that was left me, as well as to my brothers, has been taken away and sold, even to the frock that I wore.

I would implore your Highnesses to forgive my complaints. I am indeed in as ruined condition as I have related. With regard to temporal things, I have not even a *blanca*

for an offering; and in spiritual things, I have ceased here
in the Indies from observing the prescribed forms of religion. . . .

But to return to the ships: although the tempest had so
completely separated them from me as to leave me single,
yet the Lord restored them to me in His good time. The
ship for which we had the greatest fear, had put out to sea
to escape being blown toward the island. The *Gallega* lost
her boat and a part of her provisions, which latter loss indeed all of the ships suffered. With this tempest I struggled
on till I reached Jamaica, and there the sea became calm,
but there was a strong contrary current which carried me
as far as the Queen's Garden without seeing land. Hence,
as opportunity offered, I pushed on for the mainland, in
spite of the wind and a fearful contrary current, against
which I contended for sixty days. All this time I was unable
to get into harbor, nor was there any cessation of the tempest, which was one continuation of rain, thunder and
lightning. I at length reached the Cape of Gracias a Dios,
and after that the Lord granted me fair wind and tide; this
was on the twelfth of September. Twenty-eight days did
this fearful tempest continue, during which I was at sea and
saw neither sun nor stars, my ships lay exposed, with sails
torn, and anchors, rigging, cables, boats and a great quantity of provisions lost. Other tempests have been experienced, but never of so long a duration as this. I myself had
fallen sick, and was many times on the point of death, but
from a little cabin that I had caused to be constructed on
deck, I directed our course. My brother was in the ship that
was in the worst condition and the most exposed to danger;
and my grief on this account was the greater that I had
brought him with us against his will.

Such is my fate, that the twenty years of service through
which I have passed with so much toil and danger, have
profited me nothing, and at this very day I do not possess a
roof in Spain that I can call my own; if I wish to eat or

sleep, I have nowhere to go but to the inn or tavern, and most times lack wherewith to pay the bill.

I reached the land of Cariay, where I stopped to repair my vessels and take in provisions, as well as to afford relaxation to my men, who had become very weak. There I gained information respecting the gold mines of which I was in search and two Indians conducted me to Carambaru, where the people, who go naked, wear golden mirrors round their necks, which they will neither sell, give, nor part with for any consideration. They named to me many places on the sea-coast where there were both gold and mines. I started with the intention of visiting all of them. It was on the eve of St. Simon and St. Jude, which was the day fixed for our departure; but that night there arose so violent a storm, that we were forced to go wherever it drove us. I ran before the wind without power to resist it. Never was the sea seen so high, so terrific and so covered with foam; not only did the wind oppose our proceeding onward, but it also rendered it highly dangerous to run in for any headland, and kept me in that sea, which seemed to me as a sea of blood, seething like a cauldron on a mighty fire. Never did the sky look more fearful; during day and night it burned like a furnace and every instant I looked to see if my masts and my sails were not destroyed. These flashes came with such alarming fury that we all thought the ships must have been destroyed. All this time the waters from heaven never ceased, not to say that it rained, for it was like a repetition of the deluge. Twice had the ships suffered loss in boats, anchors, rigging, and were now lying bare without sails . . . still raining. The sea very tempestuous and I was driven backward under bare poles. . . .

I anchored at an island, where I lost, at one stroke, three anchors; and at midnight, when the weather was such that the world appeared to be coming to an end, the cables of the other ship broke, and it came down upon my vessel with such force that it was a wonder we were not dashed to pieces; the single anchor that remained to me was our only preservation. After six days, when the weather became calm, I resumed my journey, having already lost all my tackle; my ships were pierced with borers more than a honeycomb and the crew entirely paralyzed with fear and in despair. There the storm returned to drive me back . . . I continued beating against contrary winds, and with the ships in the worst possible condition. With three pumps, and the use of pots and kettles, we could scarcely clear the water that came into the ship, there being no remedy but this, against the shipworm, I determined on keeping the sea, in spite of the weather, when we miraculously came upon land.

Weep for me whoever has charity, truth and justice. I did not come out on this voyage to gain to myself honor and wealth; for at that time all hope of such a thing was dead. I do not lie when I say, that I went to your Highnesses with honest purpose of heart, and sincere zeal in your cause. I humbly beseech your Highnesses, that if it please God to rescue me from this place, you will graciously sanction my pilgrimage to Rome and other holy places. May the holy Trinity protect your Hignesses' lives, and add prosperity. . . .

* * *

Storms and men; the very worms of the sea were opposed to him. But if, as he instinctively, but for his insane doggedness, would have done, he had undertaken that holy pilgrimage of which he had spoken, the flower might again, in that seclusion, often have appeared to him in all its old-time loveliness, as when he himself floated with luck and in sunshine on that tropic sea toward adventure and discovery:

* * *

. . . at the third hour of Saturday night it began to blow from the N.E. and I shaped my course to the west. We took in much water over the bows, which retarded our progress and nine leagues were made during the day and night.

Sunday we made nineteen leagues, and I decided to reckon less than the number run, for should the voyage prove of long duration, the people would not be so terrified and disheartened. This day we lost sight of land, and many fearful of not seeing it again sighed and shed tears. The sailors steered badly, letting the ships fall off to N.E. and even more, of which I was forced to complain several times.

Monday . . . Tuesday we sailed on our course which was west and made twenty leagues or more. We saw a large piece of the mast of a ship of one hundred and twenty tons, but were unable to get it.

Wednesday . . . On this day, Thursday, thirteenth September, at the commencement of the night, the needles turned a half point to the north-west, and in the morning still more so. This I took to be due to a movement of the North Star which must have an orbit like the others howbeit less than they.

Friday, on the westerly course, day and night, twenty leagues, counting a little less. Here those on the caravel *Niña* reported that they had seen a tern, a bird which is never far from land.

Saturday, we made twenty-seven leagues on the west course; and in the early part of the night there fell into the sea a marvelous flame of fire, at a distance of about four or five leagues from the ship.

Sunday, the sixteenth, day and night, I steered the course west, making thirty-nine leagues but counted only thirty-six. There were some clouds and small rain. From this day and ever afterward very temperate breezes, so that there was great pleasure in enjoying the mornings, nothing being wanted but the song of nightingales. It was like April in Andalucia. Here we began to see many tufts of grass that were very green and appeared to have been quite recently torn from the land. All this I called to the attention of the men and from this I judged that we were near land, but not the mainland which I make to be more distant.

The seventeenth of September, Monday, I proceeded on the west course and made over fifty leagues in the day and night, counting only forty-seven. A favorable current aided us on our way. There was very much fine grass and herbs from rocks, which came from the west, so that it seemed for certain that land must be near. This day the pilots observed the north point and found, for the first time, that the needles turned a full point to the west of north. All this day the mariners were alarmed and dejected and would not give their reason. But I knew that it was because of the needle. At dawn I ordered that the north should be again observed. They then found that the needles were true for the cause was that the star makes the movement and not the needles. At dawn we observed much more weed appearing, like herbs from a river, in which one of the men discovered a live crab. This I kept that all might see it and believe on the land. The sea water was found to be less salt than it had been since leaving the Canaries. This I caused many to taste. The breezes were always soft. Every one was pleased and the best sailors went ahead to sight the first land. Many tunnyfish passed on all sides of us and the crew of the *Niña* killed one. All these signs came from the west in which direction I trust in that high God in whose hands are all victories that very soon we shall see land. On that morning there appeared a white bird, called boatswainbird, which is not in the habit of sleeping on the sea.

Tuesday, we made forty-five leagues, counting only thirty-eight. The sea was like the river of Seville. Martin Alonzo, with the *Pinta*, which was a fast sailer, did not wait, but said to me from his caravel, that he hoped to see land that night. A great cloud appeared to the north, a sign of the nearness of land.

Wednesday, twenty-five leagues, but it was calm, and counted only twenty-two. This day, at ten o'clock, a booby came to the ship and in the afternoon another, these birds not generally going more than twenty leagues from the land. There was also some drizzling rain without wind, which is a sure sign of land. I felt it to be certain that there were islands both to the north and south of our position and that we were passing through them. This I explained to all saying that my desire was to press on to the Indies, the weather being fine, as such it was, and that on the return we should see all. Here the pilots found their position. He of the *Niña* made the Canaries four hundred and forty leagues distant, the *Pinta* four hundred and twenty. But he of my own ship made the distance exactly four hundred leagues, which I gave out to be the true.

Thursday, twentieth of September, the course was W. by N. and as her head was all round the compass, owing to the calm that prevailed, the ship made only seven or eight leagues. Two boobies came to the ship, and afterwards another, a sign of the proximity of land. One of the men caught a bird with the hand, which was like a tern. But it was a riverbird, not a seabird, the feet being like those of a gull. At dawn two or three land birds came singing to the ship and they disappeared before sunset.

Twenty-first of September, most of the day was calm, later a little wind. During the day and night we made only thirteen leagues. At dawn we saw so much weed that the sea appeared to be covered with it. And it came from the west. A booby was seen. The sea was very smooth, like a river, and the air the best in the world. Toward midday a whale was sighted, which is a sign of land, because they always keep near the shore.

Saturday, September twenty-second, I shaped my course W.N.W. more or less, her head turning from one to the other point and made thirty leagues. This contrary wind was very necessary to me, because my people had become much excited at the thought that in these seas no wind ever blew in the direction of Spain. In the morning there was no weed but in the afternoon it was very thick.

This day, Sunday, the twenty-third of September, I shaped a course N.W. and at times more northerly; sometimes getting upon our course, which was west, and made about twenty-two leagues. A dove was seen and also another booby, another riverbird and some white birds. Great quantities of weed and crabs in it. The sea being calm and smooth, the crews began to murmur, saying that here there was no great sea and the wind would never blow so that they could return to Spain. Many were in great despair and torment of mind thinking that they would never be able to return. Afterward the sea arose very much and later adverse winds appeared. The adverseness of the wind and the high sea were very helpful to me since they freed the crew of the idea that there would be no favorable sea and winds for their return. Yet even then some objected, saying that the wind would not last.

Monday, on the west course all day and night making fourteen leagues. I counted only twelve.

Tuesday, calm and afterwards wind. On the west course till night. This day I signaled that the *Pinta* should draw near and conversed with Martin Alonzo Pinzon respecting a chart which I had sent to the caravel three days before on which I had depicted certain islands in that sea. Martin Alonzo said that the ships were in the position on which the islands were placed, with which I agreed but added that it might be that we had not fallen in with them due to the currents which had always set the ships to the N.E. and that we had not made so much as the pilots had reported. At my request the chart was sent back on a line. Thereat I plotted our position on it with the aid of the pilot and mariners that they might be reassured. At sunset Martin Alonzo went up on the poop of his ship and with joy called out that he had sighted land. I fell on my knees and gave thanks to the Lord, so heavy had been my burdens these latter days at the despair among the men and the murmurs going among them, that I should have to turn back. And Martin Alonzo said the *Gloria in Excelsis* with his people. My own crew did the same. Those of the *Niña* all went up on the mast and into the rigging and declared that it was land. It seemed distant twenty-five leagues. So it appeared until night. I ordered the course

to be altered from west to S.W. in which direction the land
had appeared. Four leagues that day on a west course and
seventeen S.W. during the night, in all twenty-one, but I
told the men that thirteen was the distance made good. The
sea was very smooth so that many sailors bathed alongside.
We saw many giltheads and other fish.

Wednesday, what had been said to be land was only clouds
and I continued on the west course till afternoon, then altered to S.W. Day and night thirty-one leagues counting
twenty-four for the people. The sea was like a river, the air
pleasant and mild. The despair of the crew redoubled at
this disappointment but I comforted them as best I could,
begging them to endure a while longer for all that would be
theirs in the end.

Thursday, the course west, and distance made good day
and night twenty-four leagues, twenty being counted for the
people. Many giltheads came. One was killed. A boatswainbird came.

Twenty-eighth September, Friday, the course was west
and the distance, owing to calms, only fourteen leagues,
counting only thirteen. Little weed but more giltheads.
Caught one.

Saturday, the course was west, twenty-four leagues,
counting only twenty-one. Calm, not much distance made
good during day and night. Today we saw a man-o-war
bird, which makes the boobies vomit what they have swallowed, and eats it, maintaining itself on nothing else. It is a
seabird but does not sleep on the sea, and does not go more
than twenty leagues from land. The sea smooth as a river.
Much weed.

Sunday, the last day of September, west fourteen leagues,
eleven being counted. Four boatswainbirds came to the ship
which I considered a great sign of land.

Monday, first of October, west twenty-five leagues,
counted twenty. A heavy shower of rain. At dawn the pilot
of our ship made the distance from Hierro five hundred
eighty-four leagues to the west. The reduced reckoning

which I showed to the crew made it five hundred seventy-eight leagues, but the truth which I kept secret was seven hundred seven. Thus the wisdom of the double reckoning was confirmed.

Tuesday, west, day and night thirty-nine leagues, counted for the crew thirty. The weed, many thanks to God, coming from east to west, contrary to the usual course. Many fish seen and one killed. A white bird like a gull.

Wednesday, still the west course, and made good forty-seven leagues, counted forty. Sandpipers appeared, and much weed, some old and some quite fresh and having fruit. No birds. So I gave it out that we had left the islands behind that were depicted on the chart. Here many called upon me to turn about and search for the land but I did not wish to keep the ships beating about, although I had certain information of islands in this region. It would not have been good sense to do this since the weather was favorable and the chief intention was to go in search of the Indies by way of the west. This was what I had promised to the King and Queen, and they had sent me for this purpose.

Thursday, west sixty-three leagues, counted forty-six. More than forty sandpipers came to the ship in a flock and two boobies. A shipsboy hit one with a stone. There also came a man-o-war bird and a white bird like a gull. The crew here became ever louder in their complaints but I gave as little heed as I was able though many were now openly mutinous and would have done me harm if they dared.

Peter Gutierrez: So that, virtually, you have staked your life and the lives of your companions, upon the foundation of a mere speculative opinion.

Columbus: So it is: I cannot deny it. But consider a little. If at present you and I, and all our companions, were not in this vessel, in the midst of this sea, in this unknown solitude, in a state as uncertain and perilous as you please; in what other condition of life should we pass these days? Perhaps more cheerfully? or should we not rather be in some greater trouble or solicitude, or else full of tedium? I care not to mention the glory and utility we shall carry back, if the enterprise succeeds according to our hope. Should no other fruit come from this navigation, to me it appears most profitable inasmuch as for a time it preserves us free from tedium, makes life dear to us, makes valuable to us many things that otherwise we should not have in consideration.

Friday, fifth of October, fifty-seven leagues, but counted forty-five. The sea smooth and quiet. To God be given thanks, the air being pleasant and temperate, with no weed, many sandpipers, and flying fish coming on the deck in numbers.

Saturday, continued the west course, forty leagues, thirty-three being counted. Martin Alonzo said that it would be best to steer west by south, that night, for the island of Cipango which the map showed but I thought it best to go at once to the continent and afterwards to the island.

Sunday, seventh October, west twenty-three leagues, counting eighteen. This day the *Niña* hoisted a flag at the masthead, and fired a gun, which was the signal I had ordered that land had been sighted. At this time also, I ordered that at sunrise and sunset, all the ships should join me, because at these times things are most proper for seeing the greatest distance, the haze clearing away. No land was seen during the afternoon as reported by the *Niña*. But we passed great numbers of birds flying from N. to S.W. This I believed to be due either to the birds going to sleep on land or that they were flying from the winter which might be supposed to be near in the land from which they were coming. And this in some measure consoled the men from their disappointment over the false news from the *Niña* since it is known that most of the islands held by the Portuguese were discovered by the flight of birds. For this reason I resolved to give up the west course and to shape a course W.S.W. for two days. We began the new course an hour before sunset, expecting to see land soon and this served to encourage the crew with renewed hope.

Monday, the course W.S.W. and twelve leagues were

made during the day and night. Thanks be to God the air is very soft like April at Seville; and it is a pleasure to be here, so balmy are the breezes. The weed this day is very fresh, there are many land birds and one was taken that was flying S.W., terns, ducks and a booby.

Tuesday, ninth October, the course S.W. The wind then changed and I steered W. by N. four leagues. Throughout the night birds were heard passing.

Wednesday, fifty-nine leagues, W.S.W., but counted no more than forty-four. Here the people could endure no longer. All now complained of the length of the voyage. But I cheered them as best I could, giving them good hopes of the advantages they might gain by it. Roused to madness by their fear, the captains declared they were going back but I told them then, that however much they might complain, I had to go to the Indies and they along with me, and that I would go on until I found them, with the help of our Lord. And so for a time it passed but now all was in great danger from the men.

Thursday, eleventh of October. The course was W.S.W. More sea than there had been during the whole of the voyage. Sandpipers and a green reed near the ship. And for this I gave thanks to God as it was a sure sign of land. Those of the *Pinta* saw a cane and a pole, and they took up another small pole which appeared to be worked with iron; also another bit of cane, a land plant and a small board. The crew of the caravel *Niña* also saw signs of land, and a small plant covered with berries.

After sunset I returned to the west course. Up to two hours past midnight we had gone ninety miles, when the *Pinta* which was the fastest sailer and had gone ahead, found the land and gave the signals. The land was first seen by Rodrigo de Triana.

Though on the night before, at ten o'clock, I saw a light and called Peter Gutierrez and said that there seemed to be a light, and that he should look at it. He did so and saw it. The same to Rodrigo Sanchez who at first could see nothing but afterward saw the light once or twice like a wax candle rising and falling. When they said the *Salve*, which all the sailors are accustomed to sing in their way, I admonished the men to keep a good lookout on the forecastle and to watch well for land and to him who should first cry out that he had seen land I would give a silk doublet besides the other rewards promised by the Sovereigns which were ten thousand *maravedis* to him who should first see it. Two hours past midnight, the moon having risen at eleven o'clock and then shining brightly in the sky, being in its third quarter and a little behind Rodrigo de Triana, the land was sighted at a distance of about two leagues. At once I ordered them to shorten sail and we lay under the mainsail without the bonnets, hove to waiting for daylight.

On Friday, the twelfth of October, we anchored before the land and made ready to go on shore. Presently we saw naked people on the beach. I went ashore in the armed boat and took the royal standard, and Martin Alonzo and Vincent Yañez, his brother, who was captain of the *Niña*. And we saw the trees very green, and much water and fruits of divers kinds. Presently many of the inhabitants assembled. I gave to some red caps and glass beads to put round their necks, and many other things of little value. They came to the ships' boats afterward, where we were, swimming and bringing us parrots, cotton threads in skeins, darts—what they had, with good will. As naked as their mothers bore them, and so the women, though I did not see more than one young girl. All I saw were youths, well made with very handsome bodies and very good countenances. Their hair short and coarse, almost like the hairs of a horse's tail. They paint themselves some black, some white, others red and others of what color they can find. Some paint the faces and others the whole body, some only round the eyes and others only on the nose. They are themselves neither black nor white.

On Saturday, as dawn broke, many of these people came to the beach, all youths. Their legs are very straight, all in one line and no belly. They came to the ship in canoes, made out of the trunk of a tree, all in one piece, and wonderfully worked, propelled with a paddle like a baker's shovel, and go at a marvelous speed.

Bright green trees, the whole land so green that it is a pleasure to look on it. Gardens of the most beautiful trees I ever saw. Later I came upon a man alone in a canoe going from one island to another. He had a little of their bread, about the size of a fist, a calabash of water, a piece of brown earth, powdered then kneaded, and some dried leaves which must be a thing highly valued by them for they bartered with it at San Salvador. He also had with him a native basket. The women wore in front of their bodies a small piece of cotton cloth. I saw many trees very unlike those of our country. Branches growing in different ways and all from one trunk; one twig is one form and another is a different shape and so unlike that it is the greatest wonder in the world to see the diversity; thus one branch has leaves like those of a cane, and others like those of a mastic tree; and on a single tree there are five different kinds. The fish so unlike ours that it is wonderful. Some are the shape of dories and of the finest colors, so bright that there is not a man who would not be astounded, and would not take great delight in seeing them. There are also whales. I saw no beasts on land save parrots and lizards.

On shore I sent the people for water, some with arms, and others with casks; and as it was some little distance, I waited two hours for them.

During that time I walked among the trees which was the most beautiful thing which I had ever seen. . . .

Eia ergo, advocata nostra, illos tuos misericordes oculos ad nos converte. Et Jesum, benedictum fructum ventris tui, nobis post hoc exsilium ostende. O clemens, o pia, o dulces Maria.

The Destruction of Tenochtitlan

UPON THE ORCHIDEAN beauty of the new world the old rushed inevitably to revenge itself after the Italian's return. Such things occur in secret. Though men may be possessed by beauty while they work that is all they know of it or of their own terrible hands; they do not fathom the forces which carry them. Spain cannot be blamed for the crassness of the discoverers. They moved out across the seas stirred by instincts, ancient beyond thought as the depths they were crossing, which they obeyed under the names of King or Christ or whatever it might be, while they watched the recreative New unfolding itself miraculously before them, before *them*, deafened and blinded. Steering beyond familiar horizons they were driven to seek perhaps self-justification for victorious wars against Arab and Moor; but these things are the surface only. At the back, as it remains, it was the evil of the whole world; it was the perennial disappointment which follows, like smoke, the bursting of ideas. It was the spirit of malice which underlies men's lives and against which nothing offers resistance. And bitter as the thought may be that Tenochtitlan, the barbaric city, its people, its genius wherever found should have been crushed out because of the awkward names men give their emptiness, yet it was no man's fault. It was the force of the pack whom the dead drive. Cortez was neither malicious, stupid nor blind, but a conqueror like other conquerors. Courageous almost beyond precedent, tactful, resourceful in misfortune, he was a man of genius superbly suited to his task. What his hand touched went down in spite of him. He was one among the rest.

Velasquez, the Cuban Governor who sent him out, traitor-
ously attacked him from the rear a week afterward. His own
captains would have deserted him, so hard was he to follow.
But the entire enterprise lived for many years on the verge
of being allowed to languish, ruin to succeed destruction,
because of the fortuitous anger which blossomed so naïvely,
so mysteriously in Fonseca, Bishop of Burgos, President of
the Council of the Indies. This the man, Cortez' most powerful enemy, already so notorious for the spiteful malevolence
with which he thwarted the views of Columbus—a logic
clearer had there been two Fonsecas instead of the one.
After a rough voyage from Cuba, across the gulf, Cortez
landed his small force safely before what is now Vera Cruz,
near the native city of Cempoal. There, lest his men should
desert him in view of the hardships which lay ahead, he had
his vessels beached, under pretext of their being no longer
seaworthy, and destroyed them.

Montezuma immediately sent gifts, at the same time begging the Spaniard not to risk coming up into the back country: a gold necklace of seven pieces, set with many gems like
small rubies, a hundred and eighty-three emeralds and ten
fine pearls, and hung with twenty-seven little bells of gold.—
Two wheels, one of gold like the sun and the other of silver
with the image of the moon upon it, made of plates of those
metals, twenty-eight hands in circumference, with figures of
animals and other things in bas relief, finished with great
skill and ingenuity.—A headpiece of wood and gold, adorned
with gems, from which hung twenty-five little bells of gold,
and, on it, instead of plume, a green bird with eyes, beak and
feet of gold.—Several shoes of the skin of deer, sewed with
gold thread, the soles of which were made of blue and white
stones of a brilliant appearance.—A shield of wood and
leather, with little bells hanging to it and covered with
plates of gold, in the middle of which was cut the image of
the god of war between four heads of a lion, a tiger, an eagle
and an owl represented alive with their hair and feathers.—

Twenty-four curious and beautiful shields of gold, of feathers and very small pearls, and four of feathers and silver only.—Four fishes, two ducks and some other birds of molten gold.—A large mirror adorned with gold, and many small.—Miters and crowns of feathers and gold ornamented with pearls and gems.—Several large plumes of beautiful feathers, fretted with gold and small pearls.—Several fans of gold and silver mixed together; others of feathers only, of different forms and sizes.—A variety of cotton mantles, some all white, others chequered with white and black, or red, green, yellow and blue; on the outside rough like shaggy cloth and within destitute of color and nap.—A number of under-waistcoats, handkerchiefs, counterpanes, tapestries and carpets of cotton, the workmanship superior to the materials of which they were composed.—And books made of tablets with a smooth surface for writing, which being joined might be folded together or stretched out to a considerable length, "the characters inscribed thereon resembling nothing so much as Egyptian hieroglyphics."—But Cortez was unwilling to turn back; rather these things whetted his appetite for the adventure. Without more ado he sent letters to his king advising him that having come to these lands to conquer them, in the royal name and that of the true church, he would forthwith proceed to take Montezuma, dead or alive, unless he should accept the faith and acknowledge himself a subject to the Spanish throne.

The advance was like any similar military enterprise: it accomplished its purpose. Surmounting every difficulty Cortez went his way into the country past the quiet Cempoalan maizefields, past the smoking summit of Popocatepetl, until, after weeks of labor, he arrived upon the great lakes and the small cities in them adjoining Tenochtitlan itself. Montezuma seeing that there was nothing else for it, sent envoys accompanied by three hundred warriors, who met the Spaniard advancing on the lake road and there welcomed him to the district with great ceremony and show of friendliness.

Noticeable among them was one young man of magnificent appearance who descended from his litter and walked to meet the Conqueror while his followers ran before him, picking up stones and other small obstructions which lay in his path. Cortez now passed over his first causeway into one of the lesser lake cities, built of well-hewn stone sheer from the water. He was overcome with wonder. The houses were so excellently put together, so well decorated with cloths and carven wood, so embellished with metalwork and other marks of a beautiful civilization; the people were so gracious; there were such gardens, such trees, such conservatories of flowers that nothing like it had ever been seen or imagined. At the house where the Conqueror was entertained that day and night he especially noted a pool built of stone into the clear waters of which stone steps descended, while round it were paven paths lined with sweet-smelling shrubs and plants and trees of all sorts. Also he noted the well-stocked kitchen garden. The following day at noon he arrived at the end of his journey.

There it lay! a city as large as Cordova or Seville, entirely within the lake two miles from the mainland: Tenochtitlan. Four avenues or entrances led to it, all formed of artificial causeways. Along the most easterly of these, constructed of great beams perfectly hewn and fitted together, and measuring two spears-lengths in width, the Christian advanced. Running in at one side of the city and out at the other this avenue constituted at the same time its principal street. As Cortez drew nearer he saw, right and left, magnificent houses and temples, close to the walls of which, each side, moved parallel rows of priests in black robes, and, between them, supported by two attendants, Montezuma, on foot, down the center of the roadway. Cortez stepped forward but the attendants interceded. The Emperor then advanced alone and with great simpleness of manner placed a golden chain about the Christian's neck. Then taking him by the hand,

and the whole procession following, he conducted him to the quarters which had been chosen for the visitors, a great building close to the royal palaces in the center of the city. Everything had been prepared in advance: all the material needs together with rich gifts, as before: precious metals, gems, male and female apparel of remarkable elegance, ornamental hangings for bedchambers, tapestries for halls and temples, counterpanes composed of feathers interwoven with cotton, and many beautiful and curious artifices "of so costly and unusual workmanship that considering their novelty and wonderful beauty no price could be set on them." Here in this large building whose great hall was to serve the Spaniards for barracks from that time until the end, Montezuma and Cortez found themselves seated at last face to face. Montezuma spoke: "They have told you that I possess houses with walls of gold and many other such things and that I am a god or make myself one. The houses you see are of stone and lime and earth."—Then opening his robe: "You see that I am composed of flesh and bone like yourselves and that I am mortal and palpable to the touch."—To this smiling sally, so full of gentleness and amused irony, Cortez could reply nothing save to demand that the man declare himself a subject to the Spanish King forthwith and that, furthermore, he should then and there announce publicly his allegiance to the new power.—Whatever the Aztec may have felt during the weeks of Cortez' slow advance upon his capital from the seashore, nothing at the present moment seemed to disturb his aristocratic reserve. He had thought and he had made up his mind. Without semblance of anger, fear or impatience; without humility or protest but with the force bred of a determination to face at any cost a situation fast going beyond his control, he spoke again. He explained that his people were not the aborigines of the land but that they had emigrated there in times past and ended by accepting the Spanish Monarch as his rightful and hereditary master. After due announcements and explanations had been made to the people Cortez became the acknowledged regent, in the name of Castile and the true church, for all that country.

Streets, public squares, markets, temples, palaces, the city spread its dark life upon the earth of a new world, rooted there, sensitive to its richest beauty, but so completely removed from those foreign contacts which harden and protect, that at the very breath of conquest it vanished. The whole world of its unique associations sank back into the ground to be reënkindled, never, Never, at least, save in spirit; a spirit mysterious, constructive, independent, puissant with natural wealth; light, if it may be, as feathers; a spirit lost in that soil. Scarcely an element in the city's incredible organization but evidenced an intellectual vigor full of resource and delicacy which had given it distinction. Half land and half water the streets were navigated by canoes and bridged at the intersections by structures of great timbers over which ten horses could go abreast. For water supply a masonry pipe, two paces broad and five feet high, ran from the mainland over one of the great causeways carrying excellent drinking water. There were two such aqueducts, side by side, each to be used alternately while the other was cleaning. There were public squares, and one of great size surrounded by porticoes where daily sixty thousand souls engaged in buying and selling under the supervision of twelve central magistrates and numbers of inspectors. Here "everything which the world affords" was offered for purchase, from the personal services of laborers and porters to the last refinements of bijouterie; gold, silver, lead, brass, copper, tin; wrought and unwrought stone, bricks burnt and unburnt, timber hewn and unhewn, of different sorts; game of every variety, fowls, quails, partridges, wild ducks, parrots, pigeons, reed-birds, sparrows, eagles, hawks, owls, likewise the skins of some birds of prey with their feathers, head, beak and claws; rabbits, hares, deer and little dogs, which they raised for eating; wood and coals in abundance and brasiers of earthenware for burning coals; mats of various kinds; all kinds of green vegetables, especially onions, leeks, watercresses, nasturtium, sorrel, artichokes and golden thistle; fruits, fish, honey, grain—either whole, in the form of flour or baked into loaves; different kinds of cotton thread of all colors; jars, jugs, pots and an endless variety of vessels, all made of fine clay, most of them glazed and painted; eggs, cakes, pâtés of birds and fish; wine from the maguey; finally everything that could be found throughout the whole country was sold there, each kind of merchandise in a separate street or quarter of the market assigned to it exclusively, and thus the best order was preserved. There was an herb street, there were shops where they shaved and washed the head, and restaurateurs who furnished food and drink at a price.

Large numbers of temples existed throughout the great city, but for grandeur and excellence of architectural detail one far surpassed the rest. Forty towers, lofty and well built, rose from within its sacred precinct, the largest of which, constructed of hewn stone remarkably hard in texture, had fifty steps leading to its main body. A mass higher than the cathedral of Seville. Three halls of wonderful extent and height, adorned with figures sculptured in wood and stone, contained the principal idols. And from these, through very small doors, opened the chapels, to which no light was admitted, nor any person except the priests, and not all of them. Decorated with curious imagery in stone, the woodwork carved in relief and painted with figures of monsters and other things, unpaved, darkened and bloodstained, it was in these chapels that the religious practices which so shocked the Christian were performed. Here it was that the tribe's deep feeling for a reality that stems back into the permanence of remote origins had its firm hold. It was the earthward thrust of their logic; blood and earth; the realization of their primal and continuous identity with the ground itself, where everything is fixed in darkness. The priests in black robes, tribal men, never cutting or combing their hair; the instinctive exclusion of women from all places of worship; the debarring of priests from female society: it was a ceremonial acknowledgment of the deep sexless urge of life itself, the hungry animal, underlying all other power; the mysterious secret of existence whose cruel beauty they, the living, inherited from the dead. The same for their sculpture. It is the mystery of the past which monsters, grotesques, beasts combined with the human, truly signify—gentle animal associations distorted by the invasions of night—and not a debased instinct whose reliance is necessarily upon oppression and fear. The earth is black and it is there: only art advances. The figures of the idols themselves were of extra-human size and composed, significantly, of a paste of seeds and leguminous plants, commonly used for food, ground and mixed together and kneaded with human blood, the whole when completed being consecrated with a bath of blood from the heart of a living victim. The chief of these idols Cortez precipitated from their pedestals and cast down the temple steps; an act of extraordinary daring; at the same time purifying the chapels and setting up in them images of Our Lady and the saints. Such a stroke could not fail to have proved of the most serious consequence to all had not Montezuma again displayed his tact, self-control and remarkable grasp of the changing situation. The new state of affairs was accepted, human sacrifice was abolished and the orderly significance of the events taking place was publicly made evident. In person, together with many of the principal citizens, he, Montezuma, assisted at the final purification of the chapels. Whether or not this be evidence on the Aztec's part of weakness or the deepest forbearance, surely nothing like it for quiet flexibility of temper and retained dignity has ever been recorded. Perhaps by a sudden, daring stroke this man might have rid himself of the intestine enemy who was each day, each week, striking deeper at the nation's life.

Perhaps fear had unmanned him. Perhaps what we call for-bearance was no more than the timidity which is an over-whelming agony of heart inspired by the sight of a resistless force aimed at our destruction. Still, if this be so, Montezuma has left no trace of cowardice upon the records. But weak-ling or genius, about the suave personality of this barbaric chieftain the liveliest, most airily expansive moods of the race did flower, just as the black permanence of tribal under-standing stood rooted in the priesthood. Perhaps it was a conscious knowledge of this that inspired and moved Monte-zuma in the present action.

Surely no other prince has lived, or will ever live, in such state as did this American cacique. The whole waking aspira-tions of his people, opposed to and completing their religious sense, seemed to come off in him and in him alone: the drive upward, toward the sun and the stars. He was the very per-son of their ornate dreams, so delicate, so prismatically color-ful, so full of tinkling sounds and rhythms, so tireless of in-vention. Never was such a surface lifted above the isolate blackness of such profound savagery. It is delightful to know that Montezuma changed his clothes four times a day, don-ning four different suits, entirely new, which he never wore again; that at meals he was served in a great clean-swept chamber on mats upon the floor, his food being kept warm in chafing dishes containing live coals; that at meals he sat upon a small cushion "curiously wrought of leather." But nowhere in his state was the stark power of beauty, the re-fined and the barbaric, so exquisitely expressed as in his smaller palaces and places of amusement. "What can be more wonderful than that a barbarous monarch, as he is, should have every object in his domain imitated in gold, sil-ver, precious stones and feathers; the gold and silver being wrought so naturally as not to be surpassed by any smith in the world; the stonework executed with such perfection that it is difficult to conceive what instruments could have been used, and the feather work superior to the finest production in wax and embroidery." "There is one palace inferior to the rest, attached to which is a beautiful garden with balconies extending over it supported by marble columns and having a floor formed of jasper elegantly inlaid. Belonging to it are ten pools, in which are kept the different species of water birds found in the country, all domesticated: for the sea birds there are pools of salt water and for the river birds, fresh water. Each species being supplied with the food natural to it when wild. Over the pools are corridors and galleries, to which Montezuma resorts, and from which he can look out and amuse himself with the sight of the birds there." "In an apartment of the same palace there are men, women and children whose faces, bodies, hair, eyebrows and eyelashes were white from birth." "The Emperor has another very beautiful palace, with a large courtyard, paved with handsome flags in the style of a chessboard. There are cages about nine feet in height and six paces square, each of which is half covered with a roof of tiles, and the other half has over it a wooden grate, skilfully made. Every cage contains a bird of prey, of all species." "In the same palace there are several large halls on the ground floor, filled with immense cages built of heavy pieces of timber, well put together, in which are kept lions, wolves, foxes and a great variety of other animals of the cat kind." "The care of these animals and birds is assigned to three hundred men." Daily the Emperor's wine cellar and larder were open to all who wished to eat and drink. His meals were served by three or four hundred youths who brought on an infinite variety of dishes; indeed, whenever he dined or supped, the table was loaded with every kind of fish, flesh, fruits and vegetables which the country afforded. Both at the beginning and end of every meal they furnished water for the hands, and the napkins used on these occasions were never employed a second time.

And then the end: Cortez had demanded gold from the first. To satisfy him, small groups of two Spaniards and two

Indians, bearing the proper credentials, had been despatched about the Aztec's domain, to distances in some cases of several hundred miles, that the tribute be collected. On one of these forays the two Christians were killed. Cortez immediately seized the person of Montezuma, together with his daughters and sons, imprisoning them in the garrison-fortress. From that time on, it was merely a matter of detail and of time as to what form the final catastrophe would take. Events shifted back and forth until in May, seven months after the Spaniards' first entrance to the city, the people laid siege to the intolerable intruders, determined to have done with them. In answer to shouts from outside, Montezuma, a prisoner within, had appeared on the ramparts of the besieged fortress whence he implored his people to give over their attacks. In reply he was struck on the head by a stone which killed him. Only the horse and the ordnance saved the Christians on that memorable retreat across the great causeway. Fighting madly to escape with some remnant of his forces through the masses of the enemy, and to retain at the same time his prisoners and treasure, Cortez lost everything. The children of Montezuma, the gold, everything perished over the sides of the breached and beleaguered avenue across the lake down which the Spaniards retreated, foot by foot, with swarms of Indians flinging themselves continually upon them. They escaped. Some months later they returned and continued the destruction, this time deliberately and with calculated malintention. Tenochtitlan surrounded, the water supply cut off, the augmented Spanish forces began to burrow forward and after weeks of desperate effort they succeeded in their plans. It was the horses the Indians feared most. At one time they had Cortez in their very hands only to have them cut off at the wrists by his followers. But nothing could bemuse them now. They knew now what it all meant and they opposed themselves to the intruder inflexibly and without murmur until the end. Neither the overwhelming means used against them, their desertion by friends of the nearby tribes, the lack of water, starvation, nor attempts to inspire them with fear, made the slightest impression. To every advance made inviting them to parley they had but the one answer: no! Cortez, dejected, seeing that it would be necessary to exterminate them before he could succeed in taking the city and dreading the horror of such a course, decided with reluctance, in order to impress them, to burn the noble edifices in the great square which had served Montezuma for aviaries. "It grieved me much but it grieved the enemy more." Each day he heard mass and returned to the city to renew the attack upon the now nearly starved inhabitants who had retreated to the market quarter and there still held out. At one time during a successful sally the Indians had killed two of the Spanish horses and in great spirits had sent the severed heads by messengers in canoes to the surrounding tribes for them to come to the rescue, but none dared. Most had already joined the Christian in his irresistible purpose. But Guatemotzin, the young nephew of Montezuma, would not give in. Women and children reduced to the last extremity by hunger and privation were wandering dazed about the streets when the Spaniards had made their final charge. But Guatemotzin, taken captive from a boat in an effort to get to the mainland, still maintained his pride and integrity of spirit. He had done all that he could and he was beaten. Placing his hand upon the hilt of Cortez' dagger, he asked the Spaniard to draw it and plunge it into his heart. Cortez refused. Later the Conqueror tried to rebuild the city. *Viva quien vence!*

The Fountain of Eternal Youth

History, history! We fools, what do we know or care? History begins for us with murder and enslavement, not with discovery. No, we are not Indians but we are men of their world. The blood means nothing; the spirit, the ghost of the land moves in the blood, moves the blood. It is we who ran to the shore naked, we who cried, "Heavenly Man!" These are the inhabitants of our souls, our murdered souls that lie... agh. Listen! I tell you it was lucky for Spain the first ship put its men ashore where it did. If the Italian had landed in Florida, one twist of the helm north, or among the islands a hair more to the south; among the Yamasses with their sharpened bones and fishspines, or among the Caribs with their poisoned darts—it might have begun differently.

When in the later years Ponce found his plantations going under for lack of slaves—no more to be trapped in Puerto Rico, *rico!* all ruined—he sought and obtained a royal patent to find more in the surrounding islands. He was granted the right to hunt out and to take the Caribs; the Caribs whom The Great Maker had dropped through a hole in the sky among their islands; they whose souls lived in their bodies, many souls in one body; they who fought their enemies, ate them; whose gods lived, Mabouya, in the forest, Oumekon, by the sea—there were other gods—

His ship came into Guadeloupe—the great sulphur cone back of the water. He had arrived straight from Spain, hot foot after niggers. Having much soiled linen aboard from the long trip, he ordered his laundresses ashore, with a body of troops to guard them, where a stream could be observed coming down to the sea.

It was a paradise. A stream of splashing water, the luxuriant foliage. A gorge, a veritable tunnel led upstream between cliffwalls covered by thick vines in flower attended by ensanguined hummingbirds which darted about from cup to cup in the green light. But the soul of the Carib was on the alert among the leaves. It was too late.

Fierce and implacable we kill them but their souls dominate us. Our men, our blood, but their spirit is master. It enters us, it defeats us, it imposes itself. We are moderns—madmen at Paris—all lacking in a ground sense of cleanliness. It is the Caribs leaping out, facing the arquebuses, thinking it thunder, looking up at the sky: No rain! No clouds! Then the second volley. Their comrades bleeding, dead. Kill! Not a Spaniard but they stretched out in the streambed. Hagh, I can hear the laundresses squeal on the shore—run hither and thither. The devils had them safe. Let old Ponce sit up in his hammock on the poop of his ship. Let him send other boats ashore. The Indians have grabbed up the women. Three naked savages shot through the chest from behind before they could gain the forest rolled over and gripped the females they had been carrying by the throat with their teeth. Worth being a laundress to be carried off that way, eh? Nice psychologic study, those women. And the damned bloodhound, Berrescien. Ponce had got his belly full. They outflanked him in canoes, ridiculed his strategy, took his chainshot in the chest and came back for more. They drove him off, so much so that they made him forget his dog, the precious Berrescien, of whom he thought more, that and his hidalgan pride, than— a population. The hound had been left behind in their scared flight. They saw him, they in the retreating boats, leap from the woods in pursuit of a flying Carib. Listen to this. The Indian swam out, the Spaniards in the boats turned back for the beast. The dog was steadily gaining on his victim. But, O Soul of the New World, the man had his bow and arrow with him as he swam. Tell that to Wilson. He stopped, turned, raised his body half out of the water, treading it, and put a bolt into the damned hound's throat —whom sharks swallowed. Then to shore, not forgetting— leaping to safety—to turn and spit back the swallowed chainshot, a derisive yell at the Christians.

They had the women and the dog. They left what they had defeated, to—us.

If men inherit souls this is the color of mine. We are, too, the others. Think of them! The main islands were thickly populated with a peaceful folk when Christ-over found them. But the orgy of blood which followed, no man has written. We are the slaughterers. It is the tortured soul of our world. Indians have no souls; that was it. That was what they said. But they knew they lied—the blood-smell proof. Ponce had been with the discoverer on his second trip. He became a planter. Sugar cane was imported from the Canaries, maize was adopted from the Indian souls. But revenues dwindled where none would work save in the traffic in girls: nine years old, reads the Italian's journal. Slaves. The Indians having no souls knew what freedom means. The Spaniards killed their kings, betrayed, raped, murdered their women and children; hounded them into the mountains. Ponce with wife and children in the *Casa Blanca* was one of the bloodthirstiest. They took them in droves, forced them to labor. It was impossible to them— not having been born to baptism. How maddening it is to the spirit to hear:—Bands of them went into the forests, their forests, and hanged themselves to the trees. What else? Islands—paradise. Surrounded by seas. On all sides "heav-enly man" bent on murder. Self-privilege. Two women and one man on a raft had gotten one hundred and fifty miles out to sea—such seamen were they—then luck again went against the Indian. Captured and back to slavery. Caravels crept along the shore by night. Next morning when women and children came down to the shore to fish—fine figures, straight black hair, high cheekbones, a language— they caught them, made them walk in bands, cut them down if they fainted, slashed off breasts, arms—women, children. Gut souls—

Thus the whole free population was brought into slavery or killed off. Aboujoubo, greatest chief in the island of San Ion, retreated in anguish to a rocky height. Ponce, now Governor, since he dare not economically murder every one, sallies out and is received by a native queen, girls dancing, gives one a gold crucifix, legend says. Two years later finds her under a bush, both hands hacked off. Belly-hurt he digs a shallow grave with his sword for her and shoves the gold symbol into his wallet. He exchanges names with a chief, sacred symbol of Indian faith and friendship. Hounds him out later: I am Juan Ponce de Leon! says the savage, standing before his followers—hanged nevertheless. The hound, Berrescien, gone ahead into a rocky place, comes spinning back, tumbling down, knocking against rocks, a gash in his forehead. Ponce defeated, embittered has the dog stretched upon a litter of leaves and branches and carried to the ship.

Do these things die? Men who do not know what lives, are themselves dead. In the heart there are living Indians once slaughtered and defrauded—Indians that live also in subtler ways: Ponce at fifty-two was rich, the murderous campaigns of his youth had subjugated the island—allayed his lust of common murder. The island was, in any case, mostly conquered.

An old Indian woman among his slaves, began to tell him of an island, Bimini, a paradise of fragrant groves, of all fruits. And in the center of it a fountain of clearest water of virtue to make old men young. Think of that!

Picture to yourself the significance of that—as revenge, as irony, as the trail of departing loveliness, *fata morgana*. Yet the real, the thing destroyed turning back with a smile. Think of the Spaniard listening. Gold. Gold. Riches. And figure to yourself the exquisite justice of it: an old woman, loose tongued—loose sword—the book, her soul already half out of her with sorrow: abandoned by a Carib who had fled back to his home having found Borequien greatly overrated. Her children enslaved—

The man, fifty-two, listened. Something has escaped him. At that moment rich, idle, he was relieved of his governorship. Vessels, three. He fitted them up at his own cost. Men enough, eager to serve the old master, rushed to his banner. Let the new governor complain that he was taking away too many able soldiers. Ponce smiled. Men whose terms of service had expired do as they please.

> *Por donde va la mar*
> *Vayan las arenas—*

They sailed north. It was March. In the wind, what? Beauty the eternal. White sands and fragrant woods, fruits, riches, truth! The sea, the home of permanence, drew them on into its endless distances. Again the new! Do you feel it? The murderer, the enslaver, the terror striker, the destroyer of beauty, drawn on by beauty across the glancing tropical seas—before Drake, before the galleons. The rhythm of the waves, birds, fish, seaweed as on the first voyage. They even put in at Guanahani for water—Columbus' first landfall; then populous, inviting; now desolate, defeated, murdered—unpeopled.

March! Spring! to the north. The argosy of the New World! In search of eternal youth. In search of the island of Bimini—an old woman's tale. The destroyer. Admonished that he had done enough, still there floated a third world to discover: no end—away from the beginning—tail chaser.

A Carne de lobo
Diente de perro

he could not halt—no end. Curious that Amino—the boy of Palos who watched Columbus prepare his vessels for the first voyage and went on the second—should be his pilot. Sea scud. The same piloted Cortez to Mexico.

Let them go. They found nothing but a row of white islands called "The Martyrs," a catch of turtles, Las Tortugas, a sandy coastline, a devil of a current that shoved them about and devilish Indians who drove them back from the watering places—flamingoes, pelicans, egrets, herons—Rousseau has it. Thickets with striped leaves, ferns emerging from the dark, palms, the heat, the moon, the stars, the sun in a pool of swampwater. Fish fly. In the water seals—back to Cuba.

Old now, heavy at heart over the death of his bloody pet, Ponce retired to his Casa Blanca and sulked for three years. Then came the news of Cortez' triumph and the wealth of Montezuma.

Ponce—

de Leon
en nombre y podesta

—the victor, now defeated, must stir again. Back to Florida thinking to find on the continent, he only then found that he had discovered, another Tehuantepec.

But this time the Yamasses put an arrow into his thigh at the first landing—and let out his fountain. They flocked to the beach, jeered him as he was lifted to the shoulders of his men and carried away. Dead.

De Soto and the New World

SHE—Courage is strength—and you are vigilant, saga-
cious, firm besides. But I am beautiful—as "a cane box,
called petaca, full of unbored pearls." I am beautiful: a city
greater than Cuzco; rocks loaded with gold as a comb with
honey. Believe it. You will not dare to cease following me
—at Apalachi, at Cutifachiqui, at Mabilla, turning from the
sea, facing inland. And in the end you shall receive of me,
nothing—save one long caress as of a great river passing
forever upon your sweet corse. Balboa lost his eyes on the
smile of the Chinese ocean; Cabeça de Vaca lived hard and
saw much; Pizarro, Cortez, Coronado—but you, Hernando
de Soto, keeping the lead four years in a savage country,
against odds, "without fortress or support of any kind,"
you are mine, Black Jasmine, mine.—

* * *

On Friday, the thirtieth day of May, in the year 1548, the
army, fresh from Cuba, landed in Florida, on the west coast,
two leagues from the town of an Indian chief named Ucita.
The ground was very fenny and encumbered with dense
thickets and high trees.

From this place, Espíritu Santo, they began their eventful
journey, having first sent a small squadron north to find a
base toward which they might travel. And they waited two
months for its return "which seemed like a thousand years,"
but finally the ships appeared and with good news. De Soto
divided his forces, sending a few back to Cuba and leaving
some others as a garrison at the place they then occupied.
With the rest he set out paralleling the coast toward
Anhaica Apalachi where they were to spend the winter that

45

year. The course was north and west, a march of about a hundred leagues—through obscure and intricate parts: native villages in the swamps, Caliquen, Napateca, Hurripa-cuxi, Paracoxi, Tocaste, Cale—outlandish names.

* * *

She—Who will recognize them? None but you. To the rest without definition but to you each a thing in itself, delicate, pregnant with sudden meanings.

* * *

The way had been difficult: through a great morass, misled, ambuscaded at the fords, fighting, swimming, starving for a month at a time, thankful for a little parched corn, not even ripe, the cob and all being eaten as it was, and the stalk, too, for want of better.

* * *

She—It is de Soto! all goes forward somehow. But I am before you. It is my country. Everything is in accordance with my wish. Eight men start from a thicket, naked and tattooed, your lancers rush upon them, but one falls to his knees crying out, "Do not kill me. I am a Christian! It is Juan Ortiz, relic of Narvaez' forces, whom I have nursed tenderly for you these twelve years, teaching him the wild language. Witness my love. But I shall take him from you when he is most needed."—

* * *

At Anhaica Apalachi, through the winter, they lived with difficulty on game and other stores, such as they could take from the natives, miserably, as best they were able.

On Wednesday, the third of March, 1549, the Governor left his winter quarters at Apalachi to seek Yupaha, of which a young slave had told them: a country toward the rising sun, governed by a woman, where there was gold in quantity.

Now the second year was starting. Led by the youth they continued to bear east and north in the hope of finding the country of which he had spoken: days, weeks, a month —with small food, such want of meat and salt that oftentimes, in many places, a sick man would say, "Now, if I had but a slice of meat, or only a few lumps of salt, I should not thus die." But the Indians, skillful with the bow, would get abundance of deer, turkeys, rabbits and other game. Crossing a stream after nine last days of forced marching they came out into a pine grove on the far bank. Here all direction was lost. "He went about for the road and returned to us desperate."

The Governor had brought thirteen sows to Florida, which had increased to three hundred swine; and the maize having failed for three days, he ordered killed daily, for each man, half a pound of pork, on which small allowance, and some boiled herbs, the people with much difficulty lived.

From Apalachi in Florida to Cutifachiqui, on the Savanna River, two days march from the sea, where presently after the greatest hardships they arrived, they had traveled northeast it may be four hundred and thirty leagues. At this place, it appeared well to all to make a settlement; but Soto, as it was his object to find another treasure like that of Atabalipa, lord of Peru, would not be content to stay. The natives were asked if they had knowledge of any great lord further on, to which they answered that twelve days' travel thence was a province called Chiaha, subject to a chief of Coca.

The Governor then resolved, having rested his army, to go at once in quest of that country, taking with him a quantity of pearls which the cacique had given him; and being an inflexible man, and dry of word, who, although he liked to know what the others all thought and had to say, after he had once made up his mind he did not like to be opposed, and as he ever acted as he thought best, all bent to his will. So they turned north and continued forward until the fall, bending about through a quiet country.

* * *

She—For you I come severally as envoys from the chief men upon the road, bearing baskets of mulberries, a honey comb, marten skins and the hides of deer, and in calabashes the oil of walnuts and bear fat, drawn like olive oil, clear and of good taste.—

* * *

And what? Silences, death, rotting trees; insects "so that the sails were black with them and the men laughed, in spite of their forlorn condition, to see each others' faces so swollen and out of shape in the morning"; alligators, reptiles, a wild rose "like that of Spain, but with less leaves, because it grew in the woods." Sun, moon, stars, rain, heat, snow; water to the neck for days; blue-butterflies among the green palmetto leaves; grapes and others that grow on vines along the ground; plums of two sorts, vermillion and gray, of the form and size of walnuts, having three or four stones in them; wolves, deer, jackals, rabbits,—

* * *

She—To make you lonesome, ready for my caresses.

* * *

"Unprepared, we believed ourselves on a footing of peace, so much so that some of us, putting our arms in the luggage, had gone without any."

Then to battle! It is Mabilla, the staked town.

* * *

She—It is I, my son, Tuscaloosa; tall of person, muscular, lean and symmetrical. All is you; I, too, am all—one either side. Men, horses, hogs—all goes down in our fury. Now you feel me. Many times I shall drive you back from the palisades. But you come again. What shall I do to govern that lust—which if it break, I am the most defeated? Those in chains having set down their burdens near the fence, my people lift them on their backs and bring them into the town. Thus, to anger you, I have possession of all the baggage, the clothes, pearls and whatever else you have besides lost in the conflagration. I am strong! I shall possess you.

Oh, but I lie. I am weak. I fail. I cannot take you. What are they but savages—who know nothing? they wound you, they wound you, and every arrow has upon its barbs a kiss from my lips. There is one in your thigh, between the edges of the armor. Thrice you fall before reaching the gate! The fools, madmen. It is into my own flesh, fifty, a hundred times deeper than into yours. And me it kills—but you, though you cannot grip the saddle because of it, you fight standing all day in the stirrups. I divide myself to take you and it is myself that wounds myself, jealous even of your injuries, furious at that sweet touch of your flesh which my tools enjoy but I have—not yet. It is all you. The young Sylvestre fainting on the back track; Pedro Moron diving from the bridge with a shower of arrows about him —swimming to safety; Don Carlos, alighting to pull an arrow from his horse's breast at the stockade, receives one himself, in at the neck, out behind—and falls prostrate.

* * *

After heaviest losses in men, beasts and possessions they prevailed and of the Indians all were killed, two thousand five hundred more or less, all having fought with the utmost bravery and devotion.

The Governor now learning that Francisco Maldonado was waiting for him at the port of Ochuse, six days' travel distant to the southward, he caused Juan Ortiz to keep the news secret, that he might not be interrupted in his purpose; because the pearls he wished to send to Cuba for show, that their fame might raise the desire of coming to Florida, had been lost, and he feared that, hearing of him without seeing gold or silver or other thing of value from that land, it would come to have such a reputation that no one would be found willing to go there when men would be wanted; so he determined to send no news of himself until he should discover a rich country. So that to Tuscaloosa must be given credit, in effect, for a great victory.

On Sunday, the eighteenth of November, the sick being found to be getting well, the Governor again set out, moving west, to Chicaca, a small town of twenty houses, but well stocked with maize. There he determined to pass the second winter. The Indians, at peace, came frequently with turkeys and rabbits and other food—but secretly they were plotting other matters.

Suddenly, on a certain night, the air above the straw roofs is filled with flame. Sentries and the enemy arrive in the town together; a terrific confusion, four columns converging upon the same point. Indians moving about freely in the town, because of the peace that existed, had that night brought the fire in little pots, not to be seen. Everything is aflame. Men come out naked from their beds. The horses strive to free themselves, some succeed. The hogs squeal and perish. Soto and one other are all that are able to mount. He drives upon an Indian with his lance and transpierces him. His saddle girth, hastily adjusted, slips and he falls. Who will straighten out the confusion in the night? Who will gather the naked and disarmed soldiers, among the smoke, the flames, the noise? The Governor is up. He directs as best he can. But, by luck, the horses dashing about through the smoke spread terror to the savages who think it the cavalry forming for an attack. Alarmed they escape from the stockade.

* * *

She—Naked, armless, acold you draw off, in the morning, to Chicacilla, protecting yourself as best you can —there to retemper the swords and await what will happen. Some are reduced to straw mats for their only cover, lying now this way, now to the fire, keeping warm as they are able.

And for this your people begin to hate you. It is my work. But again I am defeated, your last thought shall be for their safety. Because you have found no gold, only increasing hardships; because of your obstinacy, unexplained, incredible to them—you will be compared meanly with far lesser spirits. It is their revenge, making you solitary—ready for my caresses.

And if, to survive, you yourself in the end turned native,
this victory is sweetest of all. Bitter the need that at Nilco
will cause that horrid slaughter: You already sick, in grave
danger, thinking of the men. Let them talk, my Indian: I
will console you. None but you, the wise, the brave, could
have answered.

* * *

At Chicacilla, the balance of the winter over, once more
they gathered their strength and again set out to the westward, beginning the third summer. There was a town
Quizquiz. Here, after struggling seven days through a
wilderness having many pondy places with thick forests,
they came out upon the Great River.

He went to look at the river: swift and very deep; the
water, flowing turbidly, bringing from above many trees
and much timber, driven onward by its force.

The next day the chief of that country arrived.

* * *

She—It is I.

* * *

Two hundred canoes filled with men having weapons.
They were painted with ochre, wearing great bunches of
white and other plumes of many colors, having feathered
shields in their hands, with which they sheltered the oars-
men on either side, the warriors standing erect from bow to
stern, holding bows and arrows. The barge in which the
chief came had an awning at the poop under which he sat;
and there, from under the canopy, where the chief man
was, the course was directed and orders issued to the rest.
All came down together, and arrived within a stone's throw
of the ravine, whence the chief said to the Governor, who
was walking along the river bank, with others who bore
him company, that he had come to visit, serve and obey
him. The Governor expressed his pleasure, and besought
him to land, that they might the better confer; but the
chief gave no reply, ordering three barges to draw near,

wherein were great quantity of fish, and loaves like bricks, made of pulp and plums, which Soto receiving, gave him thanks and again entreated him to land.

Making the gifts had been a pretext, to discover if any harm might be done; but finding the Governor and his people on their guard, the chief began to draw off from the shore, when the crossbowmen, who were in readiness, with loud cries shot at the Indians, and struck down five or six of them.

* * *

She—Well done, Spaniard! like an Indian. Witness then my answer:

* * *

They retired with great order, not one leaving the oar, even though the one next to him might have fallen, and covering themselves they withdrew. These were fine looking men, very large and well formed; and what with the awnings, the plumes, and the shields, the pennons, and the number of people in the fleet, it appeared like a famous armada of galleys.

During the thirty days that were passed there, four piraguas were built, into three of which one morning, three hours before daybreak, the Governor ordered twelve cavalry to enter, four in each, men in whom he had confidence that they would gain the land notwithstanding the natives and secure passage or die. So soon as they had come ashore the piraguas returned and when the sun was two hours high, the people had all got over. The distance was nearly half a league: a man standing on the shore could not be told whether he were a man or something else, from the far side.

* * *

She—Now you are over, you have straddled me, this is my middle. Left to right, the end is the same. But here in the center I am not defeated. Go wander. Aquixo, Casqui, Pacaha. Take what you will. Clothe your men, yourself you will never clothe as I clothe you, in my own way. They have suffered, they have gone nearly bare. At Pacaha I have provisioned them in advance.

* * *

Shawls, deer skins, lion and bear skins, and many cat skins were found. Numbers who had been a long time badly covered here clothed themselves. Of the shawls they made mantles and cassocks. Of the deer skins were made jerkins, shirts, stockings and shoes; and from the bear skins they made very good cloaks, such as no water could get through. They found shields of raw cowhide out of which armor was made for the horses.

* * *

She—Look, then, Soto, upon this transformed army.— Here forty days and at the end I am beside you once more. Where is she now, Doña Ysobel, your helpmate, years since, in Cuba?

* * *

The chief of Pacaha bestowed on him two of his sisters telling him that they were tokens of love, for his remembrance, to be his wives. The name of one was Macanoche, that of the other Mochila. They were symmetrical, tall and full; Macanoche bore a pleasant expression; in her manners and features appeared the lady, the other was robust.

* * *

She—Ride upon the belly of the waters, building your boats to carry all across. Calculate for the current; the boats move with a force not their own, up and down, sliding upon that female who communicates to them, across all else, herself. And still there is that which you have not sounded, under the boats, under the adventure—giving to all things the current, the wave, the onwash of my passion. So cross and have done with it, you are safe—and I am desolate. But you are mine and I will strip you naked—jealous of everything that touches you. Down, down to me—in and under and down, unbeaten, the white kernel, the flame—the flame burning under water, that I cannot quench.

I will cause it to be known that you are a brute. Now it is no sea-ringed island, now it is no city in a lake: Come, here is room for search and countersearch. Come, black-beard, tireless rider, with an arrow in the thigh. I wait for you—beyond the river. Follow me—if you can. Follow me, Señor, this is your country. I give it to you. Take it. Here are carriers for your burdens; here are girls for your beds; my best men for adversaries. You have beaten them all. My time is coming: you have seen how they defend their pali-sades for me; they have driven trees into the ground about their villages. They are men, tall, slim, full of strategies; they come against you naked, with their bows and arrows; they die at the paddles but none quivers. It is me they defend. I am for the brave, for the wise, for the victor. Watch yourself at the fords, at the porches of houses.

See how I have fled you, dashing into a lake there to freeze all night, coming forth at dawn, half drowned, my brows hidden in lily leaves. At the sight of your boats, at the breath of your name, the villages are left empty. Noth-ing can induce the chief to show himself. All have gone upstream to an island, carrying their goods with them. At the sight of your men in armor, terror strikes them; they plunge into the stream, pushing their possessions on little rafts, that escaping in the haste, float downstream. I have fled, a single man, among my own people but your hounds scenting me out have dragged me down.

* * *

Now it begins to change. The third winter past, at Ali-mamu, it is the fourth year.

At Alimamu, where they learned to catch rabbits with Indian snares, Juan Ortiz died, a loss the Governor greatly regretted; for, without an interpreter, not knowing whither he was traveling, Soto feared to enter the country, lest he might get lost. The death was so great a hindrance to our going, whether on discovery or out of the country, that to learn of the Indians what would have been rendered in four words, it now became necessary to have the whole day; and oftener than otherwise the very opposite was understood to what was asked; so that many times it happened the road traveled one day, or sometimes two or three days would have to be returned over, wandering up and down, lost in the thickets.

For four days marching was impossible because of the snow. When that ceased to fall, he traveled three days through a desert, a region so low, so full of lakes and bad passages, that at one time, for a whole day, the travel lay through water up to the knees at places, in others to the stirrups; and occasionally, for the distance of a few paces there was swimming. And he came to Tutelpinco, a town untenanted and found to be without maize, seated near a lake that flowed into the river with a great current.

* * *

She—Nearer, nearer.

* * *

Cayas, Quigaltam, Guachoya—thither the Governor determined to go in a few days to learn if the sea was near. He had not over three hundred efficient men, nor more than forty horses. Some of the beasts were lame, and useful only in making out a show of a troop of cavalry.

At Guachoya he sent Juan de Anasco with eight of the cavalry down the river to discover what population might be there and get what knowledge there was of the sea. He was gone eight days and stated, when he got back, that in all that time he could not travel more than fourteen or fifteen leagues, on account of the great bogs that came out of the river, the canebrakes and thick shrubs that were along the margin, and that he had found no inhabited spot.

The river, the river.

The Governor sank into a deep despondency at sight of the difficulties that presented themselves to his reaching the sea; and, what was worse, from the way in which the men and horses were diminishing in numbers, he could not sustain himself in the country without succor. Of that reflection he pined.

But before he took to his pallet, he sent a message to the cacique of Quigaltam to say that he was the child of the sun, and whence he came all obeyed him, rendering him tribute; that he besought him to value his friendship, and to come where he was. By the same Indians the chief replied:

"As to what you say of your being the child of the sun, if you will cause him to dry up the great river, I will believe you; as to the rest, it is not my custom to visit any one, but rather all, of whom I have ever heard, have come to visit me, to serve and obey me, and pay me tribute, either voluntarily or by force. If you desire to see me, come where I am; if for peace, I will receive you with especial good will; if for war, I will await you in my town; but neither for you nor for any man, will I set back one foot."

When the messenger returned the Governor was already low, being very ill of fevers. He grieved that he was not in a state to cross the river at once to see if he could not abate that pride; though the stream was already flowing very powerfully, was nearly half a league broad, sixteen fathoms deep, rushing by in a furious torrent, and on either shore were many Indians; nor was his power any longer so great that he might disregard advantages, relying on his strength alone.

Every day the Indians of Guachoya brought fish, until they came in such plenty that the town was covered with them.

Now the Governor feared to repair the palisades that they might not suppose he stood in awe of them; and, lest the Indians rise, he ordered the slaughter at Nilco, to strike dread into the rest.

Conscious that the hour approached in which he should depart this life, Soto commanded that all the king's officers should be called before him, the captains and principal personages, to whom he made a speech. He told them that he

was about to go into the presence of God, to give account
of all his past life; and since He had been pleased to take
him away at such a time, he, His most unworthy servant,
rendered Him hearty thanks. He confessed his deep obliga-
tions to them all, for their great qualities, their love and
loyalty to his person, well tried in suffering of hardship. He
begged that they would pray for him. He asked that they
would relieve him of the charge he had over them as well
as of the indebtedness he was under to them all, and to forgive him any wrongs they may have suffered at his hands.
To prevent any divisions that might arise, as to who should
command, he begged that they elect a principal person to
be governor, and being chosen, they would swear before
him to obey; that this would greatly satisfy him, abate
somewhat the pains he suffered, and moderate the anxiety
of leaving them in a country, they knew not where.

Baltasar de Gallegos responded in behalf of all, consoling
him with remarks on the shortness of the life of this world,
attended as it was by so many toils and afflictions, saying
that whom God earliest called away, He showed particular
favor; with many other things appropriate to such an occasion; and finally since it pleased the Almighty to take him
to Himself, amid the deep sorrow which they not unrea-
sonably felt, it was necessary and becoming in him, as in
them, to conform to the Divine Will; that as respected the
election of a governor, which he ordered, whomsoever his
Excellency should name to the command, him would they
obey. Thereupon the Governor nominated Luís de Moscosco
de Alvarado to be his captain-general; when by all those
present was he straightway chosen and sworn Governor.

The next day, the twenty-first of May, departed this life
the magnanimous, the virtuous, the intrepid captain, Don
Hernando de Soto, Governor of Cuba and Adelantado of
Florida. He was advanced by fortune, in the way she is
wont to lead others, that he might fall the greater depth; he
died in a land, and at a time, that could afford him little
comfort in his illness, when the danger of being no more

heard from stared his companions in the face, each one himself having need of sympathy, which was the cause why they neither gave him companionship nor visited him, as otherwise they would have done.

Some were glad.

It was decided to conceal what had happened, lest the Indians might venture on an attack when they should learn that he whom they feared was no longer opposed to them.

So soon as death had taken place, the body was put secretly in a house, where it remained three days: thence it was taken by night to the gate of the town and buried within. The Indians having seen him ill, finding him no longer, suspected the reason; and passing by where he lay, they observed the ground loose and looking about talked among themselves. This coming to the knowledge of Luís de Moscosco he ordered the corpse to be taken up at night, and among the shawls that enshrouded it having cast abundance of sand, it was taken out in a canoe and committed to the middle of the stream.

Down, down, this solitary sperm, down into the liquid, the formless, the insatiable belly of sleep; down among the fishes: there was one called bagre, the third part of which was head, with gills from end to end, and along the sides were great spines, like very sharp awls; there were some in the river that weighed from a hundred to a hundred and fifty pounds. There were some in the shape of barbel; another like bream, with the head of a hake, having a color between red and brown. There was likewise a kind called peel-fish, the snout a cubit in length, the upper lip being shaped like a shovel. Others were like a shad. There was one called pereo the Indians sometimes brought, the size of a hog and had rows of teeth above and below.

Luís de Moscosco ordered the property of the Governor to be sold at public cry. It consisted of two male and three female slaves, three horses, and seven hundred swine. From that time forward most of the people owned and raised hogs.

Sir Walter Raleigh

OF THE PURSUIT of beauty and the husk that remains, perversions and mistakes, while the true form escapes in the wind, sing O Muse; of Raleigh, beloved by majesty, plunging his lust into the body of a new world—and the deaths, misfortunes, counter coups, which swelled back to certify that ardor with defeat. Sing! and let the rumor of these things make the timid more timid and the brave desperate, careless of monuments which celebrate the subtle conversions of sense and let truth go unrecognized. Sing! and make known Raleigh, who would found colonies; his England became a mouthful of smoke sucked from the embers of a burnt weed. And if the nations, well founded on a million hindrances, taxes, laws and laws to annul laws must have a monument, let it be here implied: this undersong, this worm armed to gnaw away lies and to release—Raleigh: if it so please the immortal gods.

Sing of his wisdom, O Muse: The truth is that all nations, how remote soever, being all reasonable creatures, and enjoying one and the same imagination and fantasy, have devised, according to their means and materials, the same things.

They all have lighted on the invention of bows and arrows; all have targets and wooden swords, all have instruments to encourage them to fight, all that have corn beat it in mortars and make cakes, baking them upon slate stones; all devised laws without any grounds had from the scriptures or from Aristotle's Politick, whereby they are governed; all that dwell near their enemies impale their villages, to save themselves from surprise. Yea, besides the same inventions, all have the same natural impulsions; they follow nature in the choice of many wives; and there are among them which, out of a kind of wolfish ferocity, eat man's flesh; yea, most of them believe in a second life, and they are all of them idolators in one kind or another—

These things, still chewing, he chewed out. And as an atheist, with Marlow, they would have burned him. It was his style! To the sea, then! mixed with soundest sense—on selling cannon to one's enemies.

But through all else, O Muse, say that he penetrated to the Queen!

Sing! O Muse and say, he was too mad in love, too clear, too desperate for her to trust upon great councils. He was not England, as she was. She held him, but she was too shrewd a woman not to know she held him as a woman, she, the Queen; which left an element. Say that he was made and cracked by majesty, knew that devotion, tasted that wisdom and became too wise—and she all eyes and wit looking through until her man, her Raleigh became thin, light, a spirit. He was the whetter, the life giver through the Queen—but wounded cruelly. In this desperate condition, will-less, inspired, the tool of a woman, flaming, falling, being lifted up, robbed of himself to feed her, caught, dispatched, starting, held again, giving yet seeking round the circle for an outlet: this was, herself; but what, O Muse, of Raleigh, that proud man?

Say, first, he was the breath of the Queen—for a few years; say, too, that he had traveled much before he knew her, that he had seen the tropics and explored the Orinoco River for a hundred miles. Then say, O Muse, that now he saw himself afar, that he became—America! that he conceived a voyage from perfection to find—an England new again; to found a colony; the outward thrust, to seek. But it turned out to be a voyage on the body of his Queen: England, Elizabeth—Virginia!

He sent out colonists, she would not let him go himself; nothing succeeded. It was a venture in the crook of a lady's finger, pointing, then curving in. Virginia? It was the nail upon that finger. O Raleigh! nowhere, everywhere—and nothing. Declare, O Muse, impartially, how he had gone with the English fleet to strike at Spain and how she called him back—Sire, do you not know, you!? These women are my person. What have you dared to do? How have you dared, without my order, to possess yourself of what is mine? Marry this woman!

Sing, O Muse, with an easy voice, how she, Elizabeth, she England, she the Queen—deserted him; Raleigh for Leicester, Essex now for Raleigh; she Spencer whom he friended, she "The Faery Queen," she Guiana, she Virginia, she atheist, she "my dear friend Marlow," she rents, rewards, honors, influence, reputation, she "the fundamental laws of human knowledge," she prison, she tobacco, the introduction of potatoes to the Irish soil: It is the body of the Queen stirred by that plough—now all withdrawn.

O Muse, in that still pasture where you dwell amid the hardly noticed sounds of water falling and the little cries of crickets and small birds, sing of Virginia floating off: the broken chips of Raleigh: the Queen is dead.

O Virginia! who will gather you again as Raleigh had you gathered? science, wisdom, love, despair. O America, the deathplace of his son! It is Raleigh, anti-tropical. It is the cold north, flaring up in ice again.

What might he have known, what seen, O Muse?—Shoal water where we smelt so sweet and so strong a smell, as if we had been in the midst of some delicate garden; and keeping good watch and keeping but slack sail—we arrived upon the coast; a land so full of grapes as the very beating and surge of the sea overflow them, such plenty, as well there as in all places else, on the sand and on the green soil on the hills, as well as every little shrub, as also climbing towards the tops of high cedars, that in all the world I think a like abundance is not to be found. And from below the hill such a flock of cranes, mostly white, arose with such a cry as if an army of men had shouted all together.— He might have seen the brother of the king, Granganimo, with copper cap, whose wife, comely and bashful, might have come aboard the ship, her brows bound with white coral; or running out to meet them very cheerfully, at Roanoak, plucked off his socks and washed his feet in warm water. A people gentle, loving, faithful, void of all guile and treason. Earthen pots, large, white and sweet and wooden platters of sweet timber.

Sing, O Muse and say, there is a spirit that is seeking through America for Raleigh: in the earth, the air, the waters, up and down, for Raleigh, that lost man: seer who failed, planter who never planted, poet whose works are questioned, leader without command, favorite deposed— but one who yet gave title for his Queen, his England, to a coast he never saw but grazed alone with genius.

Question him in hell, O Muse, where he has gone, and when there is an answer, sing and make clear the reasons that he gave for that last blow. Why did he send his son into that tropic jungle and not go himself, upon so dangerous an errand? And when the boy had died why not die too? Why England again and force the new King to keep his promise and behead him?

Voyage of the Mayflower

THE PILGRIMS were seed of Tudor England's lusty blossoming. The flamboyant force of that zenith, spent, became in them hard and little. Among such as they its precarious wealth of petals sank safely within bounds to lie dreaming or floating off while the Restoration throve, a sweltering seclusion of the hothouse, surrounded by winter's cold.

In those little pips a nadir, sure as the sun, was reached, in which lay the character of beginnings in North America. As particles stripped of wealth, mortifying as they were mortified, "*predicateurs*," greatly suffering, greatly prepared to suffer, they were the perfect sprout for the savage continent God had driven them to. But Puritans, as they were called, if they were pure it was more since they had nothing in them of fulfillment than because of positive virtues.

By their very emptiness they were the fiercest element in the battle to establish a European life on the New World. The first to come as a group, of a desire sprung within themselves, they were the first American democracy—and it was they, in the end, who would succeed in making everything like themselves. No man led them; there was none. The leaders had failed long since for them at home—if there ever had been any—and those still at home were still more removed from them than ever. Stripped and little they came resting on no authority but the secret warmth of their tight-locked hearts. But, unhappily, never had they themselves nor has any one penetrated there to see what was contained. The emptiness about them was sufficient terror for them not to look further. The jargon of God, which they used, was their dialect by which they kept themselves surrounded as with a palisade. They pleaded weakness, they called continually for help (while working shrewdly with their own hands all the while), they asked protection—but the real help had been to make them small, small and several, several and each as a shell for his own "soul." And the soul? a memory (or a promise), a flower sheared away—nothing.

Theirs is the secret of fairy tales, the descent of the "soul" into picturesque smallness: children, dwarfs, elves; the diminutive desires of the lowly for—they scarcely know what. The "God" of the Pilgrims is redolent of these mysteries. All their fears, their helplessness, the uncertainty of their force—have the quality of such lore. The pathetic detail of the rough sailor who cursed the poor people and what happened to him is strongly in this mood. It shows also the collective sense of the destiny common to lowly people.

From the outset they had had trouble, then the account goes on:—"These troubles being blowne over, and now all being compacte together in one shipe, they put to sea again with a prosperous winde, which continued diverce days together, which was some incouragement unto them; yet according to ye usuall maner many were afflicted with sea sickness. And I may not omit here a spetial worke of God's providence. Ther was a proud and very profane younge man, one of ye seamen, of a lustie body, which made him the more hauty; he would allway be contemning ye poore people in their sickness, and cursing them dayly with greeous execrations, and did not let to tell them, that he hoped to cast halfe of them over board before they came to their journey's end, and to make merry with what they had; and if he were by any gently reproved he would curse and swear most bitterly. But it pleased God before they came halfe seas over, to smite this yong man with a greeveous disease, of which he dyed in a desperate maner, and so was himself ye first yt was throwne overboard. Thus his curses light on his owne head; and it was an astonishment to all his fellows for they noted it to be ye just hand of God upon him."

The dreadful and curious thing is that men, despoiled and having nothing, must long most for that which they have not and so, out of the intensity of their emptiness imagining they are full, deceive themselves and all the despoiled of the world into their sorry beliefs. It is the spirit that existing nowhere in them is forced into their dreams. The Pilgrims, they, the seed, instead of growing, looked black at the world and damning its perfections praised a zero in themselves. The inversion of a Gothic Calvin.

For the Puritans there had been a decline of which it was their miserable fate never to know, while they raised their holy incantations. These are not the great flower of the spirit. Purged by hard experience (worn bodies from which a white dove springs), they are not all soul as they and we have imagined. Bodily suffering was more an alleviation than otherwise, a distraction that kept them mercifully blinded. They were condemned to be without flower, to sow themselves basely that after them others might know the end. Each shrank from an imagination that would sever him from the rest.

And so they stressed the "spirit"—for what else could they do?—and this spirit *is* an earthly pride which they, prideless, referred to heaven and the next world. And for *this* we praise them, instead of for the one thing in them that was valuable: their tough littleness and weight of many to carry through the cold; not their brokenness but their projection of the great flower of which they were the seed.

The Pilgrims were mistaken not in what they did, because they went hard to work with their hands and heads, but in what they imagined for their warmth. It could not have been otherwise. But it is sordid that a rich world should follow apathetically after. Their misfortune has become a malfeasant ghost that dominates us all. It is they who must have invented the "soul," but the perversion is for this emptiness, this dream, this pale negative to usurp the place of that which really they were destined to continue.

This stress of the spirit against the flesh has produced a race incapable of flower. Upon that part of the earth they occupied true spirit dies because of the Puritans, except through vigorous revolt. They are the bane, not the staff. Their religious zeal, mistaken for a thrust up toward the sun, was a stroke in, in, in—not toward germination but the confinements of a tomb.

Everything attests their despoiled condition: the pitiful care for each one, the talk of the common wealth (common to all alike, so never the proud possession of any one) and the church—that secret inversion of loveliness; their lost position, itself, in the new land, the cold, disease, starvation —inexplicable, unavoided troubles; their committing themselves not to any plan but floating on the ocean as a seed to God—to the sea and the winds—trustful, in a leaky boat. It is the weakling in us all that finds this beautiful. So with the low condition of their words themselves, the bad spelling of their journal; treated with contempt by the least of those they had to do with, so contemned that no one would lend them money "so they were forst to selle of some provisions to stop this gape"; their continually expressed love of each other, "Beloved friends, sory we are that there should be occasion of writing at all unto you," etc.

"So they comited them selves to ye will of God and resolved to proceed. In sundrie of these storms the winds were so feirce and ye seas so high, as they could not beare a knote of saile, but were forced to hull, for diverce days together. And in one of them, as they thus lay at hull in a mighty storm, a lustie young man (called John Howland) coming upon some occasion above ye gratings, was, with a

seel of ye shipe thrown into ye sea: but it pleased God yt
he caught hold of ye topesaile halliards, which hung over
board, and ran out at great length: yet he held his hould
(though he was sundrie fadomes under water) till he was
hold up by ye same rope to ye brim of ye water, and then
with a boat hooke and other means got into ye shipe again,
and his life saved; and though he was something ill with it,
yet he lived many years after, and became a profitable
member both in church and comone wealth."

This passage is perfect: the one man of it, at sea, in the
merciful guardianship of God, (washed away, howbeit),
relying on his own hands and feet saves himself by force of
himself, is hauled back by others like himself; the minute
care for detail, the note of his subsequent illness, and yet,
the moral at the end.

And this moral? As with the deformed Aesop, morals are
the memory of success that no longer succeeds.

But the enjoyment of the lust, the hidden flower, they
martyrized as the spirit or the soul, has curious turns. Pri-
marily despoiled by providence; clinging with the doggedness of a northern race, cold, close and slow to that; they
become unfit, except where there exists the same sort of
stress which brought them into being; the hard, repressive
pioneer soil of the mind. They must have relied on vigorous hypocrisy to save them—which they did. But this they
could not revere.

If the "puritan" in them could have ended with their
entry into the New World and the subtle changes of
growth at once have started (See Cotton Mather's "Wonders of the Invisible World," the prefatory remarks),
everything would have been different, but the character of
the land was not favorable. They did try to land further
south.

In fear and without guidance, really lost in the world, it
is they alone who would later, at Salem, have strayed so far
—morbidly seeking the flame,—that terrifying unknown
image to which, like savages, they too offered sacrifices of

human flesh. It is just such emptiness, revulsion, terror in all ages, which in fire—a projection still of the truth—finds that which lost and desperate men have worshiped. And it is still to-day the Puritan who keeps his frightened grip upon the throat of the world lest it should prove him—empty.

Such would the New World become. Their strength made it, but why, why the perpetual error of remaining at that low point? It is that at which the soul, dying in them, not liberated by death, but dead—is sad.

The result of that brave setting out of the Pilgrims has been an atavism that thwarts and destroys. The agonized spirit, that has followed like an idiot with undeveloped brain, governs with its great muscles, babbling in a text of the dead years. Here souls perish miserably, or, escaping, are bent into grotesque designs of violence and despair. It is an added strength thrown to a continent already too powerful for men. One had not expected that this seed of England would come to impersonate, and to marry, the very primitive itself; to creep into the very intestines of the settlers and turn them against themselves, to befoul the New World.

It has become "the most lawless country in the civilized world," a panorama of murders, perversions, a terrific ungoverned strength, excusable only because of the horrid beauty of its great machines. To-day it is a generation of gross know-nothingism, of blackened churches where hymns groan like chants from stupefied jungles, a generation universally eager to barter permanent values (the hope of an aristocracy) in return for opportunist material advantages, a generation hating those whom it obeys.

What prevented the normal growth? Was it England, the northern strain, the soil they landed on? It was, of course, the whole weight of the wild continent that made their condition of mind advantageous, forcing it to reproduce its own likeness, and no more.

The Founding of Quebec

WHY CANNOT I sit here lovingly, quietly and simply thinking of that most delightful man, Champlain, without offending you? Samuel de Champlain, of Brouage, on the Bay of Biscaye, if you remember. His father was an admiral in the navy of Henry of Navarre. Here was a man. Here *is* a man after my own heart. Is it merely in a book? So am I then, merely in a book. You see? Here at least I find the thing I love. I mean here *is* the thing, accurately, my own world, the world in which I myself breathe and walk and live—against that which you present. No, no! I insist. We live in different worlds.

There is a place among the works of Machiavelli where he says that coming home at evening from the fields dusty and tired out he doffs his outdoor clothes, dresses himself for a new part and entering his study becomes a king. It is not too rare a feeling but at least I understand it. Not that I'm a great reader; I tire of books too easily. Can anything tire like a book? But to me this Champlain is the perfection of what we lack, here. And sometimes, you know, well—it's a godsend to read a book—about such as he.

Parkman says, "Champlain was a man all for the theme and purpose, nothing for himself." Good Lord, these historians! By that I understand the exact opposite of what is written: a man all for himself—but gently, with love, with patience, unwilling to endure the smallest fracture of his way of doing. He knew Champlain and followed Champlain in everything. See if I am not right.

At the time of which I speak he had already spent three

years in North America, penetrating as far as the location of the city he would found, trading, making maps, charting the coast and drawing colored pictures of everything. And now, in France, he is ready to make his real essay. To support his project he asks one favor only of the king, a monopoly of the fur trade for three years. Good! He gets Pont Gravé to sponsor him and, all in proper time, sets out with two vessels for New France, a country almost invented, one might say, out of his single brain.

First the sea. The two ships heading for Cape St. Lawrence had lost track of each other, Pont Gravé's, as it turned out later, being in the van. Then the northern coast. It is a new world this time sure enough: high mountains with little soil, rocks and sand covered with firs and birches, icy winds, hard currents and treacherous tides. But presently he arrived at the harbor of Tadoussac, their rendezvous, outside of which he anchored in a storm.

But what has happened? Where is Pont Gravé and the other ship? The New World presses on us all; there seems no end to it—and no beginning. So too with him. They see a ship's boat coming. So Pont Gravé has gained the harbor. Good. But there's a stranger in the skiff. A Basque. There's been trouble.

To me there is a world of pleasure in watching just that Frenchman, just Champlain, like no one else about him, watching, keeping the thing whole within him with amost a woman's tenderness—but such an energy for detail—a love of the exact detail—watching that little boat drawing nearer on that icy bay. This is the interest I see. It is this man. This —me; this American; a sort of radio distributor sending out sparks to us all.

Well, here's the boat. What's happened? Ah, Pont Gravé is here, of course. Well? There was a Basque ship in the bay before him, they refused to stop their trade in furs at the King's order. A short battle. Pont Gravé wounded. This Basque with us has come to make a truce. Champlain was "greatly annoyed," his records say, at such a beginning. Greatly annoyed! Isn't that a treasure?

Well, what? What to do? Well, what's first? To plant the colony this year, *this* year, you understand. Everything else —aside. To begin with, he must see Pont Gravé. He is hurt but will recover. The Basque is content to temporize. There is a truce. The carpenters are set to work and since the ships are too unwieldy for the river a small barque is soon completed. In this, not waiting for a second one, Champlain, the gentleman, the adventurer, the enthusiast, drawer of colored pictures—is ready to go and found the City of Quebec.

Is that weakness, not to have destroyed the Spaniard on the spot, or to have died himself? Yes. Drake would not have done it, nor would Raleigh. Columbus, yes. Yes, it was a kind of weakness I suppose—a thing priceless, miraculous in that age and in such a place. It is a pride as separate from the ordinary as—Well, these things are costly.

See what it entailed. For these things show in a man. And who cares so long as a man leads, leads? I mean here is a fine energy that penetrated Canada, the cold, the isolation, the savages, but the fineness of it is all personal. It is all a fire, a lost—something that the ship, the sailors, the very theme itself does not need. It disturbs, torments, undermines the way, it is a fine difficulty to success. But you shall see.

The river ascended, they arrive at the selected place. Here Quebec shall stand. But how carefully he has noted every island, every tree almost upon the way and how his imagination has run west and south and north with the stories of the Indians, surmising peoples, mountains, lakes, some day to be discovered, with the greatest accuracy. And what care he takes, what fastidious pains to establish beyond point of controversy the exact place where Jacques Cartier wintered formerly, that it was not where popular misconception had supposed but in another place—beyond the scientific possibility of a doubt. This is Champlain.

Do not mistake me though. This was a great adventurer, a tremendous energy, one of the foremost colonizers of our continent. He knew our North Atlantic coast from end to end, had been in Boston Harbor, noted the islands and what trees grew on them, had been at Plymouth—or where it should be—fifteen years before the Pilgrims. And, in addition, had left charts, maps, colored drawings, as I told you, that are priceless now.

You remember, he had left Pont Gravé recovering from his wound at Tadoussac and the Basque there with him; one watching the other; while he himself had gone up in the barque to the place selected for his city. Immediately he set the men to work, some digging a cellar, some sawing logs and making boards of them and some doing the construction. He speaks of their energy and good spirits, saying that with such a fine *ensemble* the supplies would soon be under cover. But now the second barque comes up the river with its support. What devil is it in this land? What special hell has had this country assigned to it as a province?

"I was in a garden that I was having prepared," he writes. In a garden! that's wonderful to me. He was in this garden when the pilot of the second barque came to him with a story—for his private ear. Champlain drew the fellow off into a little wood, and there he heard: From the very day of setting out from France, it seems, there had been one at least who'd planned to murder him. That's how Quebec was planted: from the first day. It is the genius of such men as Champlain to attract such dooms. A locksmith, one Jean de Val, was the chief culprit, but by this time almost the whole company had been subverted, only the unexpected arrival of the second barque having saved the Master from his death that night. One of the company had confessed.

Is it not clarity itself? The man absorbed in his work, eager, riding ahead of his plans—and fate dogging him behind.

But now he is awakened, what does he do? What? It is

too amusing! Mind you his life is threatened. He gets the pilot, his informer, to send the four chief felons two bottles of wine from the second barque, a gift, we'll say, from their friends, the Basques, and will they come to dinner at the barque that night?

They come, of course, and there he seizes them. What then? But first he has had a session with the man himself who first disclosed the plot. I can see that puzzled face. Why? Why? Why have they wished to kill him, him Champlain? He'd pardon every one, except those four, if he could learn the motive.

Nothing, except that they had imagined that by giving up the place into the hands of the Basques and Spaniards, they might all become rich, and that they did not want to return to France.

How's that for a simple answer? Think what Champlain must have thought at that, he bred on the sea, a Frenchman —probably nowhere so much at home as by himself, out of France, carrying his own head about prying curiously into the wilderness. And now that he had them handcuffed, those four, imagine what comes next. He took them personally down the river in the barque to Tadoussac and called a council: Pont Gravé, the Captain of the vessel, the surgeon, the mate and other sailors—and himself. Can you beat it?

They decided that to kill the one man Jean de Val would be sufficient, and necessary to intimidate the Spanish who were everywhere about. The other three should be returned to France for trial. So they strangled and hanged de Val and stuck his head upon a pike. To me the whole thing's marvelous—all through.

Then he, Champlain, returned up river, carefully took stock of the provisions which the knaves had badly wasted —and goes on with his city.

(His friend replies)

To hell with all that: collecting pictures for France—or

science—or art! What for the New World? No. I know
what you mean. A spirit of resignation. Literature. Books—
a library. Good night, then. That's not you. You!

It is why France never succeeded here. It is the Latin, or
Gaelic or Celtic sense of historic continuity. Let it go back,
Roman, Greek, Phoenician, Egyptian, Arab—Jew; let it go
back with roots in every culture of the world. Chinese. It is
the weakness of you French—planting a drop of your precious blood in outlandish veins, in the wilderness and
fancying that that addition makes them French—that by
this the wilderness is converted! civilized, a new link in the
chain. Never. Great as your desire may be.

Rebellion, savagery; a force to leap up and wrench you
from your hold and force you to be part of it; the place,
the absolute new without a law but the basic blood where
the savage becomes brother. That is generous. Open. A
break through.

Champlain couldn't. The place (that more vulgar men
sensed as the strength in their arms) was outraged, that is—
if you are right—and I think you are. These men struck at
him as an impertinence. He with his maps, for France, for
science, for civilization—his gentleness, his swoons. I say, it
is marvelous—if you want it, but as against a New World—
it is inconceivable.

It claims you, you! and you resign the office for the sake
of—history. Quite so, you say.

The land! don't you feel it? Doesn't it make you want to
go out and lift dead Indians tenderly from their graves, to
steal from them—as if it must be clinging even to their
corpses—some authenticity, that which—

Here not there.

The May-Pole at Merry Mount

A MOST CONFUSING THING in American History, as we read it, is the nearly universal lack of scale. This parochialism is helped by such balanced statement as A. C. Adams' preface to Thomas Morton's *The New English Canaan*—in which the incident of the May-pole at Merry Mount is related. Adams has compared that "vulgar royalist libertine," Morton, and the Puritans of the Plymouth Colony too closely. He has seen the time too near. He has accepted the mere chance presence of Morton in the neighborhood of Plymouth as the outstanding fact, letting his mind dwell upon that, trying one party against the other, as they quarreled in the flesh—till both are worn, in our eyes, to some unrecognizable, indifferent proportion. The description, "a vulgar royalist libertine, thrown by accident into the midst of a Puritan Community, an extremely reckless but highly amusing old debauchee and tippler," is not adequate to describe a man living under the circumstances that surrounded Morton; its tone might do for a London clubman but not a New World pioneer taking his chances in the wilderness. It lacks scale.

Adams' pretty scholar humor can be very annoying. "Had Morton lived in Virginia or even in the vicinity of New York," he says, "he would not have been noticed." What of it? He did *not* live in either Virginia or New York and he *was* noticed; so he was brought to write the *Canaan*, so he has come down to us and so we recognize him. Instead of quarreling with his luck, Adams should have given us a better picture. Not that one expects or should expect, in the preface to a book of slight importance, more than a simple exposition of the facts relating to it. But

Thomas Morton was unique in our history and since Adams does attempt an evaluation of his book it is a pity he did not realize that, in history, to preserve things of "little importance" may be more valuable—as it is more difficult and more the business of a writer—than to champion a winner. It is not so much good history to present Morton with sly amusement in mortal and unmannerly combat with his betters, as it would be to relieve him from that imposition of his time and seriously to show up that lightness, his essential character, which discloses the Puritans themselves as maimed, to their advantage, for survival, the converse of which—in a crooked way, perhaps, but in a way—Morton presented.

No use, merely because he lived that way, to join Morton with the Puritans; comment upon him and his book should be laid mainly elsewhere, upon the more general scene of the New World, in his relationship with its natives—to which the Puritans so violently objected. And they were dead right in that, Adams convinces us. Such a place as Morton kept at "Ma-re Mount," the yearly rendezvous of a rough and lawless class of men, selling liquor and firearms to the savages "was a terror unto them, who lived stragglingly, and were of no strength in any place;" and it was unfair of Morton—seeing how the Indians valued guns and liquor—to use them for barter when the other settlers were not permitted to do so. This was the practical side of the desire to rid the colony of this man. But since the whites were armed with guns and had liquor, was it in the eyes of history *wrong* for Morton to use them for his trade? Another side of Puritan disgust with this brazen fellow was the moral one of his consorting with the Indian girls. It was upon this count, not the first, that they chose finally to attack him.

> *Lasses in beaver coats come away*
> *Ye shall be welcome to us night and day.*

Some of the earlier writers on the New England Indians

have spoken of the modesty of the women; Wood, in his *Prospect*, for instance, and Josselyn, in the second of his "Two Voyages." "Morton however is significantly silent on this point, and the idea of female chastity in the Indian mind, in the rare cases where it existed at all, seems to have been of the vaguest possible description. Morton was not a man likely to be fastidious, and his reference to the 'lasses in beaver coats,' is suggestive." This is as near as Adams ever gets to a full statement of the facts.

In Parkman, "Jesuits in North America," (ch. iv) there is a very graphic account of the missionary Le Jeune's experience among the Algonquins, in which he describes the interior of a wigwam on a winter's evening. "Heated to suffocation, the sorcerer, in the closest possible approach to nudity, lay on his back, with his right knee planted upright and his left leg crossed on it, discoursing volubly to the company, who, on their part, listened in positions scarcely less remote from decency." Le Jeune says, "Les filles et les jeunes femmes sont à l'extérieur très honnestement couvertes, mais entre elles leurs discours sont puants, commes des cloaques."

Parkman says that "chastity in women was recognized as a virtue by many tribes." Of the New England Indians Williams remarks,—"Single fornications they count no sin, but after marriage they count it heinous for either of them to be false." Judging by an incident mentioned by Morton, however, adultery does not seem to have been looked upon as a very grave offense among the Indians of the vicinity in which he lived. "The colour of their eies being so generally black made a salvage, that had a young infant whose eies were gray, showed him to us, and said they were English mens eies; I tould the Father that his son was *nan weeteo*, which is a bastard; hee replied *tita cheshetue squaa*, which is, he could not tell, his wife might play the whore; and his childe the father desired might have an English name, because of the liteness of his eies, which the father had in admiration because of the novelty amongst their nation."

Strachey (Historie p. 65) says of the Virginians: "Their young women goe not shadowed (clothed) amongst their own companie, until they be nigh eleven or twelve returns of the leafe old, nor are they much ashamed thereof, and therefore would the before remembered Pocahuntas, a well featured, but wanton yong girle, Powhatan's daughter, sometymes resorting to our fort, of the age of eleven or twelve years, get the boyes forth with her into the market place, and make them wheele, falling on their hands, turning up their heels upwards, whome she would followe, and wheele so her self, naked as she was, all the fort over; but being over twelve years, they put on a kind of semecinctum lethern apron before their bellies, and are very shamefaced to be seen bare.

"—wantons before marriage and household drudges after, it is extremely questionable whether they had any conception of it" (i.e. female chastity). From conflicting reports from many sources the truth seems to be that the state of affairs with respect to this trait of female chastity was a matter largely of individual inclination. Some would be chaste and others wanton as the blood ruled them or the local fashion of the moment seemed to warrant. Were a wife too flagrantly adulterous no husband would want her; thus, the case would decide itself.

And so—"Morton's inclination to boisterous revelry culminated at last in that proceeding which scandalized the Plymouth elders and passed into history." Book III, Chapter 14, of *The New English Canaan* presents it as follows: "The Inhabitants of Pasonagessit having translated the name of their habitation from the ancient Salvage name to Ma-re Mount, and being resolved to have the new name confirmed for a memorial to after ages, did devise amongst themselves to have it performed in a solemn maner, with Revels and merriment after the old English custome; (they) prepared to sett up a Maypole upon the festivall day of Philip and Jacob (1627), and therefore brewed a barrell of excellent beare and provided a case of bottles, to be spent, with other good cheare, for all commers of that day. And because they would have it in compleat forme, they had prepared a song fitting to the time and present occasion. And upon May day they brought the Maypole to the place appointed, with drumes, gunnes, pistols and other fitting instruments, for the purpose; and there erected it with the help of Salvages, that came thether to see the manner of our Revels. A goodly pine tree of 80 foot longe was reared up, with a peare of buckshorns nayled one somewhat neare unto the top of it: where it stood, as a faire sea mark for directions how to finde out the way to mine Hoste of Ma-re Mount."

Bradford's account was very different—"They also set up a May-pole, drinking and dancing about it many days together, inviting the Indian women, for their consorts, dancing and frisking together, (like so many fairies, or furies rather) and worse practices. As if they had anew revived and celebrated the feasts of the Roman Goddes Flora, or the beastly practieses of the madd Bacchinalians. Morton likewise (to shew his poetrie) composed sundry rimes and verses, some tending to lasciviousnes, and others to the detraction and scandall of some persons, which he affixed to this idle or idoll Maypolle."

This gambol on the green brought matters to a head with a vengeance. Although, as Adams says, it would not have been sufficient in itself to have caused the Puritan Elders to take action had there not been the graver matter of the sale of firearms behind it—yet it was the direct cause of Miles Standish going with eight men to arrest Morton. He was taken, his plantation destroyed, after the good, round formula: "to please the Indians"—and he himself put in the stocks, where the Indians came to look at him very much in amazement to know what it was all about.

Morton was scandalously maltreated while in the care of his captors and, due to their failure to provide food, he nearly died on the vessel which transported him back to England for trial. But as Adams smilingly remarks, had it been later in our history and on a more westerly frontier, they would just have shot him. In England, an acquaintance of Ben Jonson and others at *The Mermaid*, Morton wrote

his book. It was no great literary feat. It is, in a great measure, trivial and obscure, but as a piece from American History it has its savor which Adams dulls rather than height-
ens—which is too bad.

It seems impossible for Adams to get clearly in mind
what Morton means when he expostulates—"this harmless
mirth by younge men (that lived in hope to have wifes
brought over to them, that would save them a laboure to
make a voyage to fetch any over) was much distasted by
the precise Separatists—those moles . . . But marriage and
hanging, (they say) comes by destiny and Scogan's choice,
tis better (than) none at all. He that played Proteus (with
the help of Priapus) put their noses out of joynt, as the Prov-
erb is—"

Or: as Scogan, (famous court buffoon attached to the
household of Edward IV) ordered to be hanged, but
allowed the privilege of choosing the tree, escaped hanging
by being unable to find a tree to his liking—trying many; so
Morton and his men, awaiting wives from England, escaped
marriage by varying (Proteus) among (Priapus) the Indian
girls they took to bed with them.

This in its simplicity the Puritans lacked spirit to explain.
But spiritless, thus without grounds on which to rest their
judgments of this world, fearing to touch its bounties, a
fissure takes place for the natural mouth—and everything's
perverse to them. Forced by Morton's peccadillo they
countered with fantastic violence—and some duplicity—
having the trade in beaver skins in view.

Then their own true perversions enter in; for "ignorance
of the law is no excuse." As Morton laid his hands, roughly
perhaps but lovingly, upon the flesh of his Indian consorts,
so the Puritans laid theirs with malice, with envy, insanely,
not only upon him, but also—one thing leading to another—
upon the unoffending Quakers.

Trustless of humane experience, not knowing what to
think, they went mad, lost all direction. Mather defends the
witchcraft persecutions.

Cotton Mather's Wonders of the Invisible World

I

ENCHANTMENTS ENCOUNTERED

I

It was as long ago, as the year 1637, that a Faithful Minister of the Church of *England*, whose name was Mr. *Edward Symons*, did in a Sermon afterwards printed, thus express himself: At New England now the Sun of Comfort begins to appear, and the glorious Day-Star to show itself;—*Sed Venient Annis Sæculæ Seris*, there will come Times in after Ages, when the *Clouds will overshadow and darken the Sky there*. Many now promise to themselves nothing but successive Happiness there, which for a time through God's Mercy they may enjoy; and I pray God, they may a long time; but in this World there is no Happiness perpetual. An *Observation*, or I had almost said an *Inspiration*, very dismally now verify'd upon us! It has been affirm'd by some who best knew *New England*, That the World will do New England a great piece of Injustice, if it acknowledge not a measure of Religion, Loyalty, Honesty and Industry, in the People there, beyond what is to be found with any other People for the number of them. When I did a few years ago, publish a Book, which mentioned a few memorable Witchcrafts, committed in this Country; the excellent *Baxter*, graced the second edition of that Book, with a kind Preface, wherein he sees cause to say, If any are scandalized, that New England, a place of as serious Piety, as any I can hear of, under Heaven, should be troubled so *much with Witches; I think, 'tis no wonder; Where will the Devil show most malice, but where he is hated, and hateth most;* and I hope, the Country will still deserve and answer the Charity so expressed by that Reverend man of God. Whosoever travels over this Wilderness, will see it richly bespangled with Evangelical Churches, whose Pastors are holy, able, and painful Overseers of their Flocks, lively Preachers, and vertuous Livers;... We are still so happy, that I suppose there is no Land in the Universe more free from the debauching, and the debasing Vices of Ungodliness. The Body of the People are hitherto so disposed, that *Swearing, Sabbath-breaking, Whoring, Drunkenness, and* the like, do not make a Gentleman, but a Monster, or a Goblin, in the vulgar Estimation. All this notwithstanding, we must humbly confess to our God, that we are miserably degenerated from the first Love of our Predecessors; however we boast ourselves a little, when Men would go to trample upon us, and we venture to say, *whereinsoever any is bold (we speak foolishly) we are bold also.* The first Planters of these Colonies were a chosen Generation of Men, who were first so pure, as to disrelish many things, which they thought wanted Reformation Elsewhere; and yet withal so peaceable, that they embraced a voluntary Exile in a squallid, horrid American Desart, rather than to live in Contentions with their Brethren. Those good Men imagined that they should leave their Posterity in a place, where they should never see the Inroads of Profanity, or Superstition: And a famous Person returning hence, could in a Sermon before the Parliament, profess, *I have now been seven Years in a Country, where I never saw one Man drunk, or heard one oath sworn, or beheld one Beggar in the Streets all the while.* Such great Persons as Budaeus, and others, who mistook Sir *Thomas More's* Utopia, for a Country really existent, and stirr'd up some Divines charitably to undertake a Voyage thither, might now have certainly found a Truth in their Mistake; *New England* was a true Utopia. But, alas, the Children and Servants of those old Planters must needs afford many, degenerate Plants, and there is now risen up a Number of People, otherwise inclined than our *Joshua's*, and the Elders that out-liv'd them. Those two things our holy Progenitors, and our happy Advantages make Omissions of Duty, and such Spiritual Disorders as the whole World abroad is overwhelmed with, to be as provoking in us, as the most flagitious Wickedness committed in other places; and the Ministers of God are accordingly severe in their Testimonies: But in short, those Interests of the Gospel, which were the Errand of our Fathers into these Ends of the Earth, have been too much neglected and postponed, and the Attainments of an handsome Education, have been too much undervalued, by Multitudes that have not fallen into Exorbitances of wickedness; and some, especially of our young Ones, when they have got abroad from under the Restraints here laid upon them, have become extravagantly and abominably Vicious. Hence 'tis, that the Happiness of *New England* has been but for a time, as it was foretold, and not for a long time, as has been desir'd for us. A Variety of Calamity has long follow'd this Plantation; and we have all the Reason imaginable to ascribe it unto the Rebuke of Heaven upon us for our manifold *Apostasies;* we make no right use of our Disasters: If we do not, *Remember whence we are fallen, and repent, and do the first Works.* But yet our Afflictions may come under a further Consideration with us: There is a further Cause of our Afflictions, whose due must be given him.

2

The *New Englanders* are a People of God settled in those, which were once the *Devil's* Territories; and it may easily be supposed that the *Devil* was exceedingly disturbed, when he perceived such a People here accomplishing the Promise of old made unto our Blessed Jesus, *That He should have the Utomost parts of the earth for his Possession.* There was not a greater Uproar among the *Ephesians,* when the Gospel was first brought among them, than there was among, *The Powers of the Air* (after whom those Ephesians walked) when first the *Silver Trumpets* of the Gospel here made the *Joyful* Sound. The Devil thus Irritated, immediately try'd all sorts of Methods to overturn this poor Plantation: and so much of the Church, as was *Fled into this Wilderness*, immediately found, *The Serpent cast out of his Mouth a Flood for the carrying of it away*. I believe, that never were more Satanical Devices used for the Unsetling of any People under the Sun, than what have been Employ'd for the Extirpation of the *Vine* which God has here *Planted, Casting out the Heathen, and preparing a Room before it, and causing it to take deep root, and fill the Land, so that it sent its Boughs unto the* Atlantic *Sea Eastward, and its Branches unto the* Connecticut *River Westward, and the Hills were covered with the shadow thereof*. But, All those Attempts of Hell, have hitherto been Abortive, many an *Ebenezer* has been Erected unto the Praise of God, by his Poor People here; and, *Having obtained Help from God, we continue to this Day*. Wherefore the Devil is now making one Attempt more upon us; an Attempt more Difficult, more Surprizing, more snarl'd with unintelligible Circumstances than any that we have Encountered; an Attempt so *Critical*, that if we get well through, we shall soon Enjoy *Halcyon* Days with all the *Vultures* of Hell *Trodden under our Feet*. He has wanted his *Incarnate Legions* to Persecute us, as the People of God have in the other Hemisphere been persecuted: he has therefore drawn forth his more *Spiritual* ones to make an attacque upon us. We have been advised by some Credible Christians yet alive, that a malefactor, accused of *Witchcraft* as well as *Murder*, and Executed in this place more than Forty Years ago, did then give Notice of, *An Horrible* PLOT *against the Country by* WITCHCRAFT, *and a Foundation of* WITCHCRAFT *then laid, which if it were not seasonably discovered, would probably Blow up, and pull down all the Churches in the Country*. And we have now with Horror seen the *Discovery* of such a *Witchcraft!* An Army of *Devils* is horribly broke in upon the place which is the *Center*, and after a sort, the *First-born* of our *English* Settlements: and the Houses of the Good People there are fill'd with the doleful Shrieks of their Children and Servants, Tormented by Invisible Hands, with Tortures altogether preternatural.

.   .   .   .

II

THE TRIAL OF BRIDGET BISHOP, ALIAS OLIVER, AT THE COURT OF OYER AND TERMINER, HELD AT SALEM, JUNE 2, 1692.

1. She was Indicted for Bewitching of several Persons in the Neighbourhood, the Indictment being drawn up, according to the *Form* in such Cases usual. And pleading, *Not Guilty*, there were brought in several persons, who had long undergone many kinds of Miseries, which were preternaturally inflicted, and generally ascribed unto an *horrible Witchcraft*. There was little occasion to prove the *Witchcraft*, it being evident and notorious to all beholders. Now to fix the *Witchcraft* on the Prisoner at the Bar, the first thing used was the Testimony of the *Bewitched;* whereof several testifi'd That the *Shape* of the Prisoner did oftentimes very grievously Pinch them, Choak them, Bite them, and afflict them; urging them to write their Names in a *Book,* which the said Spectre called *Ours*. One of them did further testifie, that it was the *Shape* of this Prisoner, with another, which one day took her from her wheel, and carrying her to the Riverside, threatened there to Drown her, if she did not Sign to the *Book* mentioned; which yet she refused. Others of them did also testifie, that the said *Shape* did in her Threats brag to them that she had been the Death of sundry Persons, then by her named; that she had *Ridden* a Man then likewise named. Another testifi'd, the

Apparition of *Ghosts* unto the Spectre of *Bishop*, crying out, *You Murdered us!* About the Truth whereof there was in the Matter of Fact but too much Suspicion.

2. It was testifi'd, That at the Examination of the Prisoner before the Magistrates, the Bewitched were extremely tortured. If she did but cast her Eyes on them, they were presently struck down; and this in such a manner as there could be no collusion in the Business. But upon the Touch of her Hand upon them, when they lay in their Swoons, they would immediately Revive; and not upon the Touch of any ones Else. Moreover, upon some Special Actions of her Body, as the shaking of her Head, or the turning of her Eyes, they presently and painfully fell into the like postures. And many of the like Accidents now fell out, while she was at the Bar, One at the same time testifying, That she said, *She could not be troubled to see the afflicted thus tormented.*

3. There was Testimony likewise brought in, that a Man Striking once at the place, where a bewitched person said, the *Shape* of this *Bishop* stood, the bewitched cried out, *That he had tore her Coat*, in the place then particularly specifi'd; and the Woman's Coat was found to be Torn in that very place.

4. One *Deliverance Hobbs*, who had confessed her being a Witch, was now tormented by the Spectres, for her Confession. And she now testifi'd, That this *Bishop* tempted her to Sign the *Book* again, and to deny what she had confess'd. She affirm'd, That it was the Shape of this Prisoner, which whipped her with Iron Rods, to compel her thereunto. And she affirmed, that this *Bishop* was at a General Meeting of the Witches, in a Field at *Salem*-Village, and there partook of a Diabolical Sacrament in Bread and Wine then administered.

5. To render it further unquestionable, that the Prisoner at the Bar, was the Person truly charged in THIS *Witchcraft* there were produced many Evidences of OTHER *Witchcrafts*, by her perpetrated. For Instance, *John Cook* testifi'd, That about five or six Years ago, one Morning, about Sun-Rise, he was in his Chamber assaulted by the *Shape* of this Prisoner; which look'd on him, grinn'd at him, and very much hurt him with a Blow on the Side of the Head; and that on the same day, about Noon, the same *Shape* walked in the Room where he was, and an Apple Strangely flew out of his Hand, into the Lap of his Mother, six or eight Foot from him.

6. *Samuel Gray* testifi'd, That about fourteen Years ago, he wak'd on a Night, and saw the Room where he lay full of Light; and that he then saw plainly a Woman between the Cradle, and the Bed-side, which look'd upon him. He rose, and it vanished; tho' he found the Doors all fast. Looking out at the Entry-door, he saw the same Woman in the same Garb again; and said, *In God's Name, what do you come for?* He went to Bed, and had the same Woman again assaulting him. The Child in the Cradle gave a great Screech, and the Woman disappeared. It was long before the Child could be quieted; and tho it pined away, and, after divers months, died in a sad condition. He knew not *Bishop*, nor her Name; but when he saw her after this, he knew by her Countenance, and Apparel, and all Circumstances, that it was the Apparition of this *Bishop*, which had thus troubled him.

7. *John Bly* and his Wife testifi'd, That he bought a sow of *Edward Bishop*, the Husband of the Prisoner; and was to pay the Price agreed, unto another person. This Prisoner being angry that she was hindred from figuring the Mony quarrell'd with *Bly*. Soon after which, the Sow was taken with strange Fits; Jumping, Leaping, and Knocking her

Head against the Fence; she seem'd Blind and Deaf, and would neither Eat nor be Suck'd. Whereupon a Neighbor said, she believed the Creature was *Over-looked;* and sundry other Circumstances concurred, which made the Deponents believe that *Bishop* had bewitched it.

8. *Richard Corvan* testifi'd, That Eight Years ago, he lay awake in his Bed, with a Light burning in the Room, he was annoy'd with the Apparition of this *Bishop*, and of two more that were Strangers to him, who came and oppressed him so, that he could neither stir himself, nor wake anyone else, and that he was the Night after, molested again in the like manner; the said *Bishop*, taking him by the Throat, and pulling him almost out of the Bed. His Kinsman offered for this cause to lodge with him; and that Night, as they were awake, discoursing together, this *Corvan* was once more visited by the Guests which had formerly been so troublesome; his Kinsman being at the same time struck speechless, and unable to move Hand or Foot. He had laid his Sword by him, which these unhappy Spectres did strive much to wrest from him; only he held too fast for them. He then grew able to call the People of his House; but altho' they heard him, yet they had not power to stir or speak; until at last, one of the People crying out, *What's the matter?* The Spectres all vanished.

9. *Samuel Shattock* testifi'd, That in the Year 1680, this *Bridget Bishop*, often came to his House upon such frivolous Errands, that they suspected she came indeed with a purpose of mischief. Presently, whereupon, his Eldest Child, which was of as promising Health and Sense, as any Child of its Age, began to droop exceedingly; and the oftener that *Bishop* came to the House, the worse grew the Child. As the Child would be standing at the Door, he would be thrown and bruised against the Stones, by an invisible Hand, and in like sort knock his Face against the sides of the House, and bruise it after a miserable manner. After-

wards this *Bishop* would bring him things to Dye, whereof he could not imagin any use; and when she paid him a piece of Mony, the Purse and Mony were unaccountably conveyed out of a lock'd Box, and never seen any more. The Child was immediately, hereupon, taken with terrible Fits, whereof his Friends thought he would have dyed; Indeed he did almost nothing but Cry and Sleep for several Months together; and at length his understanding was utterly taken away. Among other Symptoms of an Inchantment upon him, one was, That there was a Board in the Garden, whereon he would walk; and all the Invitations in the World could never fetch him off. About 17 or 18 years after, there came a Stranger to *Shattock's* House, who seeing the Child, said, *This poor Child is Bewitched; and you have a Neighbor living not far off, who is a Witch.* He added, *Your Neighbor has had a falling out with your Wife; and she said, in her Heart, your Wife is a proud Woman, and she would bring down her Pride in this Child.* He then remembered, that *Bishop* had parted from his Wife in muttering and menacing Terms, a little before the Child was taken Ill. The abovesaid Stranger would needs carry the bewitched Boy with him, to *Bishop's* House, on pretense of buying a pot of Cyder. The Woman entertained him in furious manner; and flew also upon the Boy, scratching his Face till the Blood came; and saying, *Thou Rogue, what dost thou bring this Fellow here to plague me?* Now it seems the Man said, before he went, That he would fetch Blood for *her.* Ever after the Boy was follow'd with grievous Fits, which the Doctors themselves generally ascribed unto *Witchcraft;* and wherein he would be thrown still into the *Fire* or the *Water,* if he were not constantly look'd after; and it was verily believed that *Bishop* was the cause of it.

10. *John Louder* testify'd, That upon some little Controversy with *Bishop* about her Fowls, going well to Bed, he did awake in the Night by Moonlight, and did see clearly

the likeness of this Woman grievously oppressing him; in which miserable condition she held him, unable to help himself, till near Day. He told *Bishop* of this; but she deny'd it, and threatened him very much. Quickly after this, being at home on a Lord's day, with the doors shut about him, he saw a black Pig approach him; at which, he going to kick, it vanished away. Immediately after, sitting down, he saw a black Thing jump in at the Window, and come to stand before him. The Body was like that of a Monkey, the Feet like a cocks, but the Face much like a Mans. He being so extremely affrighted, that he could not speak; this Monster spoke to him, and said, *I am a Messenger sent unto you, for I understand that you are in some Trouble of Mind, and if you will be ruled by me, you shall want for nothing in this World.* Whereupon he endeavoured to clap his Hands upon it; but he could feel no substance; and it jumped out of the Window again; but immediately came in by the Porch, tho' the Doors were shut, and said, *You had better take my Counsel!* He then struck at it with a Stick, but struck only the Ground-sel, and broke the Stick: The Arm with which he struck was presently Disenabled, and it vanished away. He presently went out at the Back-door, and spied this *Bishop* in her Orchard, going toward her House; but he had not power to set one foot forward unto her. Whereupon, returning into the House, he was immediately accosted by the Monster he had seen before; which Goblin was now going to fly at him; whereat he cry'd out, *The Whole Armour of God be between me and you!* So it sprang back, and flew over the Apple-tree; shaking many Apples off the Tree, in its flying over. At its leap, it flung Dirt with its Feet against the Stomach of the Man; whereon he was then struck Dumb, and so continued for three Days together. Upon the producing of this Testimony, *Bishop* deny'd that she knew this Deponent: Yet their two Orchards joined; and they had often had their little Quarrels for some years together.

11. *William Stacy* testify'd, That receiving Mony of this *Bishop*, for work done by him; he had gone but a matter of three Rods from her, and looking for his Mony, found it unaccountably gone from him. Sometime after, *Bishop* asked him, whether his Father would grind her Grist for her? He demanded why? She reply'd, *Because Folks count me a Witch*. He answered, *No question but he will grind it for you*. Being then gone about six Rods from her, with a small Load in his Cart, suddenly the Off wheel stump'd, and sunk down into an hole, upon plain Ground; so that the Deponent was forced to get help for the recovering of the Wheel: But stepping back to look for the hole, which might give him this Disaster, there was none at all to be found. Some time after, he was waked in the Night; but it seem'd as light as day; and he perfectly saw the shape of the *Bishop* in the Room, troubling of him; but upon her going out, all was dark again. He charg'd *Bishop* afterwards with it, and she deny'd it not; but was very angry. Quickly after, this Deponent having been threatened by *Bishop*, as he was in a dark Night going to the Barn, he was suddenly taken or lifted from the Ground, and thrown against a Stonewall: After that, he was again hoisted up and thrown down a Bank, at the end of his House. After this again, passing by this *Bishop*, his Horse with a small Load, striving to draw, all his Gears flew to pieces, and the Cart fell down; and this Deponent going then to lift a Bag of Corn, of about two Bushels, could not budge it with all his Might.

Many other Pranks of this *Bishop's* this Deponent was ready to testify. He also testify'd, That he verily believ'd the said *Bishop* was the Instrument of his Daughter *Priscilla's* Death; of which suspicion, pregnant Reasons were assigned.

12. To crown all, *John Bly* and *William Bly* testify'd, That being employ'd by *Bridget Bishop*, to help to take down the Cellar-wall of the old House wherein she

formerly lived, they did in holes of said old Wall, find several *Poppets*, made up of Rags and Hogs-bristles, with headless Pins in them, the Points being outward; whereof she could give no Account unto the Court, that was reasonable or tolerable.

13. One thing that made against the Prisoner was, her being evidently convicted of *gross Lying in the Court*, several times, while she was making her Plea; but besides this, a Jury of Women found a preternatural Teat upon her Body: But upon a second search, within 3 or 4 hours, there was no such thing to be seen. There was also an Account of other People whom this Woman had Afflicted; and there might have been many more, if they had been enquired for; but there was no need of them.

14. There was one very strange thing more, with which the Court was newly entertained. As this Woman was under a Guard, passing by the great and spacious Meeting-house of Salem, she gave a look towards the House: And immediately a *Daemon* invisibly entring the Meeting-house, tore down a part of it; so that tho' there was no Person to be seen there, yet the People, at the noise, running in, found a Board, which was strongly fastned with several Nails, transported unto another quarter of the House.

*   *   *

THE TRIAL OF SUSANNA MARTIN,
AT THE COURT OF OYER AND TERMINER
HELD BY ADJOURNMENT AT SALEM, JUNE 29, 1692.

1. Susanna Martin, pleading *Not Guilty* to the Indictment of *Witchcraft*, brought in against her, there were produced the Evidences of many Persons very sensibly and grievously Bewitched; who all complained of the Prisoner at the Bar, as the Person whom they believed the cause of their Miseries. And now, as well as in the other Trials, there

was an extraordinary Endeavour by Witchcrafts, with Cruel and frequent Fits, to hinder the poor Sufferers from giving in their Complaints, which the Court was forced with much Patience to obtain, by much waiting and watching for it.

2. There was now also an account given of what passed at her first Examination before the Magistrates. The Cast of her *Eye*, then striking the afflicted People to the Ground, whether they saw the Cast or no; there were these among other Passages between Magistrates and the Examinate.

Magistrate: Pray, what ails these People?

Martin: I don't know.

Magistrate: But what do you think ails them?

Martin: I don't desire to spend my Judgement upon it.

Magistrate: Don't you think they are bewitch'd?

Martin: No, I do not think they are.

Magistrate: Tell us your thought about them then.

Martin: No, my thoughts are my own, when they are in, but when they are out they are anothers. Their Master——

Magistrate: Their Master? Who do you think is their Master?

Martin: If they be dealing in the Black Art, you may know as well as I.

Magistrate: Well, what have you done towards this?

Martin: Nothing at all.

Magistrate: Why, 'tis you or your Appearance.

Martin: I cannot help it.

Magistrate: Is it not *your* Master? How comes your Appearance to hurt these?

Martin: How do I know? He that appeared in the shape of Samuel, a glorifie'd Saint, may appear in any ones Shape.

It was then also noted in her, as in others like her, that if the Afflicted went to approach her, they were flung down to the Ground. And, when she was asked the reason of it, she said, *I cannot tell; it may be, the Devil bears me more Malice than another.*

3. The Court accounted themselves, alarum'd by these Things, to enquire further into the Conversation of the Prisoner; and see what there might occur, to render these Accusations further credible. Whereupon *John Allen* of Salisbury, testify'd, That he refusing, because of the weakness of his Oxen, to Cart some Stones at the request of this Martin, she was displeased at it; and said, *It had been as good that he had; for his Oxen should never do him much more service.* Whereupon, this Deponent said, *Dost thou threaten me, thou old Witch? I'll throw thee in the Brook.* Which to avoid, she flew over the Bridge, and escaped. But as he was going home, one of his Oxen tired, so that he was forced to Unyoke him, that he might get him home. He then put his Oxen, with many more, upon *Salisbury* Beach, where Cattle did use to get *Flesh.* In a few days, all the Oxen upon the Beach were found by their Tracks, to have run unto the Mouth of *Merrimack-River,* and not returned; but the next day they were found come ashore upon *Plum Island.* They that sought them, used all imaginable gentleness, but they would still run away with a violence, that seemed wholly Diabolical, till they came near the Mouth of *Merrimack-River;* when they ran right into the Sea, swimming as far as they could be seen. One of them swam back again, with a swiftness, amazing to the Beholders, who stood ready to receive him, and help up his tired Carcass: But the Beast ran furiously up into the Island, and from thence, through the Marshes, up into *Newbury* Town, and so up into the Woods; and there after a while found near *Amesbury.* So that, of fourteen good Oxen, there was only this saved: The rest were all cast up, some in one place, and some in another, Drowned.

4. *John Atkinson* testifi'd, That he exchanged a Cow with a Son of *Susanna Martin*'s, whereat she muttered, and was unwilling he should have it. Going to receive this Cow,

tho' he Hamstring'd her, and Halter'd her, she, of a Tame Creature, grew so mad, that they could scarce get her along. She broke all the Ropes that were fastned unto her, and though she were ty'd fast unto a Tree, yet she made her escape, and gave them such further trouble, as they could ascribe to no cause but Witchcraft.

5. *Bernard Peache* testifi'd, That being in Bed, on the Lord'sday Night, he heard a scrabbling at the Window, whereat he then saw *Susanna Martin* come in, and jump down upon the Floor. She took hold of this Deponent's Feet, and drawing his Body up into an Heap, she lay upon him near Two Hours, in all which time he could neither speak nor stir. At length, when he could begin to move, he laid hold on her Hand, and pulling it up to his Mouth, he bit three of her Fingers, as he judged, unto the Bone. Whereupon she went from the Chamber, down the Stairs, out at the Door. This Deponent, thereupon called unto the People of the House, to advise them of what passed; and he himself did follow her. The People saw her not; but there being a Bucket at the Left-hand of the Door, there was a drop of Blood found upon it; and several more drops of Blood upon the Snow newly fallen abroad: There was likewise the print of her 2 Feet just without the Threshold; but no more sign of any Footing further off.

At another time this Deponent was desired by the Prisoner, to come unto an Husking of Corn, at her House; and she said, *If he did not come, it were better that he did!* He went not, but the Night following, *Susanna Martin*, as he judged, and another came towards him. One of them said, *Here he is!* but he having a Quarterstaff, made a Blow at them. The Roof of the Barn, broke his Blow; but following them to the Window, he made another Blow at them, and struck them down; yet they got up, and got out, and he saw no more of them.

About this time, there was a Rumour about the Town, that *Martin* had a Broken Head; but the Deponent could say nothing to that.

The said *Peache* also testifi'd, the Bewitching the Cattle to Death, upon Martin's Discontents.

6. *Robert Downer* testified, That this Prisoner being some Years ago prosecuted at Court for a Witch, he then said unto her, *He believed she was a Witch*. Whereat she being dissatisfied, said, *That some She Devil would shortly fetch him away!* which words were heard by others as well as himself. The Night following, as he lay in his Bed, there came in at the Window, the likeness of a Cat, which flew upon him, and fast hold of his Throat, lay on him a considerable while, and almost killed him. At length he remembered what *Susanna Martin* had threatened the Day before; and with much striving he cried out, *Avoid, thou She-Devil! In the Name of God the Father, the Son, and the Holy Ghost, Avoid!* Whereupon it left him, leap't on the Floor, and flew out at the Window.

And there also came in several Testimonies, that before ever *Downer* spoke a word of this Accident, *Susanna Martin* and her family had related, *How this Downer had been handled!*

7. *John Kembal* testified, that *Susanna Martin*, upon a causeless Disgust, had threatned him, about a Certain Cow of his, *That she would never do him any more Good:* and it came to pass accordingly. For soon after the Cow was found stark dead on the dry Ground, without any Distemper to be discerned upon her. Upon which he was followed with a strange Death upon more of his *Cattle*, whereof he lost in one Spring to, the value of Thirty Pounds. But the said *John Kembal* had a further Testimony to give in against the Prisoner which was truly abominable.

Being desirous to furnish himself with a Dog, he applied himself to buy one of this *Martin*, who had a Bitch with

Whelps in her House. But she was not letting him have his choice, he said, he would supply himself then at one *Blezdels*. Having mark'd a Puppy, which he lik'd at Blezdel's, he met *George Martin*, the Husband of the Prisoner, going by, who asked him, *Whether he would not have one of his Wife's Puppies?* and he answered, *No*. The same Day, one *Edmond Eliot*, being at *Martin's House*, heard *George Martin* relate, where this Kembal had been, and what he had said, whereupon *Susanna Martin* replied, *If I live, I'll give him Puppies enough!* Within a few days after, this *Kembal*, coming out of the Woods, there arose a little Black Cloud in the North West and *Kembal* immediately felt a force upon him, which made him not able to avoid running upon the stumps of Trees, that were before him, albeit he had a broad, plain Cart-way, before him; but tho' he had his *Ax* also on his Shoulder, to endanger him in his Falls, he could not forbear going out of his way to stumble over them. When he came below the Meeting House, there appeared unto him, a little thing like a *Puppy*, of a Darkish Colour; and it shot backwards and forwards between his Legs. He had the Courage to use all possible Endeavours of Cutting it with his Ax; but he could not Hit it: the Puppy gave a jump from him, and went, as to him it seem'd into the Ground. Going a little further, there appeared unto him a Black Puppy, somewhat bigger than the first, but as Black as a Cole. Its Motions were quicker than those of his Ax; it flew at his Belly, and away; then at his Throat; so, over his Shoulder one way, and then over his Shoulder another way. His Heart now began to fail him, and he thought the Dog would have tore his Throat out. But he recovered himself, and called upon God in his Distress; and naming the Name of JESUS CHRIST, it vanished away at once. The Deponent spoke not one Word of these Accidents, for fear of affrighting his Wife. But the next Morning, *Edmond Eliot*, going into *Martin's* House, this Woman asked him where *Kembal* was? He replied, *At home a Bed for ought he knew*. She returned, *They say, he was frighted last Night*.

Eliot asked, *With what?* She answered, *With Puppies.* Eliot asked, *Where she heard of it, for he had heard nothing of it?* She rejoined, *About the Town.* Altho' *Kembal* had mentioned the Matter to no Creature living.

8. *William Brown* testifi'd, That Heaven having blessed him with a most Pious and Prudent Wife, this Wife of his, one day met with *Susanna Martin*; but when she approach'd just unto her, *Martin* vanished out of sight, and left her extremely affrighted. After which time, the said *Martin* often appear'd unto her, giving her no little trouble; and when she did come, she was visited with Birds, that sorely peck'd and prick'd her; and sometimes, a Bunch, like a Pullet's Egg, would rise in her Throat, ready to choak her, till she cry'd out, *Witch, you shan't choak me!* While this good Woman was in this extremity, the Church appointed a Day of Prayer, on her behalf; whereupon her Trouble ceas'd; she saw not *Martin* as formerly; and the Church, instead of their Fast, gave Thanks for her Deliverance. But a considerable while after, she being Summoned to give in some Evidence at the Court, against this *Martin*, quickly thereupon, this *Martin* came behind her, while she was milking her Cow, and said unto her, *For thy defaming her at Court, I'll make thee the miserablest Creature in the World.* Soon after which, she fell into a strange kind of distemper, became horribly frantick and uncapable of any reasonable Action; the Physician declaring, that her Distemper was preternatural, and that some Devil had certainly bewitched her; and in that condition she now remained.

9. *Sarah Atkinson* testifi'd, That *Susanna Martin* came from *Amesbury* to their House at *Newbury*, in an extraordinary Season, when it was not fit for any to Travel. She came (as she said, unto Atkinson) all that long way on Foot. She brag'd and shew'd how dry she was; nor could it be perceived that so much as the Soles of her Shoes were wet. *Atkinson* was amazed at it; and professed, that she

should herself have been wet up to the knees, if she had then come so far; but Martin reply'd, *She scorn'd to be Drabbled!* It was noted, that this Testimony upon her Trial, cast her in a very singular Confusion.

10. *John Pressy* testify'd, That being one Evening very unaccountably Bewildered, near a Field of *Martins*, and several times, as one under an Enchantment, returning to the place he had left, at length he saw a marvellous Light, about the bigness of an Half-bushel, near two Rod, out of the way. He went, and struck it with a Stick, and laid it on with all his might. He gave it near forty blows; and felt it a palpable substance. But going from it, his Heels were struck up, and he was laid with his Back on the Ground, sliding, as he thought, into a Pit; from whence he recover'd by taking hold on the Bush; altho' afterwards he could find no such Pit in the place. Having, after his Recovery, gone five or six Rod, he saw *Susanna Martin* standing on his Left-hand, as the Light had done before; but they changed no words with one another. He could scarce find his House in his Return, but at length he got home extremely affrighted. The next day, it was upon Enquiry understood, that *Martin* was in a miserable condition by pains and hurts that were upon her.

It was further testify'd by this Deponent, That after he had given in some Evidence against *Susanna Martin*, many years ago, she gave him foul words about it; and said *He should never prosper more;* particularly, *That he should never have more than two Cows; that tho' he was never so likely to have more, yet he should never have them.* And that from that very day to this, namely twenty years together, he could never exceed that number; but some strange thing or other still prevented his having any more.

11. *Jervis Ring* testify'd, That about seven years ago, he was oftentimes and grievously oppressed in the Night, but saw not who troubled him; until at last he Lying perfectly

Awake, plainly saw *Susanna Martin* approach him. She came to him, and forceably bit him by the Finger; so that the Print of the bite is now, long after, to be seen upon him.

12. But besides all these Evidences, there was a most wonderful *Account* of one *Joseph Ring*, produced on this occasion.

This Man has been strangely carried about by Daemons, from one *Witch-meeting* to another, for near two years together; and for one quarter of this time, they have made him, and keep him Dumb, tho' he is now again able to speak. There was one T. H. who having, as 'tis judged, a design of engaging this *Joseph Ring* in a snare of Devillism, contrived a while, to bring this *Ring* two Shillings in Debt unto him.

Afterwards, this poor Man would be visited with unknown shapes, and this T. H. sometimes among them; which would force him away with them, unto unknown Places, where he saw Meetings, Feastings, Dancings; and after his return, wherein they hurried him along through the Air, he gave Demonstrations to the Neighbors, that he had indeed been so transported. When he was brought unto these hellish Meetings, one of the first Things they still did unto him, was to give him a knock on the Back, whereupon he was ever as if bound with Chains, uncapable of stirring out of the place, till they should release him. He related, that there often came to him a Man, who presented him a *Book*, whereto he would have him set his Hand; promising to him, that he should then have even what he would; and presenting him with all the delectable Things, Persons, and Places, that he could imagin. But he refusing to subscribe, the business would end with dreadful Shapes, Noises and Screeches, which almost scared him out of his Wits. Once with the Book, there was a Pen offered him, and an Ink-horn with Liquor in it, that seemed like Blood: But he never toucht it.

This Man did now affirm, That he saw the Prisoner at several of those hellish Rendezvouzes.

Note, this Woman was one of the most impudent, scurrilous, wicked Creatures in the World; and she did now throughout her whole Tryal, discover herself to be such an one. Yet when she was asked, what she had to say for her self? Her chief Plea was, *That she had lead a most virtuous and holy Life.*

III

CURIOSITIES

Having thus far done the Service imposed upon me; I will further pursue it, by relating a few of those Matchless Curiosities, with which the *Witchcraft* now upon us, has entertained us. All I shall Report Nothing but with Good Authority, and what I would invite all my Readers to examine, while 'tis yet Fresh and New, that if there be found any mistake, it may be as willingly Retracted, as it was unwillingly *Committed.*

I. THE FIRST CURIOSITIE

'Tis very Remarkable to see what an Impious and Impudent *imitation* of Divine Things, is Apishly affected by the Devil, in several of those matters, whereof the Confessions of our Witches, and the Afflictions of our *Sufferers* have informed us.

That Reverend and Excellent Person, Mr. *John Higginson*, in my Conversation with him, Once invited me to this Reflection; that the Indians which came from far to settle about *Mexico*, were in their Progress to that Settlement, under a Conduct of the *Devil*, very strangely Emulating what the Blessed God gave to Israel in the Wilderness.

Acosta, is our Author for it, that the Devil in their Idol 'Vitzlipultzli, governed that mighty Nation. He commanded them to leave their Country, promising to make them *Lords* over all the Provinces possessed by *Six* other Nations of Indians, and give them a Land abounding with all precious things. They went forth, carrying their Idol with them, in a Coffer of *Reeds*, supported by Four of their Principal Priests; with whom he still Discoursed in secret, Revealing to them the Successes, and Accidents of their way. He advised them, when to *March*, and where to Stay, and without his Commandment they moved not. The first thing they did, wherever they came, was to Erect a *Tabernacle*, for their false god; which they set always in the midst of their Camp, and they placed the *Ark* upon an *Alter*. When they, Tired with pains, talked of, *proceeding no further* in their Journey, than a certain pleasant Stage, whereto they were arrived, this Devil in one Night, horribly kill'd them that had started this Talk, by pulling out their Hearts. And so they passed on till they came to *Mexico*.

The Devil which *there* thus imitated what was in the Church of the *Old Testament*, now among *Us* would Imitate the Affairs of the Church in the *New*. The *Witches* do say, that they form themselves much after the manner of *Congregational Churches;* and that they have a *Baptism* and a *Supper*, and *Officers* among them, abominably Resembling those of our Lord.

But there are many more of these Bloody *Imitations*, if the Confessions of the *Witches* are to be Received; which I confess, ought to be but with very much Caution.

What is their stricking down with a fierce *Look?* What is their making of the Afflicted *Rise*, with a touch of their *Hand?* What is their Transportation thro' the *Air?* What is their Travelling *in Spirit*, while their Body is cast into a Trance? What is their Causing of *Cattle* to run mad and perish? What is their Entring their Names in a *Book?* What is their coming together from all parts, at the Sound of a *Trumpet?* What is their Appearing sometimes Cloathed with *Light* or *Fire* upon them? What is their Covering of themselves and their Instruments with *Invisibility?* But a Blasphemous Imitation of certain Things recorded about our Saviour or His Prophets, or the Saints in the Kingdom of God.

2. A SECOND CURIOSITIE

In all the *Witchcraft* which now Grievously Vexes us, I know not whether anything be more unaccountable, than the Trick which the Witches have to render themselves, and their Tools *Invisible*. *Witchcraft* seems to be the Skill of Applying the *Plastic Spirit* of the World, unto some unlawful purposes, by means of a Confederacy with *Evil Spirits*. Yet one would wonder how the *Evil Spirits* themselves can do some things; especially at *Invisibilizing* of the Grossest Bodies. I can tell the Name of an Ancient Author, who pretends to show the *way*, how a man may come to walk about *Invisible*, and I can tell the Name of another Ancient Author, who pretends to Explode that way. But I will not speak too plainly Lest I should unawares Poison some of my *Readers*, as the pious *Herningius* did one of his Pupils, when he only by way of Diversion recited a *Spell*, which, they had said, would cure Agues. This much I will say; The notion of procuring *Invisibility* by any *Natural Expedient*, yet known, is, I Believe, a meer PLINYISM; How far it may be obtained by a *Magical Sacrament*, is best known to the Dangerous Knaves that have try'd it. But our *Witches* do seem to have the knack; and this is one of the Things, that make me think, *Witchcraft* will not be fully understood, until the day when there shall not be one Witch in the World.

There are certain people very *Dogmatical* about these matters; but I'll give them only three Bones to pick.

First, One of our bewitched people, was cruelly assaulted by a *Spectre*, that, she said, ran at her with a *spindle:* tho' no body else in the Room, could see either the *Spectre* or the *spindle*. At last, in her miseries, giving a snatch at the

Spectre, she pull'd the spindle away, and it was no sooner got into her hand, but the other people then present, behold, that it was indeed a Real, Proper Iron *spindle*, belonging they knew to whom; which when they lock'd up very safe, it was nevertheless by *Demons* unaccountably stole away, to do further mischief.

Secondly, Another of our bewitched people, was haunted with a most abusive *spectre*, which came to her, she said, with a *sheet* about her. After she had undergone a deal of Teaze, from the Annoyance of the *Spectre*, she gave a violent snatch at the sheet, that was upon it; wherefrom she tore a corner, which in her hand immediately became *Visible* to a Roomful of Spectators; a palpable Corner of a Sheet. Her Father, who was now holding her, catch'd that he might keep what his Daughter had so strangely seized, but the unseen *Spectre* had like to have pull'd his hand off, by endeavoring to wrest it from him; however he still held it, and I suppose has it, still to show; it being but a few hours ago, namely about the beginning of this *October*, that this Accident happened; in the family of one *Pitman*, at *Manchester*.

Thirdly, A young man, delaying to procure Testimonials for his Parents, who being under confinement on suspicion of Witchcraft, required him to do that service for them, was quickly pursued with odd Inconveniences. But once above the Rest, an officer going to put his *Brand* on the Horns of some *Cows*, belonging to these people, which tho' he had seiz'd for some of their debts, yet he was willing to leave in their possession, for the subsistance of the poor Family; this young man help'd in holding the Cows to be thus branded. The three first *Cows* he held well enough: but when the *Brand* entered the Cow's Horn, exactly the like burning *Brand* was clap'd upon his own Thigh; where he has exposed the lasting marks of it, unto such as asked to see them.

Unriddle these Things, ... *Et Eris mihi Magnus Apollo.*

Père Sebastian Rasles

Picasso (turning to look back, with a smile), Braque (brown cotton), Gertrude Stein (opening the doors of a cabinet of MSS.), Tzara (grinning), André Germain (blocking the door), Van der Pyl (speaking of St. Cloud), Bob Chandler (prodding Marcel), Marcel (shouting), Salmon (in a corner) and my good friends Philip and Madam Soupault; the Prince of Dahomi, Clive Bell (dressed), Nancy, Sylvia, Clotilde, Sally, Kitty, Mina and her two lovely daughters; James and Norah Joyce (in a taxi at the Place de l'Étoile), McAlmon, Antheil, Bryher, H. D. and dear Ezra who took me to talk with Léger; and finally Adrienne Monnier—these were my six weeks in Paris. Adrienne is last since it was she who by her insistence brought me one of my best moments among those days of rushing about and talking and seeing, while my bronzed faculties strove to right themselves—among the scenes and fashions of this world where all the world comes, from time to time, to shed its nerves—after my brutalizing battle of twenty years to hear myself above the boilermakers in and about New York, where I had embarked so precariously upon my literary career.

I was, during that time, with antennae fully extended, but nothing came of it save an awakened realization within myself of that resistant core of nature upon which I had so long been driven for support. I felt myself with ardors not released but beaten back, in this center of old-world culture where everyone was tearing his own meat, *warily* conscious of a newcomer, but wholly without inquisitiveness—No wish to know; they were served. I saw exhibitions and sat at a few tables, here and there. "Gaîte" told us of her sailor lover whom she would marry *if* she found that he really came from a large city, as he said. Brancusi sat us by his fire, the sheep slept about us while by constant rubbing his fingers carved the neck of his staff. This was a relief but like a fairy tale. It was not easy for me to be drunk; I had only a few weeks during which to see. I enjoyed the ballets, Derain— But it was no more than a kind of quickened sullenness. Could I have shouted out in the midst of it, could I have loosed myself to embrace this turning, shouting, rustling, colored thing, my mind would have been relieved. I could not do it. Could I have been Nancy to imagine myself a kitten and fall from a tree. I could not. It infuriated my meanness. Was it not my vanity and impotence? We did this, we did that, we drank at the Ritz bar. What did I presume? These questions made me shy. Marcel knows New York, I said, I shall investigate his drunken leer.

Adrienne Monnier pointed to a box at the *Cigale*. Look, she said, how enheartening. You will see *that* now in Paris everywhere. Look! there is a member of the Chamber of Deputies, there is a lawyer, there is a man of science, there is Cocteau, a few beautiful women and two or three pederasts. Is it not cheering? It makes me believe again that we are taking hold. H. D. listened. Adrienne Monnier seemed to be inviting my mood. It was she who, during the dark days of the war, had written her invitation to us all to come borrow and buy books of her; to read. A delicious savor it gave to the dinner she served us to have her lock the kitchen door and remain alone with her secret task of preparing the chicken—*à la Adrienne Monnier*, in the purest tradition of the Parisian art. To eat, to drink; wines, the delicious flesh, the poets—all good things of the world—these we must learn again to enjoy. Had she not wished to do with books, she would have enjoyed most to be a butcher, to kill a pig, to hear it squeal, eeeeEEEE! Bryher's eyes snapped darkly. We looked at prints of Brueghel; the great fish, cut open, discharging from its slit belly other fish and each fish, slit in turn, discharging other smaller fish, and so on to the smallest. She laughed with glee. Secretly my heart beat high. Here was invitation. When you come again, she said, I shall take you to *le désert*. You must talk to Valéry Larbaud, she told me. He wants to see you. Why should I? I insist that you go.

Already from the pot of my brain the odors of foods cooking had begun to rise. This encouraged me to move. One afternoon I mounted a bus and let it drag me through the rain. Some laborers were taking their overcoats out of a kiosk to put them on; one of the younger of the men had a mirror between his hands which he kept holding before an old fellow who had to laugh, in spite of himself, but shyly, like an embarrassed boy, at his own silly face which he saw there. Who is this man Larbaud who has so little pride that he wishes to talk with me? The lump in my breast hardened and became like the Aztec calendar of stone which the priests buried because they couldn't smash it easily, but it was dug up intact later. At least, so I prided myself that I felt. But after a few moments, seeing the man himself, I was unexpectedly confused. He is a student, I am a block, I thought. I could see it at once: he knows far more of what is written of my world than I. But he is a student while I am—the brutal thing itself.

At the bottom of an alley which opened out into a court, as of a decayed cloister, was the doorway which bore the number upon the card in my hand. It was a small room, nearly filled by a great table. He excused himself a moment to accompany a lady to the bus. We sat and looked at each other. So it was a pleasure to be sitting in this small room, in this secluded court, with this man whose totem is the hippopotamus—slumped down in his chair, smiling and looking. He knew what I had attempted. Almost at once he began to speak out of my imagination. He presumed too much. I am not a student; presently he will ask me questions I cannot answer! He spoke of Bolivar (he was engaged with a treatise upon the great Venezuelan patriot and liberator) bringing four fat volumes from the Spanish history upon the subject, out of his bookcase for me to see, and piling them one upon the other. Frightened I began to heal nevertheless.—The English appraised the New World too meanly. It was to them a carcass from which to tear pieces for their belly's sake, a colony, a place to despise a little. They gave to it parsimoniously, in a slender Puritan fashion. But the Spaniard gave magnificently, with a generous sweep, wherever he was able. (This tallies with the bounty of the New World, I said to myself.) They sought to make it in truth a New Spain, to build fine cathedrals, to found universities, to establish great estates. For this I like them, he said. They came as from the King himself to transport nobility, learning, refinement thither in one move.—Valéry Larbaud seemed cultivating my intimate earth with his skillful hands, a gracious gesture (lost perhaps in its own shadows, I thought); here is one at least of this world, moving to meet that other which is straining for release under my confining ribs—not wishing so much to understand it as to taste, perhaps, its freshness—Its freshness!

—if it exist! (John Barrymore's "Hamlet" wins first night ovation in London.) A herd of proofs moved through my mind like stumbling buffalo; ornaments of woven moosehair! There *is* the Indian. We are none. Who are we? Degraded whites riding our fears to market where everything is by accident and only one thing sure: the fatter we get the duller we grow; only a simpering disgust (like a chicken with a broken neck, that aims where it cannot peck and pecks only where it cannot aim, which a hog-plenty everywhere prevents from starving to death) reveals any contact with a possible freshness—and that only by inversion. Shall I never bring a look to bear which is not tawdry? Recruits to Pavlova's corps de ballet, from Montclair and Sacramento, fillers-in. There are—so many things, there's Edison, there's—Must I make a choice between to scream like a locomotive or to speak not at all? If it be a day of delirious heat, leave your cool retreat, rush about to find a sufferer and carry ice to him. In the din we die—and rot into the magazines and newspapers—and books by the million—Books. We had mentioned books. We have no books, I said.

There you are wrong. Two or three are enough, to have shown a beginning. Have you not yourself proven that there is meat—

Yes (so he had read what I intended!), the early records —to try to find—something, a freshness; if it exist.

I said, It is an extraordinary phenomenon that Americans have lost the sense, being made up as we are, that what we are has its origin in what *the nation* in the past has been; that there is a source in AMERICA for everything we think or do; that morals affect the food and food the bone, and that, in fine, we have no conception at all of what is meant by moral, since we recognize no ground our own—and that this rudeness rests all upon the unstudied character of our beginnings; and that if we will not pay heed to our own affairs, we are nothing but an unconscious porkyard and oil-hole for those, more able, who will fasten themselves upon us. And that we have no defense, lacking intelligent investigation of the changes worked upon the early comers here, to the New World, the books, the records, no defense save brute isolation, prohibitions, walls, ships, fortresses—and all the asininities of ignorant fear that forbids us to protect a doubtful freedom by employing it. That unless everything that is, proclaim a ground on which it stand, it has no worth; and that what has been morally, aesthetically worth while in America has rested upon peculiar and discoverable ground. But they think they get it out of the air or the rivers, or from the Grand Banks or wherever it may be, instead of by word of mouth or from records contained for us in books—and that, aesthetically, morally we are deformed unless we read.

You mean such books as the *Magnalia* of Cotton Mather. What! Startled but thrilling with pleasure, I found that he had read the *Magnalia.* No. HE had read it. I had *seen* the book and brushed through its pages hunting for something I wished to verify. *Un grand prédicateur.* THIS in Paris. Tiresome, I said I had found him. Yes, he assented, but very strong, very real. (My French became inspired, it was like a fountain when it is first turned on in the spring and all the moss and rust and loosened mud and sand are flung up with the water—I could see grotesque shapes of my desire escaping from me—and I laughed to myself in my intense pleasure.)

He saw my pleasure and he likewise smiled. *Quelle rire omnivore d'herbes sousmarins!* He had read the *India Christiana* with its two silver trumpets crying, "a joyful sound." "The American savages were men Satan had whished away (via Asia) at the beginning sound of the two silver trumpets calling from the tabernacle, announcing the advent of the gospel."

It is the Puritan.—

By the strength of religion alone, they surmounted all difficulties in which science has degraded us again today; all things they explain, with clarity and distinction. It is firm, it is solid, it holds the understanding in its true position, not beneath the surface of the facts, where it will drown, but up, fearlessly into a clear air, like science at its best, in a certain few minds. For our taste, it is perhaps a little grotesque, this explanation—but firm. There is vigor there—and by that, a beauty.

True enough, I said, there is abundant vigor. But to them it was, America, "the seat of them that shall think an evil thought"; the savages were men lost in the devil's woods, miserable in their abandonment and more especially, damned. Fiery particles, the Puritans, I said, acquainting him with my rigid tenet, seeds of Elizabethan vigor, few against the wilderness. Their sureness which you praise is of their tight tied littleness which, firm as it was, infuriates me today. It is their littleness that explains their admirable courage, close to the miraculous. It was good when through that first December they were going about in small boats in Cape Cod Bay, through rain and cold, under attack, when save for the finding of corn buried in the sand, they might not have had seed for the spring planting. Going about from place to place, seeking a lodgment, drowned, frozen, awaking to the howls of savages, dawn and the attack, rushing to the boat for their arquebuses, arrows in their hanging coats, at the mercy of chance and the wind, they were themselves the corn I speak of. The things they did were of highest order, permitted only by lack of full knowledge, things which would have been terrifying to them beyond endurance had they not been *reduced* to bear them.

Their courage, had they been gifted with a full knowledge of the New World they had hit upon, could not have stood against the mass of the wilderness; it took the form, then, for the mysterious processes of their implantation here, of a doctrinaire religion, a form, that is to say, fixed— but small. For the great task God had destined them to perform, they were clipped in mind, stripped to the physical necessities. They could not afford to allow their senses to wander any more than they could allow a member of their company to wander from the precinct of the church, even from Boston to Casco Bay, FOR WORLDLY PROFIT. This their formula condemned. For that Hannah Swanton was *punished* by captivity and TEMPTATION among the Catholics in Quebec.—I mean, that this form, this FORM ITSELF, such a religion upon *our* lips, though it have an economic, biologic basis in truth, nevertheless it is bred of brutality, inhumanity, cruel amputations and that THIS is the sum of its moral effect. You speak of Mather's books—? Yes, they were the flower of that religion, that unreasonable thing, on which they prided themselves for its PURITY. That is, its rigid clarity, its *inhuman* clarity, its steel-like thrust from the heart of each isolate man straight into the tabernacle of Jehovah without embellishment or softening. Its firmness is its beauty, it seems austere but limpid. Its virtue is to make each man stand alone, surrounded by a density as of the Lord: a seed in its shell. The Kingdom of God; the Devil at fault fighting for souls; Christ the Divine sacrifice; the Bible the guide; the Church its apostle. There it is, concise, bare, PURE: blind to every contingency, mashing Indian, child and matron into one *safe* mold.

They must have closed all the world out. It was the enormity of their task that enforced it. Having in themselves nothing of curiosity, no wonder, for the New World—that is nothing official—they knew only to keep their eyes blinded, their tongues in orderly manner between their teeth, their ears stopped by the monotony of their hymns and their flesh covered in straight habits. Is there another place than America (which inherits this tradition) where a husband, after twenty years, knows of his wife's body not more than neck and ankles, and four children to attest to his fidelity; where books are written and read counselling women that upon marriage, should they allow themselves for one moment to *enjoy* their state, they lower themselves to the level of the whore? Such is the persistence of this abortion of the mind, this purity. These were the modes of a people, small in number, beset by dangers and in terror. They dared not think. If frightened by Indians or the supernatural, they shook and committed horrid atrocities in the name of their creed, the cost of emptiness. All that they saw they lived by but denied. And *this* is overlooked.

There was a book written at that time attacking them: *New England Judged by the Spirit of the Lord:* it contains a relation of the Quakers in New England, from the time of their first arrival there, in 1656, to the year 1660. Wherein their merciless whippings, chainings, finings, imprisonments, starvings, burnings in the hands, cuttings off of ears and putting to death, with other cruelties, inflicted upon the bodies of innocent men and women only for conscience' sake, are described. And a further relation of the Quakers' cruel and bloody suffering in New England, continued from 1660 to 1665, beginning with the sufferings of one William Leddra, whom they put to death. There is also an appendix attacking Cotton Mather.

Why does one not hear Americans speak more often of these important things?

Because the fools do not believe that they have sprung from anything: bone, thought and action. They will not see that what they are is growing on these roots. They will not look. They float without question. Their history is to them an enigma.

What superb beauty! As with all histories, it begins with giants—cruel, but enormous, who eat flesh. They were giants.

No, no. True they had their magnificent logic but it was microscopic in dimensions—against the flamboyant mass of savagery. This disproportion has no representation in the contemporary Puritan imagination. The Puritan, finding one thing like another in a world destined for blossom only in "Eternity," all soul, all "emptiness" then here, was precluded from SEEING the Indian. They never realized the Indian in the least save as an unformed PURITAN. The *immorality* of such a concept, the inhumanity, the brutalizing effect upon their own minds, on their SPIRITS—they never suspected.

And Mather, a flower in mail, inhuman——

—a bee that stabs a bear. Blind seeds, I said, filled with the baleful beauty of their religion: an IMMORAL source——

A *source* at any rate, immoral or moral, religion, a blinding fury for the most part. They were seeds, a fiery concentrate of great virtues—dwarfed; the genus indistinguishable in the egg. It is that hidden, unacknowledged bias (that they were Elizabethans) that IS their strength. It is that violent bias that as with mocking, hellish whips would drive them still to change, to grow. But the direction, the objective has been *lost* in the mass of the NEW.

Never could they have comprehended that it would be, that it WAS, black deceit for them to condemn Indian sins, while *they* cut the ground from under the Indian's feet without acknowledging so much as his existence. The immorality, I say, of such an attitude never becomes apparent to them. Or, yes, up to a certain point it does: they bought their land instead of frankly stealing it and set up palisades to mark the two parts from each other; they instituted courts—but in themselves they were like pebbles. To them it was as nothing to desecrate the chief's mother's grave, in the name of sanctity pulling up the stakes, to shock the spirit of native reverence. Yet it cannot be said it was the time. For there was a Frenchman further north, a Jesuit, of different understanding. There was a maggot in them. It was their beliefs.

This THING and its effects you will detect in Mather, in him a curious blend of learning and intolerance that's illustrated when he says, "there are, they say, two hundred thousand books in the library which Ptolemy erected at Alexandria: but it was the addition of the scriptures which made it a truly LEARNED library." The turn of the word "learned" is the image of their sophistry.

Puritans, we name them, but they were not so called because of moral qualities. They were not blessed with that name by virtue of a stern but just conception of the world. That is a misconception of the name. They were called Puritans from a stripped dogma of four noncorrosive links, they thought, a saving bond in their desolation and abandonment between themselves and God.

He smiled and begged me to distinguish in my mind between the rugged English pioneers and a theoretic dogma that clung to them unevenly, doubtful how much any of it was a part of any one of them. But that is it, I answered. That is exactly what I pretend to do, to separate it out, to isolate it. It is an immorality that IS America. Here it began. You see the cause. There was no ground to build on, with a ground all blossoming about them—under their noses. Their thesis is a possession of the incomplete—like senseless winds or waves or the fire itself. I wish to drag this THING out by itself to annihilate it. He answered, That one cannot do. Yes, I insisted, it MUST be done, you do not know America. There is a "puritanism"—of which you hear, of course, but you have never felt it stinking all about you—that has survived to us from the past. It is an atrocious thing, a kind of mermaid with a corpse for tail. Or it remains, a bad breath in the room. This THING, strange, inhuman, powerful, is like a relic of some died out tribe whose practices were revolting.——

But the relic will be beautiful, he answered, sometimes. I have enjoyed the books.

Against his view I continually protested. I cannot separate myself, I said, from this ghostly miasm. It grips me. I cannot merely talk of books, just of Mather as if he were some pearl.—I began to be impatient of my friend's cultured tolerance, the beauties he saw. I grant you, I said, the stench of their narrowing beliefs has been made to cling too closely to the men of that time, but the more reason then to lift it out, to hold it apart, to sacrifice *them* if necessary, in order to disentangle this "thing."

Very well, he assented, you are from that place. You are caught by a smell. It is good that you struggle to appreciate it. Proceed. Mather. *What* a force, still to interest you; it is admirable. But I find your interest "très théorique."

What! I cried. Wait a bit. These men are not the only ones of these times.

It is of books that we were speaking.

It is of books that I wish to tell you.

Then they live still, those books?

I could not assure him that they did, those books of Mather's. As books, no, I said to him. But what is in them lives and there hides, as in a lair from whence it sallies now and then to strike terror through the land.

And you would be the St. George? Are they then in such a bad state in America, in such a swamp? I thought——

As always, I answered him. This fiery breath, as of a dragon, is to us a living thing. Our resistance to the wilderness has been too strong. It has turned us anti-American, anti-literature. As a violent "puritanism" it breathes still. In these books is its seed. I cannot discuss Mather with you like that! I must grow angry. I must be disturbed. It lies in wait there to defeat a beginning to morality. Cotton Mather's books, to you an enchanting diversion, a curious study, to me they are a vessel that vomits up a thing that obsesses my quiet, that allows me no tranquillity, a broken, a maimed, a foul thing—that they tell me is sweet, PURE.

This interests me greatly because I see you brimming—you, yourself—with those three things of which you speak: a puritanical sense of order, a practical mysticism as of the Jesuits, and the sum all those qualities defeated in the savage men of your country by the first two. These three things I see still battling in your heart. This interests me greatly—and it pleases me still more that you show a taste for books. Does this indicate, I say to myself, a new force in your country? Are you today presenting me with a new spectacle, a man, no matter what his qualities may be, who has *begun* to reach a height but who still retains his warmth; that moment when all greatness is conceived. It is no more than a moment, it is the birth of a civilized interest in the world.

No, no, no, I cried. I speak only of sources. I wish only to disentangle the obscurities that oppress me, to track them to the root and to uproot them——

Continue, he said. Adding, with a smile, You wish to uproot history, like those young men of the Sorbonne.

No, I seek the support of history but I wish to understand it aright, to make it SHOW itself.

Continue, continue.

There was, to the north, another force, equal to the Puritans but of opposite character, the French Jesuits; two parties with the Indians between them, two sources opposite.

But first, can you enlighten me, he now broke in, what was in the middle? Who were these Indians of whom you speak? What sort of men were they? What were their qualities?

Good, I said, take Brookfield, then, scene of the famous massacre, in 1680. The history (which we do not know) says first the whites and natives lived peaceably in this lovely, fertile valley, side by side cultivating and breeding cattle. Only after repeated evidence to the Indian of perfidy on the part of the white man—that he intended "by peaceful methods" to take and hold the land—to supplant the Indian, did he *gradually* withdraw, *later* to strike, in fair battle, for his country. But even so, even granted, as a consequence of all this, that "King Philip" erred—if he did, it was war, open and above board on the Indians' part and according to their methods, fairly begun, fairly prosecuted —had it not been for white savagery, a determination to exterminate man, woman and child of the disaffected natives—and ended by a proper treaty. Terror killed more of King Philip's people than Puritan bullets. Shocking scenes took place. Indian women found lying naked on the ground, heads cut off and stuck on poles, a relentless lust for extermination of the "bad" savages—because they fought, believing the whites had, in time of peace, tricked them. It was true.

And there is the story of the capture of a group of French Indians under a Sachem Bommaseen who being brought to Boston, prisoners, asked that they might see an English Divine. Questioned as to what the French had taught them, the Indian replied, that the French had taught them that the Lord Jesus Christ was of the French nation; that his mother, the Virgin Mary, was a French lady; that they were the English who had murdered him; and that, whereas he rose from the dead, and ascended into heaven, all who would recommend themselves to his favor, must avenge him on the English as far as they could.

Told that this was not so, the Indians replied that if what the French taught them was false, what then had the English to offer them that was good in its place?

The minister knowing their custom to use much similitude in their talk, looked about for some agreeable object. His eye lit upon a tankard of drink which happened to be standing on the table. He said: Christ has given us a good religion which might be compared to the good drink in the cup on the table. If we take that good drink into our hearts it will do us good and preserve us from death. That God's Book, the Bible, is the cup. The French having the cup of good drink, put poison in it and had made the Indians drink poison liquor, by which they run mad and begin to kill the English.

It was plain that the English had not put poison in it for they had set the cup wide open and invited all men, for they had translated the Bible into the Indian language. But the French kept the cup shut fast, the Bible in an unknown tongue, the Latin, and so kept their hands on the eyes of the Indians when they put it to their mouths to drink.

At this the Indian asked for him to show what was the good drink in the cup and what the poison the French put into it.

He then stated to them distinctly the chief articles of the Christian religion, "with all the simplicity and sincerity of a Protestant"; adding upon each, "This is the good drink in the Lord's cup of life." He further demonstrated to them how the Papists had, "in their idolatrous papery," in some way or other depraved every one of these articles, with base ingredients of their own invention, adding upon each, This is the poison which the French have put into the cup.

You need confess your sins to none but God and none but God can forgive them, said the minister. To confess your sins to a priest and submit to penance enjoined by a priest—there is no need of all this ceremony. It is nothing but French poison, all of it.——

The Indians, in a rapture of admiration and surprise to

find one who had put them in the way of obtaining "pardon for their sins" without paying beaver skins for it, fell on their knees, and, taking the minister's hand in theirs, began to kiss it in an extreme show of affection. But he shook them off with marked dislike of their posture.

He would not suffer the contrite Indians to lay their hands upon him, as the Catholic fathers in the north had done, but drew back and told them to address themselves to God alone. Ah, very fine, you say. But it is very ugly—and it is *that* which has persisted: afraid to touch! But being forced to it every day by passion, by necessity—a devil of duplicity has taken possession of us.

You know, I asked him, do you not, how other means being denied them, the Puritans ran madly to OFFICIAL sexual excess—during the long winters? It was a common thing for men to have had as many as seven wives. Few had less than three. The women died under the stress of bearing children, they died like flies under the strains and accidents of childbirth PLUS the rigors of primitive labors: carrying water, wood, etc., lugging brats up and down.

Add to this the fury against unofficial sexual indulgence and the plight of the women, at least, is heavily shadowed. It is pleasant to think of the beginning decadence of the cruel régime when some years later at Groton, I think it was—the lady who unearthed the record lives in Chicago—the women had begun to put ribbons in their hitherto plain bonnets. The elders met in solemn conclave and forbade the practice but the women met in another church and as solemnly told the men, in a word, to hush! They continued to wear their ribbons. One young lady, of this time, went to her wedding upon a white horse and in a dress of scarlet satin with a purple velvet shoulder cloak over it, bless her unknown pride.

What a beautiful country where all these simple forces have so much weight and vitality—but you were speaking of the Indians.

Yes, but I shall tell you more of that along with the story

of "those terrible priests" to the north of whom the English were so afraid and whom they accused of all evil while they themselves practiced hypocrisy, bigotry, encroachment, fraud, violence and bloodshed. "When we fought we were driven back and when peace returned we multiplied."

There was Père Rasles, a spirit, rich, blossoming, generous, able to give and to receive, full of taste, a nose, a tongue, a laugh, enduring, self-forgetful in beneficence—a new spirit in the New World.

All that will be new in America will be anti-Puritan. It will be of another root. It will be more from the heart of Rasles, in the north. There the French priests, good and bad, had penetrated a border ground, Maine, disputed between the English to the south and the French in Canada. The Indians were caught between the two factions, Catholic and Protestant. The English were at the mouths of the rivers, as in the case of Hannah Swanton at Casco bay. Père Rasles was in the Interior, living with his "cher troupeau." It is from the *Lettres Édifiantes* that I am speaking.

Contrary to the English, Rasles recognized the New World. It stands out in all he says. It is a living flame compared to their dead ash.

But the Puritans were infuriated at the progress the Priests were making and cried out against "the true character of Catholic bigotry" about them and "the danger experienced by the first settlers of Maine from this spirit."

Rasles lived thirty-four years, October 13, 1689 to October 12, 1723, with his beloved savages, drawing their sweet like honey, TOUCHING them every day.

A Catholic, a Jesuit, he was of those by whom the head of logic is beautifully relegated to its place—in heaven. To mystery, rightly reasoned, logic is consigned. Thus we put that all aside. The Church remains. Relieved of dogmatic bitterness, the priest with a fresh mind could open eyes and heart to the New World.

Nothing shall be ignored. All shall be included. The world is parcel of the Church so that every leaf, every vein in every leaf, the throbbing of the temples is of that mysterious flower. Here is richness, here is color, here is form. Consigning his creed to a worldly flower in Rome whose perfume should draw all bees, Rasles labored to have them know that garden. Contrasted with the Protestant *acts*, dry and splitting, those of Père Rasles were striking in their tenderness, devotion, insight and detail of apprehension. This was luscious fruit. The deed was for humanity,—his passion held him a slave to the New World, he strove to sound its mettle.

He was a great MAN. Reading his letters, it is a river that brings sweet water to us. THIS is a moral source not reckoned with, peculiarly sensitive and daring in its close embrace of native things. His sensitive mind. For everything his fine sense, blossoming, thriving, opening, reviving—not shutting out—was tuned. He speaks of his struggles with their language, its peculiar beauties, "*je ne sais quoi d'énergique*," he cited its tempo, the form of its genius with gusto, with admiration, with generosity. Already the flower is turning up its petals. It is *this* to be *moral:* to be *positive*, to be peculiar, to be sure, generous, brave—TO MARRY, to *touch*—to *give* because one HAS, not because one has nothing. And to give to him who HAS, who will join, who will make, who will fertilize, who will be like you yourself: to create, to hybridize, to crosspollenize,—not to sterilize, to draw back, to fear, to dry up, to rot. It is the sun. In Rasles one feels THE INDIAN emerging from within the pod of his isolation from eastern undestanding, he is released AN INDIAN. He exists, he is—it is an AFFIRMATION, it is alive. Père Rasles, often suffering the tortures of the damned as the result of an early accident—fracture of both thighs, badly mended—lived with his village—alone, absorbed in them, LOST in them, swallowed, a hard yeast——

For his presentation of the Indian point of view toward the raids on the English settlements alone, his letters are invaluable. If the Puritans feared the savage—his admirable enthusiasm for their high merit as warriors is very beautiful.

"The way they make war, these people, renders a handful of their warriors more redoubtable than would be a corps of two or three thousand European soldiers." *During the war* they carried desolation to all the country inhabited by the English. It is an enthusiasm that possesses him. I care not for the injury.

And you want to make Americans see that, you want to make them comprehend this generous spirit, as you call it? Well, come to France and make us understand it.—He laughed.

(It is the quality of this impact upon the native phase that *is* the moral source I speak of, one of the sources that has shaped America and must be recognized.)

The Indians in Maine at that time were no more than a few thousand, the Abnaki tribe. Their life was hard. Sometimes they had little to eat, often, in certain seasons, nothing. The hardships that Hannah Swanton endured following her captivity, were little more than those of any Indian woman on the march. Speed, speed, or disaster. She must walk or die. So it was with them too. Walk, carry, fight or die. The wild world touched them, always, under their cloaks. She tells of her agony, under a heavy load; she crossed swamps on logs, stepping for an hour always from one to two feet from the ground. On this trip they had little to eat for days at a time. Once she had part of a turtle they had killed. Once an Indian gave her a piece of moose liver. Once, on an island in the river with her Indian mistress, she had hailed a passing canoe filled with squaws, who, seeing her condition, gave her a roast eel to feed upon. Whortleberries, roots, and acorns were her fare, "or fish if they could catch any." But this was the life of the savage. It was also his habit, his school. By it he grew round, he grew tough. The wounded were killed. To accept torture with equanimity was a proof of virtue. Skill and courage were revered.

These things Père Rasles accepted and shared, with

difficulty in some respects at first but in the end with admiration and enthusiasm. "*Ce qui me revolta le plus,*" etc.

A price sterling was offered by the English for his head; his village—two days march from Portland—was burned and the church along with it. He stuck staunchly to his tribe and they to him. Twice he was rescued from assassination by his followers, once there was a false alarm and already the braves were on their way to attack the English fort when the mistake and his safety were discovered. It is a new picture. *Vous jugerez sans doute, que c'est de la part de Messieurs les Anglais de notre voisinage, que j'ai le plus à craindre. Il est vrai que depuis longtemps ils ont conjuré ma porte; mais ni leur mauvaise volonté pour moi, ni la mort dont ils me ménacent ne pourront jamais me séparer de mon cher Troupeau. Je le récommande à vos saintes Prières.*

Once when the English would have captured him two of his young men came to the chapel-tent in the night and whisked him away. It was winter, they had not had time to provide themselves with sufficient provisions. It was several days to the village. The three suffered side by side. They ate the dog that was with them. Then they ate their sacks of *loup marins*, boiled at a fire, though Rasles had great trouble to swallow his share, *tripes des rocher, excréscences de bois*. They ate a certain sort of wood that was cooked and so made partly soft in the center,—as Hannah had found and eaten wild pusley at another season. Crossing a lake that had begun to thaw, their showshoes became water-logged. He himself sank up to the knees in the mushy ice. His companion on the right went in to his hips. Going to help each other all managed to flounder through. He was at their side——

These were his children. He tells of how they laughed at his early attempts at the language. Failing to catch certain gutturals at first, he pronounced but half the words. He speaks of the comparative beauty of the Huron tongue.

In the spring the fish come up the river solidly packed,

two feet deep—with flesh of the most delicious taste. They gather the fish, eat all they can and dry the rest—that serves them until the corn is ready to harvest. In the spring also, celebrating the Eucharist, Rasles saw the corn planted. In August this was ready to be plucked. When that was finished there must be other food.

For this it was the habit of the Indians to go to the sea-shore. It was always, says Rasles, the same formula. He knew what was about to happen. They would gather about their spiritual counselor and offer him a speech, saying that the corn was low, that the tribe must have food and that they begged him to come with them to the shore that they might not be deprived of his spiritual comfort while they were gone. Always he answered with the one word,—

Kekiberba (I am listening, my children).

When all cried together, *8ri8rie!* (We thank you). (Note, the figure 8 is used by Rasles in his alphabet of the Abnaki language to signify the unique guttural sound characteristic of the Indian dialects.) Then they would break camp. Leaving the church he had built, he would take up his altar of a pine board with him and all would set out upon the trail.

He complains to his Jesuit brothers that the reason he is not a more constant correspondent is that he never has a moment to himself among his duties to the tribe; not only must he carry on his religious duties but they demand that he comfort them when they are ill, he must bleed them, advise them, settle their disputes, and he must hear their confessions.

In the hallowed, tender light of Rasles' love for him, the Indian stands out strangely revealed as a child, a passionate friend, a resourceful man and—a genius in attack, another music than the single horror of his war-whoop terrifying the invader.

But we are used only to the English attitude bred of the Indian raid. This is FIXED in us without realization of the

EFFECT that such a story, such a tradition, entirely the product of the state of mind that it records, has had upon us and our feeling toward the country. We scarcely know that there can be EFFECTS—that anything has a *cause*. It is of *this* our moral fiber has been made up in the past—we do not know even that moral fiber HAS a quality that is caused by something, something almost pure tradition. It is of this our conception of the New World has been fabricated.

The English, with an eye upon Maine, did everything to detach Rasles from his children, knowing that he, by keeping them in the Catholic faith, kept them united to France. They offered them everything to kill him or to send him back to Quebec and to take one of their own ministers in his stead. No success.

About this time war between France and England was threatening. The English and the Indians being at peace the new Governor of Massachusetts, envoy of the King, sought an interview with the men of Rasles' tribe. The place appointed was an island a short distance off the coast. The English were there in a barque of war when the Indians, in canoes, arrived and drew their craft up on the beach. Rasles was with them, at *their* request, to advise them—though not once throughout the following proceedings did he take part.

All this occurred, I wish you to observe, *before* an act of war on either side. But the English came *armed with one of their Ministers*, for what purpose Rasles well knew, though upon sight of the Jesuit, the English preacher was kept strictly in the background.

As the Indians stepped from their canoes, Rasles was caught in the press and forced up the beach before them, in spite of himself, he says. The English, seeing him, were taken aback; but the Governor, advancing, greeted him and then prepared to address the savages.

He told them that before long it was expected that England and France would be at war. He pleaded with the

Indians to remain neutral should this war arrive. The Indians listened. Having heard his words, they drew off to talk among themselves before giving a reply—inadvertently leaving Rasles alone, facing the English at the head of the beach.

At this the English Governor, speaking to Rasles in private, asked him, should there be war, if he would send his savages against them.—*Je lui repondis,* says the Jesuit, *que mon réligion et mon caractère de Prètre, ne m'engageoint a ne leur donner que des conseils de paix.*—But suddenly while speaking, he saw himself surrounded by twenty young braves, who feared the English might attempt to do him an injury.

And now the tribe returned with their reply: Know that the Frenchman is my brother, we have the same prayer, he and I, and we live in the same cabin of two fires. If I see you come into the cabin near the fire of my brother, I watch you from my mat. If I see that you carry a hatchet, I would think, what does this Englishman want to do with that hatchet? I get up from my mat to consider what you will do. If he raise the hatchet to strike my brother, I will run to help him.

A short time after this, a French man-of-war came up the river to Quebec announcing that France and England had commenced hostilities. At once the two hundred and fifty of Rasles' men "killed the dogs" and prepared to take the war path. Kindling the traditional fire, they performed their wild dance and then, next morning, came to him for his blessing and advice. He says: I told them to remember their prayers and to do no cruelty, to kill no one save in the heat of battle and to treat humanely all those taken prisoners.—After that he thinks of them as soldiers.

Were England and France at it, what then exceptional that the savages should wish also to indulge themselves in battle? Rasles' measured pride of them, his unexpected candor, is most refreshing. Frontier villages will suffer from an enemy. If the English waste their time blaming the priests or setting the savages upon them, Rasles does not even think of such excuses. Instead he thinks of QUALITIES.

He speaks with enthusiasm of the Indian as a fighter. He outlines their mode of approach upon a doomed village.— When they have drawn near to the point of attack they say, twenty here, thirty there. To this party that village is given to be *eaten!* It is their term. (He speaks with appreciation of their term.) What relief here from the reverent duplicity of the English, with their surprise and horror that ever THEY should suffer. And still the Puritans would poke the heads of dead Indian women on poles outside their villages. "When we fight we are beaten, at peace we multiply." At whose expense? Did one expect the Indians *not* to be fighters? Not Rasles at any rate.

The war finished with the peace of Ryswick; the Indians, as soon as they heard of it, ceased to battle. The English sought a new parley and that peace also was concluded. But the English, to appease the savages, sought to rebuild the church at Norridgewock, which they had burned during hostilities, in the hope of getting Indians to work in Boston as laborers. Yet in secret, they tried without ceasing to kill the offending Jesuit.

He was killed by them at last—at the foot of his rude cross which he had erected in the center of his village— seeking to draw the fire of the enemy upon himself in order that the women and the children might escape—and they mangled him besides, leaving him disfigured and with his bones all crushed within him.

What a curious thing it is, this American religion which we have inherited so largely from the Puritans. I find, I said, so many sources traceable today. But Père Rasles was, of course, a good man. Let it be said that all he did was due to that, as Eliot was a good man on the other side. Let it be acknowledged that much the Puritans complained of in the Jesuits was justified. And let us say that much that Père Rasles might have said against the Puritan-English was also true.

So one thing cancels the other. A good man is a good man.

This leaves two things, two flaming doctrines. As contrasting influences, I said, in shaping the aesthetic and the moral fiber of the growing race they must be weighed (not for themselves) the Catholic and Protestant, the qualities each one has lent in forming our morale.—I think these early battles have a great importance for the student of today.

They are remote, he answered.

One should read the *Lettres Édifiantes*, I think one would understand better how much we are like the Indians and how nicely Catholicism fits us. What would Mather think today of Catholic Boston? It is inevitable, I said. THIS is America. If the Puritans have damned us with their abstinence, removal from the world, denial, slowly we are forced within ourselves upon an emptiness which cannot be supplied,—this IS the soul, according to their tenets. Lost in this (and its environments) as in a forest, I do believe the average American to be an Indian, but an Indian robbed of his world—unless we call machines a forest in themselves. I would be diverting to believe, if it were so, as I think it's proving, that despite its obvious benefits, such Protestantism, in America, would have Catholicism, as its consequence. This and the accumulation of great staying wealth.

From lack of touch, lack of belief. Steadily the individual loses caste, then the local government loses its authority; the head is more and more removed. Finally the center is reached—totally dehumanized, like a Protestant heaven. Everything is Federalized and all laws become prohibitive in essence.

Such, the trail of Puritanism, is the direct cause of the great growth of the Catholic Church with us today, this dehumanization. It offers to a headless mob a government and THAT is its appeal (to take immediately the place of that lost local one that used to touch), a government in opposition to the general evil of our civil one; that is at least humane against the other (morally) that's merely stupid.

Only the negro, with a keen necessity to find an equivalent, for the voodooism, the mystery of his African jungles, where one cannot see far, has been able to make a vital thing of our religion. For the rest of us the influence is degenerative. It is largely a persistence of the stasis of the early beliefs, together with their vigor.

If enamored of the gospel, the Puritans in a wild New World by that pure stare into the center of their souls excluded terrors each for himself, and so, in effect, blocked all ingress and all egress (in theory) to the tenderer humanities, the frailties in which beauty lives entangled, rendering their lives hard, unproductive of that openness which would have been to them as a flower to the stalk; so the Catholics to the north, equally lost, would achieve the same end of escape by the equivalent of a blow on the head at the start, that relieved them of responsibility. Thus stunned and benumbed to terror, the Church comes at least with gentleness to aid. So that they could approach the Indians who, if they were *lost*, still had their apt sensual touch which the Puritan occluded.

And so America is become the greatest proselytizing ground for the Catholic in the world today—in spite of everything. The difficulty, from lack of sensual application, removed from without by an authority that represents the mystery itself—leaves hands freed for embraces, a field where tenderness may move, love may awaken and (save by the one blocked door) a way is offered.

Certain it is that the New World suffered greatly from both Puritans and Catholics; but as Père Rasles touched it nearer than his southern neighbors, and as the ghost of Puritanism still binds us by its horrid walls, so, as a corollary, Catholicism gains in that it offers us ALLEVIATION from the dullness, the lack of touch incident upon the steady withdrawal of our liberty.

The Discovery of Kentucky

THERE WAS, thank God, a great voluptuary born to the American settlements against the niggardliness of the damming puritanical tradition; one who by the single logic of his passion, which he rested on the savage life about him, destroyed at its spring that spiritually withering plague. For this he has remained since buried in a miscolored legend and left for rotten. Far from dead, however, but full of a rich regenerative violence he remains, when his history will be carefully reported, for us who have come after to call upon him.

Kentucky, the great wilderness beyond the western edge of the world, "the dark and bloody ground" of coming years, seemed to the colonists along the eastern North-American seaboard as far away, nearly, and as difficult of approach as had the problematical world itself beyond the western ocean to the times prior to Columbus. "A country there was, of this none could doubt who thought at all; but whether land or water, mountain or plain, fertility or barrenness, preponderated; whether it was inhabited by men or beasts, or both or neither, they knew not." But if inhabited by men then it was the savage with whom the settlers had had long since experience sufficient to make them loth to pry further, for the moment, beyond the securing mountain barrier.

Clinging narrowly to their new foothold, dependent still on sailing vessels for a contact none too swift or certain with "home," the colonists looked with fear to the west. They worked hard and for the most part throve, suffering the material lacks of their exposed condition with intention. But they suffered also privations not even to be estimated, cramping and demeaning for a people used to a world less primitively rigorous. A spirit of insecurity calling upon thrift and self-denial remained their basic mood. Opposed to this lay the forbidden wealth of the Unknown.

Into such an atmosphere, more or less varied, more or less changed for better or worse in minds of different understanding, was born Daniel Boone, the foremost pioneer and frontiersman of his day. A man like none other about him Boone had for the life of his fellow settlers, high or low, no sympathy whatever. Was it his ancestry, full of a rural quietness from placid Dorset or the sober Quaker training of his early associations that bred the instinct in him, made him ready to take desperate chances with his mind for pleasure? Certainly he was not, as commonly believed, of that riff-raff of hunters and Indian killers among which destiny had thrown him—the man of border foray— a link between the savage and the settler.

His character was not this. Mild and simple hearted, steady, not impulsive in courage—bold and determined, but always rather inclined to defend than attack—he stood immensely above that wretched class of men who are so often the preliminaries of civilization. Boone deliberately chose the peace of solitude, rather than to mingle in the wild wranglings and disputings of the society around him— from whom it was ever his first thought to be escaping—or he would never have penetrated to those secret places where later his name became a talisman.

Three years the junior of George Washington, Boone was taken while still a child from his birthplace on the upper waters of the Schuylkill River near Philadelphia to the then comparatively wild country of western Pennsylvania. Here he grew up. Soon a hunter, even as a boy men stepped back to contemplate with more than ordinary wonder the fearlessness with which he faced the fiercer wild beasts that prowled around. It was the early evidence of his genius. At eighteen, with his love of the woods marked for good, and his disposition for solitude, taciturnity and a hunter's life determined, the family moved again this time from the rapidly settling country of Pennsylvania to the wild Yadkin, a river that takes its rise among the mountains that form the western boundary of North Carolina.

With his arrival on the Yadkin, Daniel Boone married a neighbor's daughter, Rebecca Bryan, and together the young couple left the world behind them. Boone at once traversed the Yadkin Valley at a point still more remote from the seaboard and nearer the mountain; here he placed his cabin. It was a true home to him. Its firelight shone in welcome to the rare stranger who found that riverside. But he was not to remain thus solitary! The lands along the Yadkin attracted the notice of other settlers, and Boone, at thirty, found the smoke of his cabin no longer the only one that floated in that air. These accessions of companionship, however, congenial to the greatest part of mankind, did not suit Boone. He soon became conscious that his time on the Yadkin was limited.

The fields for adventure lay within his reach. The mountains were to be crossed and a new and unexplored country, invested with every beauty, every danger, every incident that could amuse the imagination or quicken action, lay before him, the indefinite world of the future. Along the Clinch River and the Holston River hunting parties pursued their way. As they went, the mysteries of forest life grew more familiar. Boone learned even better than before that neither roof, nor house, nor bed was necessary to existence. There were, of course, many things to urge him on in his natural choice. It was the time just preceding the Revolution. The colonial system of taxation was iniquitous to the last degree; this the pioneer could not fathom and would not endure. Such things Boone solved most according to his nature by leaving them behind.

At this point Boone's life may be said really to begin. Facing his first great adventure Boone was now in his best years. His age was thirty-six. He is described by various writers as being five feet ten inches high, robust, clean limbed and athletic, fitted by his habit and temperament, and by his physique, for endurance—a bright eye, and a calm determination in his manner. In 1769, John Finley returned from a hunting trip beyond the mountain. He talked loud and long of the beauty and fertility of the country and Daniel Boone was soon eagerly a listener. It touched the great keynote of his character, and the hour and the man had come.

"It was on the first of May, in the year 1769, that I resigned my domestic happiness for a time and left my family and peaceful habitation on the Yadkin River in North Carolina, to wander through the wilderness of America, in quest of the country of Kentucky, in company with John Finley, John Stewart, Joseph Holden, James Monay, and William Cool. We proceeded successfully and after a long and fatiguing journey through a mountain wilderness, in a westward direction on the seventh day of June following, we found ourselves on Red River, where John Finley had formerly been trading with the Indians, and from the top of an eminence, saw with pleasure the beautiful level of Kentucky."

Thus opens the so-called autobiography, said to have been written down from Boone's dictation, late in his life by one John Filson. But the silly phrases and total disregard for what must have been the rude words of the old hunter serve only, for the most part, to make it a keen disappointment to the interested reader. But now, from everything that is said, all that Boone is known to have put through and willingly suffered during the next two years, there ensued a time of the most enchanting adventure for the still young explorer. For a time the party hunted and enjoyed the country, seeing buffalo "more frequent than I have seen cattle in the settlements, browsing on the leaves of the cane, or cropping the grass on those extensive prairies, . . . abundance of wild beasts of all sorts through this vast forest; and the numbers about the salt springs were amazing." Here the party practised hunting till the twenty-second day of December following.

"On this day John Stewart and I had a pleasant ramble; but fortune changed the scene in the close of it. We had passed through a great forest, Nature was here a series of wonders and a fund of delight, and we were diverted with innumerable animals presenting themselves prepetually to our view. In the decline of the day, near the Kentucky River, as we ascended the brow of a small hill, a number of Indians rushed out of a thick canebrake upon us and made us prisoners." Escaping later the two returned to their camp to find it plundered and the others of their party gone.

But now, by one of those determining chances which occur in all great careers Squire Boone, Daniel's brother, who with another adventurer had set out to get news of the original party if possible, came accidentally upon his brother's camp in the forest. It was a meeting of greatest importance and unbounded joy to Daniel Boone. For a short time there were now four together, but within a month, the man Stewart was killed by Indians while Squire Boone's companion, who had accompanied him upon his quest, either wandered off and was lost or returned by himself to the Colonies. Daniel and Squire were left alone.

"We were then in a dangerous and helpless situation, exposed daily to perils and death amongst the savages and wild beasts—not a white man in the country but ourselves. Thus situated many hundred miles from our families, in the howling wilderness, I believe few would have equally enjoyed the happiness we experienced. We continued not in a state of indolence but hunted every day, and prepared to defend ourselves against the winter's storms. We remained there undisturbed during the winter. . . . On the first day of May, following, my brother returned home to the settlement by himself, for a new recruit of horses and ammunition, leaving me by myself, without bread, salt or sugar, without company of my fellow creatures, or even a horse or a dog.

"I confess I never was under greater necessity of exercising philosophy and fortitude. A few days I passed uncomfortably: The idea of a beloved wife and family, and their anxiety upon the account of my absence, and exposed situation, made sensible impressions on my heart. A thousand dreadful apprehensions presented themselves to my view and had undoubtedly disposed me to melancholy if indulged. One day I undertook a tour through the country, and the diversity and beauty of nature I met with in this charming season expelled every gloom and vexatious thought. Not a breeze shook the most tremulous leaf. I had gained the summit of a commanding ridge, and looking around with astonishing delight, beheld the ample plain, the beauteous tracts below. All things were still; I kindled a fire near a fountain of sweet water and feasted on a loin of a buck which a few hours before I had killed. Night came and the earth seemed to gasp after the hovering moisture.——" But only impatience is kindled by the silly language of the asinine chronicler.

But when Filson goes on to declare Boone's loneliness "an uninterrupted scene of sylvan pleasures" it is a little too much to bear. Constant exposure to danger and death, a habitation which he states had been discovered by the savages, the necessity of such stratagems as the resort to the canebrake rather than to take the risk of being found in his cabin, have nothing of sylvan pleasures in them. Boone had too much strong sense to feel anything but patience amidst the scenes of his solitude. And yet, having sounded the depth of forest life, and having considered and weighed all it had to offer, he felt secure enough to brave the perils of an exploring tour. He saw the Ohio, and unquestionably, from the results of this excursion, strengthened his determination to establish himself in such a land of delight.

For three months he was alone. It was an ordeal through which few men could have passed. Certain it is that nothing but a passionate attachment of the most extraordinary intensity could have induced even him to undergo it. If there were perils there was a pleasure keener, which bade him stay on, even in solitude, while his day was lasting. Surely he must have known that it was the great ecstatic moment of his life's affirmation.

By instinct and from the first Boone had run past the difficulties encountered by his fellows in making the New World their own. As ecstasy cannot live without devotion and he who is not given to some earth of basic logic cannot enjoy, so Boone lived to enjoy ecstasy through his single devotion to the wilderness with which he was surrounded. The beauty of a lavish, primitive embrace in savage, wild beast and forest rising above the cramped life about him possessed him wholly. Passionate and thoroughly given he avoided the half logic of stealing from the immense profusion.

Some one must have taken the step. He took it. Not that he settled Kentucky or made a path to the west, not that he defended, suffered, hated and fled, but because of a descent to the ground of his desire was Boone's life important and does it remain still loaded with power,—power to strengthen every form of energy that would be voluptuous, passionate, possessive in that place which he opened. For the problem of the New World was, as every new comer soon found out, an awkward one, on all sides the same: how to replace from the wild land that which, at home, they had scarcely known the Old World meant to them; through difficulty and even brutal hardship to find a ground to take the place of England. They could not do it. They clung, one way or another, to the old, striving the while to pull off pieces to themselves from the fat of the new bounty.

Boone's genius was to recognize the difficulty as neither material nor political but one purely moral and aesthetic.

Filled with the wild beauty of the New World to over-brimming so long as he had what he desired, to bathe in, to explore always more deeply, to see, to feel, to touch—his instincts were contented. Sensing a limitless fortune which daring could make his own, he sought only with primal lust to grow close to it, to understand it and to be part of its mysterious movements—like an Indian. And among all the colonists, like an Indian, the ecstasy of complete possession of the new country was his alone. In Kentucky he would stand, a lineal descendant of Columbus on the beach at Santo Domingo, walking up and down with eager eyes while his men were gathering water.

With the sense of an Indian, Boone felt the wild beasts about him as a natural offering. Like a savage he knew that for such as he their destined lives were intended. As an Indian to the wild, without stint or tremor, he offered himself to his world, hunting, killing with a great appetite, taking the lives of the beasts into his quiet, murderous hands as they or their masters, the savages, might take his own, if they were able, without kindling his resentment; as naturally as his own gentle son, his beloved brother, his nearest companions were taken—without his rancor being lifted. Possessing a body at once powerful, compact and capable of tremendous activity and resistance when roused, a clear eye and a deadly aim, taciturn in his demeanor, symmetrical and instinctive in understanding, Boone stood for his race, the affirmation of that wild logic, which in times past had mastered another wilderness and now, renascent, would master this, to prove it potent.

There must be a new wedding. But he saw and only he saw the prototype of it all, the native savage. To Boone the Indian was his greatest master. Not for himself surely to be an Indian, though they eagerly sought to adopt him into their tribes, but the reverse: to be *himself* in a new world, Indianlike. If the land were to be possessed it must be as the Indian possessed it. Boone saw the truth of the Red Man, not an aberrant type, treacherous and anti-white to be feared and exterminated, but as a natural expression of the place, the Indian himself as "right," the flower of his world

Keen then was the defeat he tasted when, having returned safe to the Colonies after his first ecstatic sojourn, and when after long delay having undertaken to lead a party of forty settlers to the new country, his eldest son, among five others of his own age, was brutally murdered by the savages at the very outset. It was a crushing blow. Although Boone and others argued against it, the expedition turned back and with his sorrowing wife Boone once more took up his homestead on the Yadkin. And this is the mark of his personality, that even for this cruel stroke he held no illwill against the Red Men.

Disappointed in his early hopes and when through subsequent years of battle against the wild tribes, when through losses and trials of the severest order, he led at last in the establishment of the settlers about the fort and center of Boonesborough, he never wavered for a moment in his clear conception of the Indian as a natural part of a beloved condition, the New World, in which all lived together. Captured or escaping, outwitted by or outwitting the savages, he admired and defended them always, as, implacable and remorseless enemy to the Red Man that he proved, they admired and respected him to the end of his days.

You have bought the land, said an old Indian who acted for his tribe in the transaction which now made Kentucky over to the white man, but you will have trouble to settle it. It proved true. An old lady who had been in the forts was describing the scenes she had witnessed in those times of peril and adventure, and, among other things, remarked that during the first two years of her residence in Kentucky, the most comely sight she beheld, was seeing a young man die in his bed a natural death. She had been familiar with blood, and carnage, and death, but in all those cases the sufferers were the victims of the Indian tomahawk and scalping knife; and that on an occasion when a young man was taken sick and died, after the usual manner of nature, she and the rest of the women sat up all night, gazing upon him as an object of beauty.

It was against his own kind that Boone's lasting resentment was fixed, "those damned Yankees," who took from him, by the chicanery of the law and in his old age, every last acre of the then prosperous homestead he had at last won for himself after years of battle in the new country.

Confirmed in his distrust for his "own kind," in old age homeless and quite ruined, he must turn once more to his early loves, the savage and the wild. Once more a wanderer he struck out through Tennessee for "more elbowroom," determined to leave the young nation which he had helped to establish, definitely behind him. He headed for Spanish territory beyond the Mississippi where the Provincial Governor, having gotten wind of the old hunter's state of mind, was glad to offer him a large tract of land on which to settle. There he lived and died, past ninety, serving his traps as usual.

In the woods he would have an Indian for companion even out of preference to his own sons, and from these men, the Indians, he had the greatest reverence, enjoying always when afield with them the signal honor of disposing them in the order of the hunt.

Too late the American Congress did follow him with some slight recognition. But that was by then to him really a small matter. He had already that which he wanted: the woods and native companions whom, in a written statement of great interest, he defends against all detractors and in that defense establishes himself in clear words: the antagonist of those of his own blood whose alien strength he felt and detested, while his whole soul, with greatest devotion, was given to the New World which he adored and found, in its every expression, the land of heart's desire.

George Washington

WASHINGTON was, I think, the typically good man: take it as you please. But, of course, a remarkable one. No doubt at all he, personally, was ninety percent of the force which made of the American Revolution a successful issue. Know of what that force consisted, that is, the intimate character of its makeup, that is, Washington himself, and you will know practically all there is to understand about the beginnings of the American Republic. You will know, also, why a crown was offered this great hero at the conclusion of hostilities with Great Britain, and with what a hidden gesture he rejected the idea. Therein you have it: it was unthinkable—or he might have taken it.

Here was a man of tremendous vitality buried in a massive frame and under a rather stolid and untractable exterior which the ladies somewhat feared, I fancy. He must have looked well to them, from a distance, or say on horseback—but later it proved a little too powerful for comfort. And he wanted them too; violently. One can imagine him curiously alive to the need of dainty waistcoats, lace and kid gloves, in which to cover that dangerous rudeness which he must have felt about himself. His interest in dress at a certain period of his career is notorious.

The surveying contract which took him to Duquesne and the wilderness thereabouts was, however, the other side of the question. In this he must have breathed a more serious air which cannot but have penetrated to the deepest parts of his nature. The thing is, however, that in his case it did not, as it might have done, win him permanently to that kind of an existence. There was in his nature a profound spirit of resignation before life's rich proposals which disarmed him. As he expressed it, to him it was always his "vine and figtree," home and quiet, for which he longed. Stress he could endure but peace and regularity pleased him better. There must have been within him a great country whose wild paths he alone knew and explored in secret and at his leisure.

Patience, horses or a fine carriage, a widow to wive, a sloping lawn with a river at the bottom, a thriving field, an adopted daughter—that was as far as his desire wandered. All the rest he accepted as put upon him by chance.

Resistance was, I believe, his code. Encitadeled. A protector of the peace, or at least, keeper of the stillness within himself. He was too strong to want to evade anything. That's his reputation for truthtelling. It was a good scratching to him to take it on and see himself through. He knew he would come through.

There was his club life in Alexandria, as a Mason; the ten-mile ride to Church: it warmed him up a little.

As for rebellion, I don't think it entered his mind. I don't see how it could, except from the rear, subconsciously—that fire was too subdued in him. As commander of the troops he resisted, struck and drew back, struck and doubled on his tracks and struck and struck again, then rested.

He couldn't give in. He couldn't give in without such a ruffling within himself that he had no choice but to continue. That's the secret of Valley Forge and the valor and patience of his battle, as great as the other, against an aimless, wavering Congress at Philadelphia. He couldn't give in. I believe he would have gone out and battled it alone if he had felt his army wasted from under him or even left the country. Or else—

Well, there is the night he wandered off alone near Morristown, I think, off toward the British lines on horseback, impatient of warning—to air himself, so to speak, under the stars. Something angry was stirred there.

But seven days in the week it was for him: resist, be prudent, be calm—with a mad hell inside that might rise, might one day do something perhaps brilliant, perhaps joyously abandoned—but not to be thought of.

Such men suffering thus a political conversion of their emotions are, I suppose, always the noteworthy among us. Battle to them must be the expression of that something in themselves which they fear. Washington's calmness of demeanor and characteristics as a military leader were of that cloth.

Some girl at Princeton, was it? had some joke with him about a slipper at a dance. He was full of it. And there was the obscene anecdote he told that night in the boat crossing the Delaware.

But apparently the one man who got it full, who saw him really roused was General Lee—the one who wanted to replace him in command. That was all right. Washington could understand that and forgive it in another. He forgave Lee and restored him to his division with full trust after his return from capture by the British. But when, subsequently, Lee, in direct disobedience of orders, forgetting his position and risking his own whim on an important decision before Monmouth, lost the chance for an important victory —that was different. Immediately after, Washington met him by chance at a country cross road and Lee got it.

It is said no man, before or after, saw Washington in such a rage. This sort of thing Lee had done, he, Washington, knew from top to bottom. It was the firmly held part of himself which had broken loose—in another. Should he, Washington, stop that resistance in himself, what would happen?

No use to ask that now. Here it was: disaster. To Lee then in a fury, he opened the gates of his soul and Lee saw such hell fire that it was the end of him—retired muttering and half silly to his farm in Virginia where he stayed.

The presidency could not have meant anything to Washington. I think he spoke the candid truth about it when he said he neither desired it nor sought it. He merely did his duty. He did it with wisdom since he couldn't do it any other way. He wasn't enough interested to be scheming. Resist and protect: that was the gist of most that he said. Don't go looking for trouble. Stay home. In his very face, even, it was said in Congress he had turned monster under the name of prudence: "a sort of non-describable chameleon-colored thing called prudence." Alexander Hamilton, a type that needed power, found all this quite to his liking. Washington let him do. He wanted to get back to Mt. Vernon.

America has a special destiny for such men, I suppose, great wench lovers—there is the letter from Jefferson attesting it in the case of Washington, if that were needed—terrible leaders they might make if one could release them. It seems a loss not compensated for by the tawdry stuff bred after them—in place of a splendor, too rare. They are a kind of American swan song, each one.

The whole crawling mass gnaws on them—hates them. He was hated, don't imagine he was not. The minute he had secured their dung heap for them—he had to take their dirt in the face.

From deep within, you may count upon it, came those final words when, his head in a friend's lap, he said with difficulty: "Doctor, I am dying, and have been dying for a long time,..." adding to reassure them, "but I am not afraid to die."

He is the typical sacrifice to the mob—in a great many ways thoroughly disappointing.

Poor Richard

Information to Those Who Would Remove to America:

MANY PERSONS in Europe having by letters expressed to the writer of this, who is well acquainted with North America, their desire of transporting and establishing themselves in that country, but who appear to have formed, through ignorance, mistaken ideas and expectations of what is to be obtained there, he thinks it may be useful, and prevent inconvenient, expensive, and fruitless removals and voyages of improper persons, if he gives some clearer and truer notions of that part of the world than appear to have hitherto prevailed.

He finds it is imagined by numbers that the inhabitants of North America are rich, capable of rewarding, and disposed to reward, all sorts of ingenuity; that they are at the same time ignorant of all the sciences, and, consequently, that strangers possessing talents in the belles-lettres, fine arts, etc., must be highly esteemed, and so well paid as to become easily rich themselves, that there are also abundance of profitable offices to be disposed of, which the natives are not qualified to fill; and that, having few persons of family among them, strangers of birth must be greatly respected, and of course easily obtain the best of those offices, which will make all their fortunes; that the governments too, to encourage emigration from Europe, not only pay the expense of personal transportation, but give lands gratis to strangers, with negroes to work for them, utensils of husbandry, and stocks of cattle. These are all wild imaginations; and those who go to America with expectations founded upon them will surely find themselves disappointed.

The truth is, that though there are in that country few people so miserable as the poor of Europe, there are also very few that in Europe would be called rich; it is rather a general happy mediocrity that prevails. There are few great proprietors of the soil, and few tenants; most people cultivate their own lands, or follow some handicraft or merchandise; very few rich enough to live idly upon their rents or incomes, or to pay the highest prices given in Europe for painting, statues, architecture, and the other works of art that are more curious than useful. Hence the natural geniuses that have arisen in America with such talents have uniformly quitted that country for Europe, where they can be more suitably rewarded. It is true that letters and mathematical knowledge are in esteem there; but they are at the same time more common than is appreciated; there being already existing nine colleges or universities, viz., four in New England, and one in each of the provinces of New York, New Jersey, Pennsylvania, Maryland, and Virginia, all furnished with learned professors; besides a number of smaller academies. These educate many of their youth in the languages, and those sciences that qualify men for the professions of divinity, law or physic. Strangers indeed are by no means excluded from exercising those professions; and the quick increase of inhabitants everywhere gives them a chance to employ, which they have in common with the natives. Of civil offices, or employments, there are few; no superfluous ones, as in Europe; and it is a rule established in some states, that no office shall be so profitable as to make it desirable. The thirty-sixth article of the Constitution of Pennsylvania runs expressly in these words: "As every freeman, to preserve his independence (if he has not a sufficient estate) ought to have some profession, calling, trade or farm, whereby he may honestly subsist, there can be no necessity for, nor use in, establishing offices of profit, the usual effects of which are dependence and servility unbecoming freemen, in the possessors and expectants; faction, contention, corruption, and disorder among the people; Wherefore, whenever an office, through increase of fees or otherwise, becomes so profitable as to occasion many to apply for it, the profits ought to be lessened by the Legislature."

These ideas prevailing more or less in all the United States, it cannot be worth any man's while, who has a means of living at home, to expatriate himself, in hopes of obtaining a profitable civil office in America; and as to military offices, they are at an end with the war, the armies being disbanded. Much less is it advisable for a person to go thither who has no other quality to recommend him but his birth. In Europe it has indeed its value; but it is a commodity that cannot be carried to a worse market than that of America; where people do not inquire of a stranger, *What is he?* but, *What can he do?* If he has any useful art he is welcome; and if he exercises it, and behaves well, he will be respected by all that know him; but a mere man of quality, who, on that account, wants to live upon the public, by some office or salary, will be despised and disregarded. The husbandman is in honor there, and even the mechanic; because their employments are useful. The people have a saying, that God Almighty is himself a mechanic, the greatest in the universe; and he is respected and more admired for the variety, ingenuity, and utility of his handiworks, than for the antiquity of his family. They are pleased with the observation of a negro, and frequently mention it, that *Boccarora* (meaning the white man) *make de black man workee, make de horse workee, make de ox workee, make ebery ting workee, only the hog. He, de hog, no workee; he eat, he drink, he walk about, he go to sleep when he please, he live like a gempleman.* According to these opinions of the Americans one would think himself more obliged to a genealogist, who could prove for him that his ancestors and relations for ten generations had been ploughmen, smiths, carpenters, turners, weavers, tanners, or even shoemakers, and consequently that they were useful members of society, than if he could only prove that they were gentlemen, doing nothing of value, but living idly on the labor of others, mere *fruges consumere nati*,* and otherwise good for nothing, till by their death their estates, like the carcass of the negro's gentleman-hog, come to be cut up.

With regard to encouragements for strangers from government, they are really only what are derived from good laws and liberty. Strangers are welcome, because there is room enough for them all, and therefore the old inhabitants are not jealous of them; the laws protect them sufficiently, so that they have no need of the patronage of great men; and every one will enjoy securely the profits of his industry. But, if he does not bring a fortune with him, he must work and be industrious to live. One or two years' residence gives him all the rights of a citizen; but the government does not, at present, whatever it may have done in former times, hire people to become settlers, by paying their passages, giving land, negroes, utensils, stock, or any other kind of emolument whatsoever. In short, America is the land of labor, and by no means what the English call *Lubberland*, and the French *Pays de Cocagne*, where the streets are said to be paved with half-peck loaves, the houses tiled with pancakes, and where the fouls fly about ready to be roasted, crying, *Come eat me!*

Who then are the kind of persons to whom an emigration to America may be advantageous? And what are the advantages they may reasonably expect?

Land being cheap in that country, from the vast forests still void of inhabitants, and not likely to be occupied in an age to come, insomuch that the propriety of a hundred acres of fertile soil full of wood may be obtained near the frontiers, in many places, for eight or ten guineas, hearty young laboring men, who understand the husbandry of

*" . . . born
Merely to eat up the corn."
                    —WATTS.

corn and cattle, which is nearly the same in that country as in Europe, may easily establish themselves there. A little money saved of the good wages they receive there, while they work for others, enables them to buy the land and begin their plantation, in which they are assisted by the good will of their neighbors, and some credit. Multitudes of poor people from England, Ireland, Scotland and Germany, have, by this means, in a few years become wealthy farmers, who, in their own countries, where all the lands are fully occupied, and the wages of labor low, could never have emerged from the poor condition wherein they were born.

From the salubrity of the air, the healthiness of the climate, and plenty of good provisions, and the encouragement to early marriages by the certainty of subsistence in cultivating the earth, the increase of inhabitants by natural generation is very rapid in America, and becomes still more so by the accession of strangers; hence there is a continual demand for more artisans of all the necessary and useful kinds, to supply those cultivators of the earth with houses, and with furniture and utensils of the grosser sorts, which cannot so well be brought from Europe. Tolerably good workmen in any of those mechanic arts are sure to find employ, and to be well paid for their work, there being no restraints preventing strangers from exercising any art they understand, nor any permission necessary. If they are poor, they begin first as servants or journeymen; and if they are sober, industrious, and frugal, they soon become masters, establish themselves in business, marry, raise families, and become respectable citizens.

Also, persons of moderate fortunes and capitals, who, having a number of children to provide for, are desirous of bringing them up to industry, and to secure estates for their posterity, have opportunities of doing it in America, which Europe does not afford. There they may be taught and practise profitable mechanic arts, without incurring disgrace on that account, but, on the contrary, acquiring respect by such abilities. There small capitals laid out in lands, which daily become more valuable by the increase of people, afford a solid prospect of ample fortunes thereafter for those children. The writer of this has known several instances of large tracts of land, bought, on what was then the frontier of Pennsylvania, for ten pounds per hundred acres, which when the settlements had been extended far beyond them, sold readily, without any improvement made upon them, for three pounds per acre. The acre in America is the same with the English acre, or the acre of Normandy.

Those who desire to understand the state of government in America, would do well to read the Constitutions of the several States, and the Articles of Confederation that bind the whole together for general purposes, under the direction of one assembly, called the Congress. These Constitutions have been printed, by order of Congress, in America; two editions of them have also been printed in London; and a good translation of them into French has lately been published in Paris.

Several of the princes of Europe, of late, from an opinion of advantage to arise by producing all commodities and manufactures within their own dominions, so as to diminish or render useless their importations, have endeavored to entice workmen from other countries by high salaries, privileges, etc. Many persons, pretending to be skilled in various great manufactures, imagining that America must be in want of them, and that the Congress would probably be disposed to imitate the princes above mentioned, have proposed to go over, on condition of having their passage paid, lands given, salaries appointed, exclusive privileges for terms of years, etc. Such persons, on reading the Articles of Confederation, will find that the Congress have no power committed to them, nor money put into their hands, for such purposes; and that, if any such encouragement is given, it must be by the government of some separate State. This, however, has rarely been done in America; and when it has been done, it has rarely succeeded, so as to establish a manufacture, which the country was not yet so ripe for as to encourage private persons to set it up; labor being generally too dear there, and hands difficult to be kept together, every one desiring to be a master, and the cheapness of lands inclining many to leave trades for agriculture. Some, indeed, have met with success, and are carried on to advantage; but they are generally such as require only a few hands, or wherein great part of the work is performed by machines. Goods that are bulky, and of so small value as not well to bear the expense of freight, may often be made cheaper in the country than they can be imported; and the manufacture of such goods will be profitable wherever there is a sufficient demand. The farmers in America produce, indeed, a good deal of wool and flax; and none is exported, it is all worked up; but it is in the way of domestic manufacture, for the use of the family. The buying up of quantities of wool and flax, with the design to employ spinners, weavers, etc., and form great establishments, producing quantities of linen and woolen goods for sale, has been several times attempted in different provinces; but those projects have generally failed, goods of equal value being imported cheaper. And when the governments have been solicited to support such schemes by encouragements in money, or by imposing duties on importation of such goods, it has been generally refused, on this principle, that, if the country is ripe for the manufacture, it may be carried on by private persons to advantage; and if not, it is a folly to think of forcing nature. Great establishments of manufacture require great numbers of poor to do the work for small wages; those poor are to be found in Europe, but will not be found in America till the lands are all taken up and cultivated, and the excess of people, who cannot get land, want employment. The manufacture of silk, they say, is natural in France, as that of cloth in England, because each country produces in plenty the first material; but if England will have a manufacture of silk as well as that of cloth, and France of cloth as well as that of silk, these unnatural operations must be supported by mutual prohibitions, or high duties on the importation of each other's goods; by which means the workmen are enabled to tax the home consumer by greater prices, while the higher wages they receive makes them neither happier nor richer, since they only drink more and work less. Therefore, the governments in America do nothing to encourage such projects. The people, by this means, are not imposed on, either by the merchant or by the mechanic. If the merchant demands too much profit on imported shoes, they buy of the shoemaker; and if he asks too high a price, they take them of the merchant; thus the two professions are checks on each other. The shoemaker, however, has, on the whole, a considerable profit upon his labor in America, beyond what he had in Europe, as he can add to his price a sum nearly equal to all the expenses of freight and commission, risk or insurance, etc., necessarily charged by the merchant. And the case is the same with the workmen in every other mechanic art. Hence it is that artisans generally live better and more easily in America than in Europe; and such as are good economists make a comfortable provision for age, and for their children. Such may, therefore, remove with advantage to America.

In the long-settled countries of Europe, all arts, trades, professions, farms, etc., are so full, that it is difficult for a poor man, who has children, to place them where they may gain, or learn to gain a decent livelihood. The artisans, who fear creating future rivals in business, refuse to take apprentices, but upon conditions of money, maintenance, or the like, which the parents are unable to comply with. Hence the youth are dragged up in ignorance of every gainful art, and obliged to become soldiers, or servants, or thieves, for subsistence. In America, the rapid increase of inhabitants takes away that fear of rivalship, and artisans willingly receive apprentices from the hope of profit by their labor, during the remainder of the time stipulated, after they shall be instructed. Hence it is easy for poor families to get their children instructed; for the artisans are so desirous of apprentices, that many of them will even give money to the parents, to have boys from ten to fifteen years of age bound apprentices to them till the age of twenty-one; and many poor parents have, by that means, on their arrival in the country, raised money enough to buy land sufficient to establish themselves, and to subsist the rest of their family by agriculture. These contracts for apprentices are made before a magistrate, who regulates the agreement according to reason and justice, and, having in view the formation of a future and useful citizen, obliges the master to engage by a written indenture, not only that, during the time of service stipulated, the apprentice shall be duly provided with meat, drink, apparel, washing, and lodging, and, at its expiration, with a complete new suit of clothes, but also that he shall be taught to read and write and cast accounts; and that he shall be well instructed in the art or profession of his master, or some other, by which he may gain a livelihood, and be able in his turn to raise a family. A copy of this indenture is given to the apprentice or his friends, and the magistrate keeps a record of it, to which recourse may be had, in case of failure by the master in any point of performance. This desire among the masters, to have more hands employed in working for them, induces them to pay the passages of young persons, of both sexes, who, on their arrival, agree to serve them one, two, three, or four years; those who have already learned a trade agreeing for a shorter term, in proportion to their skill and the consequent immediate value of their service; and those who have none agreeing for a longer term, in consideration of being taught an art their poverty would not permit them to acquire in their own country.

The almost general mediocrity of fortune that prevails in America obliging its people to follow some business for subsistence, those vices that arise usually from idleness are in a great measure prevented. Industry and constant employment are great preservatives of the morals and virtue of a nation. Hence bad examples to youth are more rare in America, which must be a comfortable consideration to parents. To this may be truly added, that serious religion, under its various denominations, is not only tolerated, but respected and practised. Atheism is unknown there; infidelity rare and secret; so that persons may live to a great age in that country, without having their piety shocked by meeting with either an atheist or an infidel. And the Divine Being seems to have manifested his approbation of the mutual forbearance and kindness with which the different sects treat each other, by the remarkable prosperity with which He has been pleased to favor the whole country.

(B. FRANKLIN)

NOTES FOR A COMMENTARY ON FRANKLIN

"He's sort of proud of his commonness, isn't he?"

He was the balancer full of motion without direction, the gyroscope which by its large spinning kept us, at that early period of our fate, upon an even keel.

The greatest winner of his day, he represents a voluptuousness of omnivorous energy brought to a dead stop by the rock of New World inopportunity. His energy never attained to a penetrant gist; rather it was stopped by and splashed upon the barrier, like a melon. His "good" was scattered about him. This is what is called being "practical." At such "success" we smile to see Franklin often so puffed up.

In the sheer mass of his voluptuous energy lies his chief excuse—a trait he borrowed without recognition from the primitive profusion of his surroundings.

Relaxed in a mass of impedimenta he found opportunity for thought.

Franklin, along with all the responsible aristocrats of his period, shows the two major characteristics of a bulky, crude energy, something in proportion to the continent, and a colossal restraint equalizing it. The result must have been a complete cancellation, frustration or descent to a low plane for release, which latter alternative he chose shiningly.

He played with lightning and the French court.

The great force (which was in him the expression of the New World) must have had not only volume but a quality, the determination of which will identify him. It was in Franklin, as shown characteristically in this letter, a scattering to reconnoitre.

Poor Richard's Almanac was as important in founding the nation as Paine's *Age of Reason*—he adaged them into a kind of pride in possession.

By casting scorn at men merely of birth while stressing the foundation of estates which should be family strongholds he did the service of discouraging aristocracy and creating it—the qualifying condition being that he repelled that which was foreign and supported that which was native—on a lower level FOR THE TIME BEING. He sparred for time: he was a diplomat of distinction with positive New World characteristics.

His mind was ALL out of the New World. Feeling a strength, a backing which was the New itself, he could afford to be sly with France, England or any nation; since, to live, he had to be sly with the massive strength of that primitive wilderness with whose conditions he had been bred to battle: thus, used to a mass EQUAL to them, he could swing them too. So again he asserted his nativity.

Strong and New World in innate strength, he is without beauty. The force of the New World is never in these men open; it is sly, covert, almost cringing. It is the mass that forces them into praise of mediocrity to escape its compulsions: so there is a kind of nastiness in his TOUCHING the hand of the Marchioness, in his meddling with the lightning, a resentment against his upstart bumptiousness in advising London how to light its stupidly ill-lit streets.

There has not yet appeared in the New World any one

with sufficient strength for the open assertion. So with Franklin, the tone is frightened and horribly smug—at his worst; it flames a little in de Soto; it is necessary to Boone to lose himself in the wilds; there are no women—Houston's bride is frightened off; the New Englanders are the clever bone-men. Nowhere the open, free assertion save in the Indian: this is the quality. Jones has to leave the American navy, we feel, to go to Russia, for release.

It is necessary in appraising our history to realize that the nation was the offspring of the desire to huddle, to protect —of terror—superadded to a new world of great beauty and ripest blossom that well-nigh no man of distinction saw save Boone.

Franklin is the full development of the timidity, the strength that denies itself.

Such is his itch to serve science.

"Education" represented to these pioneers an *obscure* knowledge of the great beauty that was denied them, but of the great beauty under their feet no man seems to have been conscious, to appreciable degree; the foundation they must *first* appraise.

Nowhere does the full assertion come through save as a joke, jokingly, that masks the rest.

The terrible beauty of the New World attracts men to their ruin. Franklin did not care to be ruined—he only wanted to touch.

"I wish he hadn't gone fooling with lightning; I wish he'd left it alone—the old fool." Sure enough, he didn't dare let it go in at the top of his head and out at his toes, that's it; he *had* to fool with it. He sensed the power and knew only enough to want to run an engine with it. His fingers itched to be meddling, to do the little concrete thing—the barrier against a flood of lightning that would inundate him. Of course he was the most useful, "the most industrious citizen that Philadelphia or America had ever known." He was the dike keeper, keeping out the wilderness with his wits. Fear drove his curiosity.

Do something, anything, to keep the fingers busy—not to realize—the lightning. Be industrious, let money and comfort increase; money is like a bell that keeps the dance from terrifying, as it would if it were silent and we could hear the grunt,—thud—swish. It is small, hard; it keeps the attention fixed so that the eyes shall not see. And such is humor: pennies—that see gold come of copper by adding together, shrewd guesses hidden under the armament of an humble jest.

Poor Richard.

Don't offend.

His mighty answer to the New World's offer of a great embrace was THRIFT. Work night and day, build up, penny by penny, a wall against that which is threatening, the terror of life, poverty. Make a fort to be secure in.

The terrific energy of the new breed is its first character; the second is its terror before the NEW.

As a boy, he had tentatively loosed himself once to love, to curiosity perhaps, which was the birth of his first son. But the terror of that dare must have frightened the soul out of him. Having dared that once, his heart recoiled; his teaching must have smitten him. But Franklin, shrewd fellow, did not succumb to the benumbing judgment and go branded, repentant or rebellious. He trotted off gaily to Philly and noticed Bettsy in the shop on Arch Street, the first day.

He is our wise prophet of chicanery, the great buffoon, the face on the penny stamp.

The shock his youth got went into the fibre of the Constitution: he joked himself into a rich life—so he joked the country into a good alliance: to fortify, to buckle up—and reserve a will to be gay, to BE—(on the side).

Poor Richard: Save, be rich—and do as you please—might have been his motto, with an addendum: provided your house has strong walls and thick shutters.

Prince Richard in the lamb's skin: with a tongue in the

cheek for aristocracy, humbly, arrogantly (that you may wish to imitate me) touching everything.

To want to touch, not to wish anything to remain clean, aloof—comes always of a kind of timidity, from fear.

The character they had (our pioneer statesmen, etc.) was that of giving their fine energy, as they must have done, to the smaller, narrower, protective thing and not to the great, New World. Yet they cannot quite leave hands off it but must TOUCH it, in a "practical" way, that is a joking, shy, nasty way, using "science" etc., not with the generosity of the savage or scientist but in a shameful manner. The sweep of the force was too horrible to them; it would have swept them into chaos. They HAD to do as they *could* but it can be no offense that their quality should be *named*. They could have been inspired by the new QUALITY about them to yield to loveliness in a fresh spirit.

It is the placing of his enthusiasm that characterizes the man.

It is not to mark Franklin, but to attempt to appraise the nature of the difficulties that molded him, the characteristic *weight of the mass;* how nearly all our national heroes have been driven back—and praised by reason of their shrewdness in making walls: not in bursting into flower.

To discover the NEW WORLD: that there is something there: what it has done to us, its quality, its weight, its prophets, its—horrible temper.

The niggardliness of our history, our stupidity, sluggishness of spirit, the falseness of our historical notes, the complete missing of the point. Addressed to the wrong head, the tenacity with which the fear still inspires laws, customs, —the suppression of the superb corn dance of the Chippewas, since it symbolizes the generative processes,—as if morals have but one character, and that,—SEX: while morals are deformed in the name of PURITY; till, in the confusion, almost nothing remains of the great American New World but a memory of the Indian.

Battle Between the Bon Homme Richard and the Serapis

On board the ship "Serapis," at anchor without the Texel, in Holland, October 3d, 1779.

HIS EXCELLENCY BENJAMIN FRANKLIN.

Honored and Dear Sir:—When I had the honor of writing to you on the 11th of August, previous to my departure from the Road of Groaix, I had before me the most flattering prospect of rendering essential service to the common cause of France and America. I had a full confidence in the voluntary inclination and ability of every captain under my command to assist and support me in my duty with cheerful emulation; and I was persuaded that every one of them would pursue glory in preference to interest.

Whether I was or was not deceived will best appear by a relation of circumstances.

The little squadron under my orders, consisting of the *Bon homme Richard* of 40 guns, the *Alliance* of 36 guns, the *Pallas* of 32 guns, the *Cerf* of 18 guns, and the *Vengence* of 12 guns, joined by two privateers, the *Monsieur* and the *Granville*, sailed from the Road of Groaix at daybreak on the 14th of August. The same day we spoke with a large convoy bound from the southward to Brest.

On the 23rd we saw Cape Clear and the S.W. part of Ireland. That afternoon, it being calm, I sent some armed boats to take a brigantine that appeared in the N.W. quarter.

Soon after in the evening it became necessary to have a boat ahead of the ship to tow, as the helm could not prevent her from laying across the tide of flood, which would have driven us into a deep and dangerous bay, situated between the rocks on the south called the Skallocks and on the north called the Blaskets. The ship's boats being absent, I sent my own barge ahead to tow the ship. The boats took the brigantine. She was called the *Fortuned*, and bound with a cargo of oil, blubber, and staves from Newfoundland for Bristol. This vessel I ordered to proceed immediately for Nantes or St. Malo. Soon after sunset the villains who towed the ship cut the tow rope, and decamped with my barge. Sundry shots were fired to bring them to without effect. In the mean time the master of the *Bon homme Richard*, without orders, manned one of the ship's boats, and with four soldiers pursued the barge in order to stop the deserters. The evening was clear and serene, but the zeal of that officer, Mr. Cutting Lunt, induced him to pursue too far; and a fog, which came on soon afterward, prevented the boats from rejoining the ship, although I caused signal guns to be frequently fired. The fog and calm continued the next day till toward evening. In the afternoon Captain Landais came on board the *Bon homme Richard*, and behaved towards me with great disrespect, affirming in the most indelicate manner and language that I had lost my boats and people through my imprudence in sending boats to take a prize! He persisted in his reproaches, though he was assured by Messrs. de Weibert and de Chamillard that the barge was towing the ship at the time of elopement, and that she had not been in pursuit of the prize. He was affronted because I would not the day before suffer him to chase without my orders and to approach the dangerous shore I have already mentioned, where he was an entire stranger and when there was not sufficient wind to govern a ship. He told me he was the only American in the squadron, and was determined to follow his own opinion in chasing when and where he thought proper, and in every other matter that concerned the service, and that, if I continued in that situation three days longer, the squadron would be taken, &c. By the advice of Captain de Cottineau, and with the free consent and approbation of M. de Verage, I sent the *Cerf* in to reconnoitre the coast, and endeavor to take the boats and people the next day, while the squadron stood off and on in the S.W. quarter, in the best possible situation to intercept the enemy's merchant ships, whether outward or homeward bound. The *Cerf* had on board a pilot well acquainted with the coast, and was ordered to join me again before night. I approached the shore in the afternoon but the *Cerf* did not appear. This induced me to stand off again in the night in order to return and be rejoined by the *Cerf* the next day; but to my great concern and disappointment, though I ranged the coast along and hoisted our private signals, neither the boats nor the *Cerf* joined me. The evening of that day, the 26th, brought with it stormy weather, with an appearance of a severe gale from the S.W., yet I must declare I did not follow my own judgment, but was led by the assertion that had fallen from Captain Landais, when I in the evening made a signal to steer to the northward and leave that station, which I wished to have occupied a week longer. The gale increased in the night with thick weather. To prevent separation, I carried a top light, and fired a gun every quarter of an hour. I carried, also, a very moderate sail, and the course had been clearly pointed out by a signal before night; yet, with all this precaution, I found myself accompanied only by the brigantine *Vengence* in the morning, the *Granville* having remained astern with a prize. As I have since understood the tiller of the *Pallas* broke after midnight, which disabled her from keeping up, but no apology has yet been made in behalf of the *Alliance*.

On the 31st we saw the Flamie Islands situated near the Lewis, on the N.W. coast of Scotland; and the next morning, off Cape Wrath, we gave chase to a ship to windward, at the same time two ships appearing in the N.W. quarter, which proved to be the *Alliance* and a prize ship which she had taken, bound, as I understood, from Liverpool to Jamaica. The ship which I chased brought to at noon. She proved to be the Union letter of marque, bound from London to Quebec, with a cargo of naval stores on account of government, adapted for the service of the British armed vessels on the lakes. The public despatches were lost, as the *Alliance* very imprudently hoisted American colors, though English colors were then flying on board the *Bon homme Richard*. Captain Landais sent a small boat to ask whether I would man the ship or he should, as in the latter case he would suffer no boat nor person from the *Bon homme Richard* to go near the prize. Ridiculous as this appeared to me, I yielded to it for the sake of peace, and received the prisoners on board the *Bon homme Richard*, while the prize was manned from the *Alliance*. In the afternoon another sail appeared, and I immediately made the signal for the *Alliance* to chase; but, instead of obeying, he wore and laid the ship's head the other way. The next morning I made signal to speak with the *Alliance*, to which no attention was shown. I then made sail with the ships in company for the second rendezvous, which was not far distant, and where I fully expected to be joined by the *Pallas* and the *Cerf*.

The second of September we saw a sail at daybreak, and gave chase. That ship proved to be the *Pallas*, and had met with no success while separated from the *Bon homme Richard*.

On the 3d the *Vengence* brought to a small Irish brigantine, bound homeward from Norway. The same evening I sent the *Vengence* in the N.E. quarter to bring up the two prize ships that appeared to me to be too near the islands of Shetland. While with the *Alliance* and *Pallas*, I endeavored to weather Fair Isle, and to get into my second rendezvous, where I directed the *Vengence* to join me with the three prizes. The next morning, have weathered Fair Isle, and not seeing the *Vengence* nor the prizes, I spoke the *Alliance*, and ordered her to steer to the northward, and bring them up to the rendezvous.

On the morning of the 4th the *Alliance* appeared again, and had brought to two very small coasting sloops in ballast, but without having attended properly to my orders of yesterday. The *Vengence* joined me soon after, and informed me that in consequence of Captain Landais' orders to the commanders of the two prize ships they had refused to follow him to the rendezvous. I am to this moment ignorant of what orders these men received from Captain Landais, nor know I by virtue of what authority he ventured to give his orders to prizes in my presence and without either my knowledge or approbation. Captain Ricot further informed me that he had burnt the prize brigantine because that vessel proved leaky; and I was sorry to understand afterward that, though the vessel was Irish property, the cargo was property of the subjects of Norway.

In the evening I sent for all the captains to come on board the *Bon homme Richard* to consult on future plans of operation. Captains Cottineau and Ricot obeyed me, but Captain Landais obstinately refused, and, after sending me various uncivil messages, wrote me a very extraordinary letter in answer to a written order which I had sent him on finding that he had trifled with my verbal orders. The next day a pilot boat came on board from Shetland, by which means I received such advices as induced me to change a plan which I otherwise meant to have pursued; and, as the *Cerf* did not appear at my second rendezvous, I determined to steer towards the third in hopes of meeting her there.

In the afternoon a gale of wind came on, which continued four days without intermission. In the second night of that gale the *Alliance*, with her two little prizes, again separated from the *Bon homme Richard*. I had now with me only the *Pallas* and the *Vengence*, yet I did not abandon the hopes of performing some essential service. The winds continued contrary, so that we did not see the land till the evening of the 13th, when the hills of Cheviot in the S.E. of Scotland appeared. The next day we chased sundry vessels, and took a ship and a brigantine, both from the Firth of Edinburgh, laden with coal. Knowing that there lay at anchor in Leith road an armed ship of 20 guns, with two or three fine cutters, I formed an expedition against Leith, which I purposed to lay under a large contribution, or otherwise to reduce it to ashes. Had I been alone, the wind being favorable, I would have proceeded directly up the Firth, and must have succeeded, as they lay there in a state of perfect indolence and security, which would have proved their ruin. Unfortunately for me, the *Pallas* and *Vengence* were both at a considerable distance in the offing, they having chased to the southward. This obliged us to steer out of the Firth again to meet them. The captains of the *Pallas* and *Vengence* being come on board the *Bon homme Richard*, I communicated to them my project, to which many difficulties and objections were made by them. At last, however, they appeared to think better of the design after I had assured them that I hoped to raise a contribution of 200,000 pounds sterling on Leith, and that there was no battery of cannon there to oppose our landing. So much time, however, was unavoidably spent in pointed remarks and sage deliberations that night that the wind became contrary in the morning.

We continued working to windward up the Firth without being able to reach the road of Leith, till on the morning of the 17th, when being almost within cannon-shot of the town, having everything in readiness for a descent, a very severe gale of wind came on, and being directly contrary, obliged us to bear away, after having in vain endeavored for some time to withstand its violence. The gale was so severe that one of the prizes that had been taken on the 14th sunk to the bottom, the crew being with difficulty saved. As the alarm by this time had reached Leith by means of a cutter that had watched our motions that morning, and as the wind continued contrary (though more moderate in the evening), I thought it impossible to pursue the enterprise with a good prospect of success, especially as Edinburgh, where there is always a number of troops, is only a mile distant from Leith, therefore I gave up the project.

On the 21st we saw and chased two sail off Flamborough Head, the *Pallas* in the N.E. quarter, while the *Bon homme Richard* followed by the *Vengence* in the S.W. The one I chased, a brigantine collier in ballast belonging to Scarborough was soon taken, and sunk immediately afterward, as a fleet then appeared to the southward. It was so late in the day that I could not come up with the fleet before night. At length, however, I got so near one of them as to force her to run ashore between Flamborough Head and the Spurn. Soon after I took another, a brigantine from Holland, belonging to Sunderland; and at daylight the next morning, seeing a fleet steering toward me from the Spurn, I imagined them to be a convoy, bound from London for Leith, which had been for some time expected. One of them had a pendant hoisted, and appeared to be a ship of force. They had not, however, courage to come on, but kept back, all except the one which seemed to be armed, and that one also kept to windward very near the land and on the edge of dangerous shoals, where I could not with safety approach. This induced me to make a signal for a pilot, and soon afterward two pilot boats came off. They informed me that the ship that wore a pendant was an armed merchant ship, and that a king's frigate lay there in sight at anchor within the Humber, waiting to take under convoy a number of merchant ships bound to the northward. The pilots imagined the *Bon homme Richard* to be an English ship of war, and consequently communicated to me the private signal which they had been required to make. I endeavored by this means to decoy the ships out of the port, but the wind then changing, and with the tide becoming unfavorable for them, the deception had not the desired effect, and they wisely put back. The entrance of the Humber is exceedingly difficult and dangerous; and, as the *Pallas* was not in sight, I thought it not prudent to remain off the entrance. I therefore steered out again to join the *Pallas* off Flamborough Head. In the night we saw and chased two ships until 3 o'clock in the morning, when, being at a very small distance from them, I made the private signal of recognizance which I had given to each captain before I sailed from Groaix; one-half of the answer only was returned. In this position both sides lay to till daylight, when the ships proved to be the *Alliance* and the *Pallas*.

On the morning of that day, the 23d, the brig from Holland not being in sight, we chased a brigantine that appeared laying to to windward. About noon we saw and chased a large ship that appeared coming around Flamborough Head from the northward, and at the same time I manned and armed one of the pilot boats to sail in pursuit of the brigantine, which now appeared to be the vessel that I had forced ashore. Soon after this a fleet of 41 sail appeared off Flamborough Head, bearing N.N.E. This induced me to abandon the single ship which had then been anchored in Burlington Bay. I also called back the pilot boat, and hoisted a signal for a general chase. When the fleet discovered us bearing down, all the merchant ships crowded sail toward the shore. The two ships of war that protected the fleet at the same time steered from the land, and made the disposition for the battle. In approaching the enemy, I crowded every possible sail, and made the signal for the line of battle, to which the *Alliance* showed no attention. Earnest as I was for the action, I could not reach the commodore's ship until seven in the evening. Being then within pistol shot, when he hailed the *Bon homme Richard*, we answered him by firing a whole broadside.

The battle, being thus begun, was continued with unremitting fury. Every method was practised on both sides to gain an advantage and rake each other; and I must confess that the enemy's ship, being much more manageable than the *Bon homme Richard*, gained thereby several times an advantageous situation, in spite of my best efforts to prevent it. As I had to deal with an enemy of greatly superior force, I was under the necessity of closing with him, to prevent the advantage which he had over me in point of manoeuvre. It was my intention to lay the *Bon homme Richard* athwart the enemy's bow, but, as that operation required great dexterity in management of both sail and helm, and some of our braces being shot away, it did not exactly succeed to my wishes. The enemy's bowsprit, however, came over the *Bon homme Richard's* poop by the mizzen mast, and I made both ships fast together in that situation which by the action of the wind on the enemy's sails forced her stern close to the *Bon homme Richard's* bow, so that the ships lay square alongside of each other, the yards being all entangled, and the cannon of each ship touching the opponent's side. When this position took place, it was 8 o'clock, previous to which the *Bon homme Richard* had received sundry eighteen-pound shots below the water, and leaked very much. My battery of 12-pounders, on which I had placed my chief dependence, being commanded by Lieut. Dale and Col. Weibert, and manned principally with American seamen and French volunteers, were entirely silenced and abandoned. As to the six old eighteen-pounders that formed the battery of the lower gun-deck, they did no service whatever. Two out of three of them burst at the first fire, and killed almost all the men who were stationed to manage them. Before this time, too, Col. de Chamillard who commanded a party of 20 soldiers on the poop, had abandoned that station after having lost some of his men. These men deserted their quarters. I had now only two pieces of cannon, nine-pounders, on the quarter deck, that were not silenced; and not one of the heavier cannon was fired during the rest of the action. The purser, Mr. Mease, who commanded the guns on the quarter deck, being dangerously wounded in the head, I was obliged to fill his place, and with great difficulty rallied a few men, and shifted over one of the quarterdeck guns, so that we afterward played three pieces of 9-pounders upon the enemy. The tops alone seconded the fire of this little battery, and held out bravely during the whole of the action, especially the main top, where Lieut. Stack commanded. I directed the fire of one of the three cannon against the main-mast, with double-headed shot, while the other two were exceedingly well served with grape and canister shot to silence the enemy's musketry, and clear her decks, which was at last effected. The enemy were, as I have since understood, on the instant of calling for quarters when the cowardice or treachery of three of my under officers induced them to call to the enemy. The English commodore asked me if I demanded quarters; and, I having answered him in the most determined negative, they renewed the battle with double fury. They were unable to stand the deck; but the fire of their cannon, especially the lower battery, which was entirely formed of 18-pounders, was incessant. Both ships were set on fire in various places, and the scene was dreadful beyond the reach of language. To account for the timidity of my three under officers,—I mean the gunner, the carpenter, and the master-at-arms,—I must observe that the two first were slightly wounded; and, as the ship had received various shots under water and one of the pumps being shot away, the carpenter expressed his fear that she would sink, and the other two concluded that she was sinking, which occasioned the gunner to run aft on the poop without my knowledge to strike the colors. Fortunately for me, a cannon ball had done that before by carrying away the ensign staff. He was therefore reduced to the necessity of sinking as he supposed, or of calling for quarter; and he preferred the latter.

All this time the *Bon homme Richard* had sustained the action alone, and the enemy, though much superior in force, would have been very glad to have got clear, as appears by their own acknowledgments, and by their having let go an anchor the instant that I laid them on board, by which means they would have escaped, had I not made them well fast to the *Bon homme Richard*.

At last, at half-past nine o'clock, the *Alliance* appeared, and I now thought the battle at an end; but, to my utter astonishment, he discharged a broadside full into the stern of the *Bon homme Richard*. We called to him for God's sake to forbear firing into the *Bon homme Richard;* yet he passed along the off side of the ship and continued firing. There was no possibility of his mistaking the enemy's ship for the *Bon homme Richard*, there being the most essential difference in their appearance and construction; besides, it was then full moonlight, and the sides of the *Bon homme Richard* were all black, while the sides of the prizes were yellow; yet, for the greater security, I showed the signal of our reconnoissance by putting out three lanthorns, one at the head (bow), another at the stern (quarter), and the third in the middle in a horizontal line. Every tongue cried that he was firing into the wrong ship, but nothing availed. He passed round, firing into the *Bon homme Richard's* head, stern, and broadside; and by one of his volleys killed several of my best men, and mortally wounded a good officer on the forecastle. My situation was really deplorable. The *Bon homme Richard* received various shot under the water from the *Alliance*, the leak gained on the pumps, and the fire increased much on both ships. Some officers persuaded me to strike, of whose courage and good sense I have high opinion. My treacherous master-at-arms let loose all my prisoners without my knowledge and my prospect became gloomy indeed. I would not however, give up the point. The enemy's main-mast began to shake, their firing decreased, ours rather increased, and the British colors were struck at half an hour past 10 o'clock.

This prize proved to be the British ship of war the *Serapis*, a new ship of 44 guns, built on their most approved construction, with two complete batteries, one of them of 18-pounders, and commanded by the brave Commodore Richard Pearson. I had yet two enemies to encounter far more formidable than the Britons,—I mean fire and water. The *Serapis* was attacked only by the first, but the *Bon homme Richard* was assailed by both. There were five feet of water in the hold, and though it was moderated from the explosion of so much gunpowder, yet the three pumps that remained could with difficulty only keep the water from gaining. The fire broke out in various parts of the ship, in spite of all the water that could be thrown to quench it, and at length broke out as low as the powder magazine, and within a few inches of the powder. In that dilemma I took out the powder upon deck, ready to be thrown overboard at the last extremity; and it was ten o'clock the next day, the 24th, before the fire was entirely extinguished. With respect to the situation of the *Bon homme Richard*, the rudder was cut entirely off the stern frame, and the transoms were almost entirely cut away; the timbers, by the lower deck especially, from the main-mast to the stern, being greatly decayed with age, were mangled beyond my power of description; and a person must have been an eye-witness to form a just idea of the tremendous scene of carnage, wreck, and ruin that everywhere appeared. Humanity cannot but recoil from the prospect of such finished horror, and lament that war should produce such fatal consequences.

After the carpenters, as well as Capt. de Cottineau, and other men of sense, had well examined and surveyed the ship (which was not finished before five in the evening), I found every person to be convinced that it was impossible to keep the *Bon homme Richard* afloat so as to reach a port if the wind should increase; it being then only a moderate breeze. I had but little time to remove my wounded, which now became unavoidable, and which was effected in the course of the night and the next morning. I was determined to keep the *Bon homme Richard* afloat, and, if possible, to bring her into port. For that purpose the first lieutenant of the *Pallas* continued on board with a party of men to attend the pumps, with boats in waiting ready to take them on board in case the water should gain on them too fast. The wind augmented in the night and the next day, on the 25th, so that it was impossible to prevent the good old ship from sinking. They did not abandon her till after 9 o'clock. The water was then up to the lower deck, and a little after ten I saw with inexpressible grief the last glimpse of the *Bon homme Richard*. No lives were lost with the ship, but it was impossible to save the stores of any sort whatsoever. I lost even the best part of my clothes, books, and papers; and several of my officers lost all their clothes and effects.

Having thus endeavored to give a clear and simple relation of the circumstances and the events that have attended the little armament under my command, I shall freely submit my conduct therein to the censure of my superiors and the impartial public. I beg leave however, to observe that the force that was put under my command was far from being well composed; and, as the great majority of the actors in it have appeared bent on the pursuit of interest only, I am exceedingly sorry that they and I have been at all concerned. I am in the highest degree sensible of the singular attentions which I have experienced from the Court of France, which I shall remember with perfect gratitude until the end of my life, and will always endeavor to merit while I can, consistent with my honor, continue in the public service. I must speak plainly. As I have been always honored with the full confidence of Congress, and as I also flattered myself with enjoying in some measure the confidence of the Court of France, I could not but be astonished at the conduct of M. de Chaumont, when, in the moment of my departure from Groaix, he produced a paper, a concordat, for me to sign in common with the officers whom I had commissioned but a few days before. Had that paper, or even a less dishonorable one, been proposed to me at the beginning, I would have rejected it with just contempt, and the word deplacement among others should have been necessary. I cannot, however, even now suppose that he was authorized by the court to make such a bargain with me, nor can I suppose that the minister of the marine meant that M. de Chaumont should consider me merely as a colleague with the commanders of the other ships, and communicate to them not only all he knew, but all he thought, respecting our destination and operations. M. de Chaumont has made me various reproaches on account of the expense of the *Bon homme Richard*, wherewith I cannot think I have been justly chargeable. M. de Chamillard can attest that the *Bon homme Richard* was at last far from being well fitted or armed for war. If any person or persons who have been charged with the expense of that armament have acted wrong, the fault must not be laid to my charge.

I had no authority to superintend that armament, and the persons who had authority were so far from giving me what I thought necessary that M. de Chaumont even refused among other things, to allow me irons for securing the prisoners of war.

In short, while my life remains, if I have any capacity to render good and acceptable services to the common cause, no man will step forth with greater cheerfulness and alacrity than myself; but I am not to be dishonored, nor can I accept of the half confidence of any man living. Of course, I cannot, consistent with my honor and a prospect of success, undertake future expeditions, unless when the object and destination is communicated to me alone, and to no other person in the marine line. In cases where troops are embarked, a like confidence is due alone to their commander-in-chief. On no other condition will I ever undertake the chief command of a private expedition; and, when I do not command in chief, I have no desire to be in the secret.

Captain Cottineau engaged the *Countess of Scarborough*, and took her after an hour's action, while the *Bon homme Richard* engaged the *Serapis*. The *Countess of Scarborough* is an armed ship of 20 six-pounders, and was commanded by a king's officer. In the action the *Countess of Scarborough* and the *Serapis* were at a considerable distance asunder; and the *Alliance*, as I am informed, fired into the *Pallas*, and killed some men. If it should be asked why the convoy was suffered to escape, I must answer that I was myself in no condition to pursue, and that none of the rest showed any inclination, not even M. Ricot, who had held off at a distance to windward during the whole action, and withheld by force the pilotboat with my lieutenant and 15 men. The *Alliance*, too, was in a state to pursue the fleet, not having had a single man wounded or a single shot fired at her from the *Serapis*, and only three that did execution from the *Countess of Scarborough*, at such a distance that one stuck in the side, and the other two just touched and then dropped into the water. The *Alliance* killed one man only on board the *Serapis*. As Captain de Cottineau charged himself with manning and securing the prisoners of the *Countess of Scarborough*, I think the escape of the Baltic fleet cannot so well be charged to his account.

I should have mentioned that the main-mast and the mizzen-top-mast of the *Serapis* fell overboard soon after the captain had come on board the *Bon homme Richard*.

Upon the whole, the captain of the *Alliance* has behaved so very ill in every respect that I must complain loudly of his conduct. He pretends that he is authorized to act independent of my command. I have been taught to the contrary; but, supposing it to be so, his conduct has been base and unpardonable. M. de Chamillard will explain the particulars. Either Captain Landais or myself is highly criminal and one or the other must be punished. I forbear to take any steps with him until I have the advice and approbation of your excellency. I have been advised by all the officers of the squadron to put M. Landais under arrest; but, as I have postponed it so long, I will bear with him a little longer until the return of my express.

We this day anchored here, having since the action been tossed to and fro by contrary winds. I wished to have gained the road of Dunkirk on account of our prisoners, but was overruled by the majority of my colleagues. I shall hasten up to Amsterdam; and there, if I meet with no orders for my government, I will take the advice of the French ambassador. It is my present intention to have the *Countess of Scarborough* ready to transport the prisoners from hence to Dunkirk, unless it should be found more expedient to deliver them to the English ambassador, taking his obligation to send to Dunkirk, &c., immediately an equal number of American prisoners. I am under strong apprehensions that our object here will fail, and that through the imprudence of M. de Chaumont, who has communicated everything he knew or thought on the matter to persons who cannot help talking of it at a full table. This is the way he keeps state secrets, though he never mentioned the affair to me.

I am ever, &c.,

John P. Jones.

Jacataqua

TERROR enlarges the object, as does joy. "The whole forest seemed to open," says the hunter of his first tiger, "I don't know what its exact size may have been; but, to me, it seemed thirty feet high." So, by emotional grandeur, were the heroes of antiquity conceived; and so, to the joyful eye of the lover seems the object of his delight, bringing such wonder and awe, that each motion—each look—is exaggerated, filled with power and significance, intensified to a degree that puts colder measurements aside. From this, the lore of romance has grown. In America, the legend of a horror before the war-whoops of the Indians gives some inkling of a great dread the colonists experienced—but there is rarely a countering legend of joy.

We believe that life in America is compact of violence and the shock of immediacy. This is not so. Were it so, there would be a corresponding beauty of the spirit—to bear it witness; a great flowering, simple and ungovernable as the configuration of a rose—that should stand with the gifts of the spirit of other times and other nations as a standard to humanity. There is none.

"The United States, without self-seeking, has given more of material help to Europe and to the world in the last ten years in time of need, than have all other nations of the world put together in the entire history of mankind. It has stamped out yellow fever from the coasts of South America, etc."

It is our need that is crying out, that and our immense wealth, the product of fear,—a torment to the spirit; we sell—but carefully—to seek blessings abroad. And this wealth, all that is not pure accident—is the growth of fear.

It is this which makes us the flaming terror of the world, a Titan, stupid (as were all the giants), great, to be tricked or tripped (from terror of us) with hatred barking at us by every sea—and by those most to whom we give the most. In the midst of wealth, riches, we have the inevitable Coolidge platform: "poorstateish"—meek. THIS is his cure before the world: our goodness and industry. THIS will convince the world that we are RIGHT. It will not. Make a small mouth. It is the acme of shrewdness, of policy. It will work. We shall have more to give. Logical reasoning it is: generous to save and give. It is bred of fear. It is as impossible for a rich nation to convince any one of its generosity as for a camel to pass through the eye of a needle. Puritanical; pioneer; "out of the small white farm-house"—the product of delay. The characteristic of American life is that it holds off from embraces, from impacts, gaining, by fear, safety and time in which to fortify its prolific carcass —while the spirit, with tongue hanging out, bites at its bars —its object just out of reach. Wilson grazed heaven by his lewdness; the door stood open till it was slammed closed. I relish the back door gossip that made him impossible.

Delay, all through youth, halt and cessation, not of effort, but of touch, all through life as it is learned: no end save accumulation, always upon the way to BIGGER opportunity; we keep realization from the mind with a purpose till men are trained never to possess fully but just to SEE. This makes scientists and it makes the masochist. Keep it cold and small and under the cold lens. It is bastardization as of astronomy that has no counterpart with us in the aspirations or the conceits of the flesh; a passion equal to the straining of a telescope. Digressions—The American character is acquisitive, but mediate, like the Morgan interests, Mr. Franklin at the helm, the International Mercantile Marine that owns, as mortgager, the White Star, the Red Star, the Atlantic Transport lines, etc. American lines but English ships. We own them. But who HAS them? A more practical race used to holding India. Crude as iron.

What would be better to-night than a long hour of music, at ease and away from disturbance, a friend or two of the same humor with a little talk now and again when the musician, since it should be a woman, rested,—the pause before the sexual act, that interruption from desire that piles up a weight of energy behind it like stones do a river. The impossibility to attain is the source of all good in the world, the real reason for the Puritan. No, not *all good*, though so it seems to Americans. There is a kind of piling of experience upon experience that is not bound to satiety, but to wisdom, the highest knowledge of all, to Buddha, if one likes, to release, to relief, to the dangerous ground of pleasure: *Jenseits des lust princip*, Freud sees it, beyond the charmed circle. It is no matter, since it is unknown in the province I am discussing. Here, through terror, there is no direct touch; all is cold, little and discreet:—save just under the hide.

There are no American servitors. An American will not serve another man. This is a fear. Nothing is so delightful as to serve another. Instead of that, we have "service," the thing that Rabindranath Tagore so admired, telling us we did not know we had it: Sending supplies to relieve the cyclone sufferers in Indiana. It is a passion. But to serve another, with a harder personal devotion is foreign to us: a trick for foreigners, a servant's trick. We are afraid that we couldn't do it and retain our self-esteem. We couldn't. Thus we see of what our self-esteem is made.

"Don't let's have any poor," is our slogan. And we do not notice that the chief reason for this is that it offends us to believe that there are the essentially poor who are far richer than we are who give. The poor are ostracized. Cults are built to abolish them, as if they were cockroaches, and not human beings who may not want what we have in such abundance. THAT would be an offense an American could not stomach. So down with them. Let everybody be rich and so EQUAL. What a farce! But what a tragedy! It rests upon false values and fear to discover them. Do not serve another for you might have to TOUCH him and he might be a JEW or a NIGGER.

Do you realize the fascination the story of the white woman who had twin nigger babies has for us? They accused the woman of having had intercourse with the apartment's colored elevator boy. Her husband abandoned her at once, of course,—charming man. But you know Mendel's law; they discovered there had been a darky in *his* family six generations before! There's the dénouement for every good American. Be careful whom you marry! Be careful for you can NEVER know. Watch, wait, study.

Deanimated, that's the word; something the sound of "metronome," a mechanical means; Yankee inventions. Machines were not so much to save time as to save dignity that fears the animate touch. It is miraculous the energy that goes into inventions here. Do you know that it now takes just ten minutes to put a bushel of wheat on the market from planting to selling, whereas it took three hours in our colonial days? That's striking. It must have been a tremendous force that would do that. That force is fear that robs the emotions; a mechanism to increase the gap between touch and thing, *not* to have a contact.

America adores violence, yes. It thrills at big fires and explosions. This approaches magnificence! The finest fire-fighters in the world. We live not by having less fires but more, by the excitement of seeing torturing things done well, with light ease even. But we have violence *for service,* mark it. Battleships *for peace.* The force of enterprise *for bringing bananas* to the breakfast table. Massive mining operations to transport us—whither? Bathrooms, kitchens, hospitals with a maximum of physical convenience and a minimum of waste to spare us—for what? We never ask. It is all a bar to more intimate shocks. Everything is for "generosity" and "honor." *It has to be* for us to get away with it. Therefore, we cannot acknowledge, really, downright, thievery in our friends. We can't get to it. Did we do so, we should know many things most disturbing to our peace of mind.

Atlanta, Georgia, is far worse than Paris for girls on the streets soliciting, but there is no good in it,—I don't suppose there has ever been an American woman like Kiki or that delightful Baroness who paraded Fifth Avenue one day with a coal-scuttle for a chapeau. Naturally they arrested her. Naturally. She would have been arrested in any city, but not, I imagine, with quite such a sense of duty as in America. To permit such a thing would cast a very awkward light on us all.

The impact of the bare soul upon the very twist of the fact which is our world about us, is un-American. *That* we shun and rush off to the laboratory, the wheatfield (hiding our indecent passion in meddling, playing) in a spirit of service—our chemistry is all that—salt away the profits, and boast of our saving, stabilizing *Constitution* in dread, as of a glass heart, fiercely aligning ourselves in its defense as if it were something else than a mechanical shift.

Men weaving women, women spouting men—colleges and streets torturing and annealing the machinery to cure cancer and kill mosquitoes, to carry fish in proper cars and fruit in others, to kill the *Aedes Egyptus* in the domestic water supply of Quito by the use of minnows in the house tanks—Our life is tortuous and grotesque, huge fetishes by which we are ruled in utter darkness—or we fly abroad for sensation: Anything to escape—we fear simplicity as the plague. NEVER to allow touch. What are we but poor doomed carcasses, any one of us? Why then all this fury, this multiplicity we push between ourselves and our desires? Twisting and bending; that nervous habit of wanting to be thought pleasant—tortuous and grotesque.

It is the women above all—there never have been women, save pioneer Katies; not one in flower save some moonflower Poe may have seen, or an unripe child. Poets?

Where? They are the test. But a true woman in flower, never. Emily Dickinson, starving of passion in her father's garden, is the very nearest we have ever been—starving.

Never a woman: never a poet. That's an axiom. Never a poet saw sun here.

Oh, men have had women, millions of them, of course: good, firm Janes. But one that spouted any comprehensive joy? Never. Dolly Madison was a bright doll. At best they want to be men, sit and be a pal. It's all right. How could they do anything else with the men brutally beaten by the life—

Do you know that the old town-records in Massachusetts show few men without two and many with as many as seven wives? Not at all uncommon to have had five. How? The first ones died shooting children against the wilderness like cannon balls. There's a reason for traditional cleverness! And we talk about the wilderness with affection. We are blind asses, with our whole history unread before us and helpless if we read it. Nothing noticed. Nothing taught in the academies. You'd think that THAT would force us into some immediacy. NEVER. We write books deploring the post-war hilarity of our present-day girls. Mr. Hungerford assures me the girls are no different now than they were before the Rebellion. But shh! Ben Franklin, who started black with an illegitimate son, was forced to turn white, poor Richard, to save himself later. He saw the hell and warned us, warned us to save our pennies. So, too, spendthrift Cleveland who became economist.

Our life drives us apart and forces us upon science and invention—away from touch. Or if we do touch, our breed knows no better than the coarse fiber of football. Though Bill Bird says that American men are the greatest business men in the world: the only ones who understand the passion of making money: absorbed, enthralled in it. It's a game. To me, it is because we fear to wake up that we play so well. Imagine stopping money making. Our whole conception of reality would have to be altered. But to keep a just balance between business and another object is to spoil the intoxication, the illusion, the unity even. It's very hard on the poet who must be something or other in order to live. To live against the stream, Emily Dickinson, about the only woman one can respect for her clarity, lived in her father's back yard.

Our breed knows no better than the coarse fibre of football, the despair we have for touching, the cheek, the breast —drives us to scream in beaten frenzy at the great spectacle of violence—or to applaud coldness and skill.

Who is open to injuries? Not Americans. Get hurt; you're a fool. The only hero is he who is not hurt. We have no feeling for the tragic. Let the sucker who fails get his. What's tragic in that? That's funny! To hell with him. He didn't make good, that's all.

It's a kind of celluloid of gayety (I am speaking of the theaters), a numbing coat that cuts us off from touch. Did you see the expression on Coolidge's face when Al Jolson did his stuff before him on the White House lawn? embarrassment, shame, fear to seem not to be amused, desire to get away—very bad taste on everybody's part. But it was really funny to see. That jazz dose and the Puritan: something akin: both removed from simplicity, really, and touch: each his own way, that shaky shimmy and the—shame.

What is the result? The result is the thing that results, of course.

Anyhow, it's curious to pick up results, you'll find tail ends of New England families—all burnt out; charming people: an old man marries a girl: male sons aplenty who sew and wash and make pies; embroider, select their mother's hats and dress fabrics—and paint pictures: long skinny men with emotional wits who have smelt losses. A bastard aristocracy. Men who, when their friends disappoint them, grow nervous and cry all night. It is because there are no women. These men are more out of place in pushing young America than a Chinaman—or a Tibetan.

Women—givers (but they have been, as reservoirs, empty) perhaps they are being filled now. Hard to deal with in business, more conservative, closer to earth—the only earth. They are our cattle, cattle of the spirit—not yet come in. None yet has raised benevolence to distinction. Not one to "wield her beauty as a scepter." It is a brilliant opportunity.—But the aesthetic shown by American artists (the test of the women) is discouraging: the New England eunuchs,—"no more sex than a tapeworm"—faint echoes of England, perhaps of France, of Rousseau, as Valéry Larbaud insists,—Ryder: no detail in his foregrounds just remote lusts, fiery but "gone,"—Poe: moonlight. It is the annunciation of the spiritual barrenness of the American woman.

Violence—the newspapers are full of murder, but it is for the papers: that's not immediacy but FEAR. It is the hysteria of cheated folk, similar to the outbreaks of murder and suicide in the Germanic countries after the war—The old man that murdered the woman with a Polish name in Perth Amboy. It is so clear: A man without a woman finds one. She immediately starts to torture him. It's all they can do. "Take it out of the son of a bitch"—he's put himself in a compromising position and deserves to be castrated. Every force is piled against him. So he murders her. But is THAT a deed of passion? Surely not. Or the motion picture murders. It's the shriek of starvation. As Charlot said after his first abortive attempt to get a wife: "Such is life in the Great West," that land of wealth and promise. As Roosevelt said of Roosevelt after this last gubernatorial campaign in New York: "He's a *promising* young man." Yes, it's a promising country. It's what the French say of our women in Paris: *promising* young women.

Dr. Gaskins sensed it cynically: The ideal woman should end at the eyebrows and have the rest filled in with hair. It is the practical answer to the immediate American need. Pragmatism. It's inevitable that men shall go down the scale until they strike what they want—or can get. There was the young medical fellow, a New Englander, in the State Asylum at Worcester, a periodic maniac; his history fascinated me. He is a clever physician, and a man of excellent antecedents. Shortly after college (and a medical education takes so long that a man is in his late twenties before he can afford to marry) he married a woman far below his class,—he had to to get her. Shortly realizing his fatal error, he promptly, being a sensitive man, went insane,—and was as promptly divorced and committed to the asylum by his wife, proving the soundness of his mind—fundamentally. He has married three times since and has always gone mad: a little like Strindberg. But the reasoning here is truly American. Trained a Puritan, he was bursting for lack of sexual satisfaction. Unwilling to commit the sin of fornication and being unable to get a wife of his own class, due to poverty, or what not—he married someone below his scale of aesthetic or emotional relief. Thus the greater was sacrificed to the lesser. Now he was overcome with anguish. His life was ruined. He bitterly assailed himself for his folly and lost all control. In the hospital, he worked well in the laboratory—but he was truly insane. There is no class to absorb this stress.

There is a story told of George Moore the last time he was in New York. Meeting at a tea some well shaped American woman, who was apparently intent upon showing herself to the world (though the poor thing probably didn't mean it), Moore asked her to go upstairs and undress for him that he might see her naked. She indignantly refused of course. But I like his gesture. Naturally she didn't HAVE to do as he wanted her to; yet he nailed her. And he nailed us. I think he was sufficiently distinguished for her to have satisfied him.

Or, if a girl is—(not generous, bah!) but discerning with her whole body—that's it, a woman must see with her whole body to be benevolent.—If in the eighth grade she begins to discern the depth of her necessity—she is made to feel that there is something *wrong* about her, not reckless but fundamentally *wrong*. In contradistinction, a woman from Adrianople might be taught not that it is *wrong* to give herself but that murder will follow it, or that it is a dangerous gift to be given *rarely*, but a GIFT. So she is shut up, like a French girl of better family, say; as we do wheat or a case of fine fruit. But the American girl who can run free must be protected in some other way so she is *frightened*—if possible. She is a low thing (they tell her), she is made to feel that she is vicious, evil—It really doesn't do anything save alter the *color* of her deed, make it unprofitable, it scrapes off the *bloom* of the gift— it is puritanical envy. When she gives, it will be probably to the butcher boy—since she has been an apt pupil and *believes* that she is *evil*, believes even that her pleasure is evil.

It's the central lie! but she is sure of it and gives her virginity to the butcher boy instead of having at least a decent romance. As Ken. says: we get (that is, presuming we are poets) the daughters of the butcher. In the boarding school at Burlington, my friend, a teacher, was on the alert. The tension was horrible in this fashionable school. Several of the women were watching at points of vantage—with what feelings in their own hearts it would be easy to say. Soon a soft whistle, then the window opened and the conventional knotted sheet ladder dropped out. There was a buggy down the road. Just as the second of the two girls reached the ground, they were both seized. In a wild scramble the young fellows escaped. Yes, the butcher boy and his pal. Of course, these things cannot be permitted.

Our girls have excellent physiques, really superb. I have often watched, as who has not—for they are coming out— some bather in the little stuff they wear to-day with acid passion. And there you are. They are fit only to be seen in shows, or, in the train of a launch, on aquaplanes, six at a time, the swift motion only serving to give the authentic sense of slipperiness, pseudo-naiads without the necessary wildness and the chill—fit only to be seen by the box, like Oregon apples, bright and round but tasteless—wineless, wholesale.

Why one of the hottest women that I know, lascivious in what might have been the sense in which I speak of it, but too timid, unable to stem the great American tide inimical to women, spent almost the whole war period in Washington. She was a yeomanette but employed her spare time spying on middle-aged men, Majors with wives in Omaha, who were giving the nights to their stenographers—as it was done during the war. This girl's passion was horrible to behold. It turned slightly later, though she didn't perhaps perceive it, to other women. She wrote to me from time to time of her experiences. I liked her and enjoyed her letters. In one letter, among other things, she said that no one could *imagine* what it meant to a girl to lose her virginity. But yes, I could imagine it, better than she. It means *everything* in America. Well, of course, it has meant more than it does today but I am tracing the tendency. It means that she gets such a violent jolt from her past teaching and such a sense of the hatred of the world (as she conceives it must be) against her that she is ready to commit suicide. Or "go to the dogs." That it might be the opening of wonders, of freedom to "save the nation," that it might at least be an opportunity for practical use to the half of humanity that needs just that, never occurs to her. She is crushed. Or one imagines she is. As a matter of fact, Wally Gould tells of the two Lewiston girls who were coming home by moonlight from a rendezvous in the woods with two boy friends; one was crying, but the other sighed, and said, "Well, *that's* over with"—and next day when the old fool of a neighbor was sending a box of candy to the widow, she dumped the sweets out and filled the box with horse manure.

Intelligent, our girls are, their minds are whip-like, if they don't rot, as did Martha's, she who beat the record of all years at Cornell; was secretary to Altman; was graduated as a trained nurse and, what a volcano of energy!—taught Greek in a school till she went mad at the slowness of the pupils—and married that marvelous little lame Irishman, Darby—who has the moods of a rose. What a woman! spending her life now as servitor to women in the Insane Hospital on Ward's Island—after being an inmate for years there herself—and recovering. What an energy wasted there! No place for it in the world save among the insane. Especially no place for it in the United States.

Whip-like intelligences, lost after a few years. Perverse, they "*deraille*," as Brancusi says, too easily. To them, Paris is bizarre, a "place to spill the nerves," a bewildering surprise. They cannot carry a weight, as French women do their men; under the release of Paris, they are just useless, often coarse, lewd, drunk. What's that but unsatisfying. I salute them, because only for American women, have I any deep fellow feeling, or at least they are the only ones that seem to me satisfying. Great experimenters with the emotions, "Paris" appears in so many literatures and there are so many appearances that are "Paris," heaven knows whom they are influencing. I wish they could live at home. Imagine fleeing from the world to a woman—and leaving her—strengthened, fortified, above all *free* to GO! That costs money here! Of course men should spend money upon women, especially American men.

Of course, our history has been short and comparatively obscure, for the most part. There must be character in out-of-the-way places, naturally, but none has raised the point of which I speak, to distinction. They existed, we know, degraded and demeaned in the pioneer camps, as in Maine —discredited save in a few bad narrative verses and short stories—oh, any number of stories: drunk and waking up in a whore's bed, etc. Many men tell of that primitive kindness and *savoir faire* in the frontier camps, the purse returned with money intact. To that understanding one must bow. But there has been no genius in a women, to see a man's talent and coax it up, as did Miss Li, let us say, in the Chinese legend. Never a character to raise into story.

The incidents of our lives are too completely surrounded by delays—the violence of our athletic games is mostly a delay. Of course, it is fortunate that we are so active and fearless. The youth must be "taken up" somehow. It is taken up *completely* in a great many cases, though. A good many college athletes are "burnt out" in their three years of competition; it is too much. They frequently find it impossible to breed, if that were all.

Poets, through their energy, receive such a stamp of the age upon their work, that they are marked, in fact, even in the necessities of their defeat, as having lived well in their time. Poets are defeated but in an essential and total defeat at any time, that time is stamped in character upon their work, they give shape to the formless age as by a curious die,—and so other times recognize them, the positives that created the forms which give character and dignity to the damp mass of the overpowering but characterless resistance. So Jacataqua gave to womanhood in her time, the form which bitterness of pioneer character had denied it.

At the left, with the company but not of it, silent in the midst of noise and laughter, one group accorded well with the wooded hill and quiet river, twenty or more Abenaki braves from Swan Island, picturesque in hunting garb. Perhaps none of all the company felt more interest and curiosity than did those dusky warriors, but their stolid faces and occasional guttural ejaculations gave no sign of the fire within.

Three paces in front of these silent braves stood their Sachem, Jacataqua, a girl scarce eighteen, in whom showed the best traits of her mixed French and Indian blood.

"These Anglese for whom we watch, who are they?" she asked Squire Holworth, near her.

"Soldiers who go to fight the English at Quebec under Arnold."

As the transports began to arrive and the eleven hundred disembarked, Captain Howard, commandant of Fort Westward, came up from the landing with the most notable of the guests. It was upon the reckless, dashing Arnold that all eyes were turned. Jacataqua's Abenakis stood in the same stolid silence, still a group apart, but the maiden herself, for once yielding to the wild pulses of her heart, stepped between the sturdy squires to a point of vantage whence she might gaze upon the warrior whom all men seemed to honor.

One swift glance she gave the hero, then her black eyes met a pair as dark and flashing as her own, met and were held. She turned to the man at her side.

"That, that Anglese! Who?"

"Thet? Thet's young Burr, the one Cushing said got off a sick bed to come."

Startled, she stepped back among her people.

Young Burr but waited to gain his genial host's attention to ask, excitedly:

"Who is that beauty?"

"Jacataqua, Sachem of the Indians of Swan Island; you passed the wigwams of her people on the way up the river."

In a moment, Burr was standing before the Indian princess, for the first and last time at a loss before a woman. Primitive and direct, it was she who opened the conversation and opened it with a challenge:

"These," with a wave of her brown hand toward Howard and the group of officers, "these want meat. You hunt with me? I win."

The Virtue of History

As IN WRITING of some men it should be a pageant of wild beasts, so in writing or, better, speaking of Aaron Burr, one could not begin better than by saying, "there is nothing on earth divine beside humanity."

And more especially the female part of it.

He was admired by women; yet, even his most violent detractors acknowledge him a great soldier; he had men's admiration also.

If distrust, jealousy and hatred can be called so, yes.

A secret admiration appears often under those names. But you speak there of other things than military reputation. I say, in matters of war, he was widely acknowledged a leader.

A pity, then, he did not stick to soldiering instead of entering politics.

That's the question.

I think not. On that his critics are to a man agreed.

Then just there one should look closest.

Not so.

Indeed it is so, for if there is agreement on one point in history, be sure there's interest there to have it so and that's not truth.

In governments, at least, I shall agree with you—nothing is divine.

But history follows governments and never men. It portrays us in generic patterns, like effigies or the carvings on sarcophagi, which say nothing save, of such and such a man, that he is dead. That's history. It is concerned only with the one thing: to say everything is dead. Then it fixes up the effigy: there that's finished. Not at all. History must stay open, it is all humanity. Are lives to be twisted forcibly about events, the mere accidents of geography and climate?

It is an obscenity which few escape—save at the hands of the stylist, literature, in which alone humanity is protected against tyrannous designs.

But how small is the sum of good writing against the mass of poisonous stuff that finds its way into the history books; for the dead can be stifled like the living.

That's metaphysical.

Never. That of the dead which exists in our imaginations has as much fact as have we ourselves. The premise that serves to fix us fixes also that part of them which we remember.

If history could be that which annihilated all memory of past things from our minds it would be a useful tyranny.

But since it lives in us practically day by day we should fear it. But if it is, as it may be, a tyranny over the souls of the dead—and so the imaginations of the living—where lies our greatest well of inspiration, our greatest hope of freedom (since the future is totally blank, if not black) we should guard it doubly from the interlopers.

You mean, tradition. Yes, nothing there is metaphysical. It is the better part of all of us.

It is the fountain! But men, never content in the malice with which they surround each living moment, must extend their illwill backward, jealous even of a freedom in the past, to maim and to destroy there too. Better to be a Mexican and take food to the graves on feast days.

When a man dies what can remain to us, even from the best records, save a few facts—and a mass of prejudice since he, though he were the greatest man in the world, was only one among the others of his time?

History that should be a left hand to us, as of a violinist, we bind up with prejudice, warping it to suit our fears as Chinese women do their feet.

What can we do? Facts remain but what is the truth?

We can begin by saying: No opinion can be trusted; even the facts may be nothing but a printer's error; but if a verdict be unanimous, it is sure to be a wrong one, a crude rush of the herd which has carried its object before it like a helpless condoning image. If we cannot make a man live again when he is gone, it is boorish to imprison him dead within some narrow definition, when, were he in his shoes before us, we could not do it. It's lies, such history, and dangerous. Just there may lie our one hope for the future, beneath that stone of prejudice. Perhaps Burr——

A prophet?

Perhaps Burr carried into politics an element of democratic government, even a major element, those times were slighting—no matter what, an element so powerful and so rare that he was hated for it, feared—and loved.

"A dangerous man, one who ought not to be trusted with the reins of government," said Hamilton.

How dangerous, and to whom? To usurpers? Why did the Senate weep so uncontrolledly at his farewell address? Perhaps he had somebody's number. The hateful deed he spoke of had been done already, and, in their subtler apprehensions, they wept a vital loss.

"As to Burr," it says, "these things are admitted and indeed cannot be denied, that he is a man of extreme and irregular ambition,—"

He wanted to be President, an ambition both extreme and —to his enemies—irregular.

"—that he is selfish to a degree which excludes all social affection and that he is decidedly profligate."

Hamilton again. But the man is a balloon of malice. What has this slatternly talk to do with Burr's ability in matters of public trust? It is an attempt to maim the man by loose talk of his traits and private life where his reputation cannot be attacked by pat facts marshaled in the open.

Not his ability but his reliability is questioned.

But where are the facts?

His enterprise in Mexico.

Not yet. That one thorn on which they did impale him was a later growth. It did not come until the end of years of vicious enmity by Hamilton and might well be called a deed of desperation.

It proved the soundness of their logic.

They hounded him to it to prove their logic. So for the rest of the denunciation: Burr, seldom talkative in public (a rare point in a politician and one dangerous to an opponent) but a marvelous listener (most disquieting) becomes, out of malice, "selfish to a degree that excludes all social affection,"—but the accusation falls apart itself in the last of it, that Burr was profligate—which hardly goes with one devoid of all social affection. In fact the last is a pure lie, proven fifty times over by the man's life. Incurably generous he was dearly loved by his friends. No. It is all loose talk. Or rather talk well aimed to do a damage. They feared him. Or he was out of their control; out of their understanding most likely.

"A brilliant lawyer, ranked by nearly all men of his time," it says, "only second to their favorite, his friends placed him at the head. Calm, a persuasive speaker with an unusual power of condensation, he never spoke long but swiftly to the point. He knew no fatigue. As long as an enterprise appeared not impossible he was never discouraged but his insuperable fortitude accomplished what others conceived utterly impracticable."

Is this a man to be thrown lightly into the discard? It looks mightily as if there were something there a government might conserve.

"A great man in little things while he is really small in great ones."

That's Jeffersonian rhetoric: a well turned phrase, but what does it mean? It means that in the things Burr set his hand to they found him great—he had no chance for more, they would not give him way. Would he be Governor of New York? No. Would he be Ambassador in Paris? No, though the committee three times unanimously recommended his appointment. Would he be Brigadier General when in 1798 the war with France threatened? Again, no. No, no; they were envious of this courteous, well-bred, able silent man whom no enemy could down and so they sought to do away with him by any means. We should suspect the motives of those who malign him.

Did they, or did they speak the truth of a relentless enemy to law and order?

They malign him, I assert, because of something strange in his composition, a weighty element—that in democracies is often called an enemy to law and order.

They suspected him.

Of what? They never can quite say. They say, this man must not be trusted. That is all. And that is ALL. So "history" has recorded him a blackguard.

And that women loved him.

Royally, yes; especially his daughter, his Theodosia. But that's a sop, a trick of history—

Wait. Here's splendid reading. "I contemplate you," she says, "with such a mixture of humility, admiration, reverence, love and pride that very little superstition would be necessary to make me worship you as a superior being."

By all that is divine on earth, by children, women, soldiers, he was loved.

An infatuated woman.

And by half the population to boot, since so they voted. There was something there, an element—hated and loved; suppressed; resurgent. What will history reveal? Little, count upon it, save through violent means: an egg, you must smash it to have it.

The shell only you will break.

The rigid part.

Come, then, let's look inside; to most of us, I think, Burr's life presents a travesty on greatness.

We'll take the whole period to begin with. But if we examine it, not as history, that lie! but as a living thing, something moving, undecided, swaying—Which way will it go?—something on the brink of the Unknown, as we are today,—shall we not see it (not as history has pictured it)— in no sense a period of revolution—such uprisings are for old states where senility has become ingrained—but as a half-wild colony, young, shooting out green wood? England? A dry skin to be cast off, an itch, that's all. There was a deeper matter, a yeast in the sap, an untracked force that might lead anywhere; it was springtime in a new world when all things were possible.

Freedom of conscience, a new start, and to be quit of Europe.

The Revolution came with Washington, the pin about which all hearts revolved. Most were satisfied with the obvious: England the oppressor, from whom freedom must be won. So when the war is over, why—there you are! But where are they? Sooner or later it must have been the same awakening without the Revolution. The war was nothing.

It was a war to the death that absorbed all loyal hearts.

And nearly all wits.

They were at their wits' ends.

But there were some saving minds. I say, compared to the great burst of a reawakened sense of life in the spirit of the New World, the war was nothing. But in those agonies that spirit nearly died! It had been a sense of rebirth, not so much a declaration of independence against little England as an announcement to heaven itself, full of pride and of deep feeling. England must be beaten; but, under that, there was a deeper and a stronger force passing through the moment.

There would be few to realize that undersong.

England, by chance, stood in the way. But the defeat of England was the obvious false end. And now, a race in the making, America must remember what in its hour of excitement it had promised, its declarations, its pronouncements, its Patrick Henry speeches. Were these just expedients of war to spur to battle or was it serious? There will be two opinions; and, if the small attempt to absorb the great—

Much will be left over.

The most perhaps,—two parts, a greater and a less, the lesser biting on the larger. The war won, all fatigued, would not the way be smoothed for the easy deception that—the obvious thing—liberty had triumphed?

And so it had.

And would there not be a shrewd party, one way or another, to step in and profit by the moment to say it had; and still another, opposite, to see a danger: liberty not won but lost anew in the mêlée?

Shea's rebellion.

Shea was an inspired ass. Our fate is in the air wavering which way it will go, a Junto on one side, Burr (maybe) on the other.

This is a philosophical division to be admitted if it present the facts.

I speak of fiercely contested things, practical in the extreme, that tortured the souls of the founders: "the original principle of state vitality, the most important element in our Constitution, and one steadily undermined by Federal encroachment." The sense of the individual, the basis on which the war was fought, instantly the war was over began to be debauched. Randolph sensed it. Burr sensed it. Hamilton was the Federalist champion. Washington, as President, "a monster of prudence," was the helpless mother.

All very well, yet let us recognize that there are those in the world who will throw themselves into any subversive act for sheer love of violence.

We are admonished to seek nothing but the good.

Seek, yes, but how if you do not find it?

I say, unless a land conserve this yeast, it will not raise much bread.

Burr was a subversive force.

Granted, granted.

Then?

He was a subversive force where liberty was waning.

They nearly hanged him for it.

Hang him? They tried to torture him to death with their small slanders on his private life and would have done so had he not known how to make them fail. So now they laugh and say his genius was to keep himself amused. They could not kill it in him.

His vanity they could not.

His profound refinement, his sense of the deeper forces working in his world that demanded freedom; things the others were beginning to stamp out, to whittle away, down to the common level. Gutted by their own phrases.

Is this the nation that made Washington?

It made him a cripple.

Protector of liberty.

Whose, Hamilton's?—to harness the whole, young, aspiring genius to a treadmill? Paterson he wished to make capital of the country because there was waterpower there which to his time and mind seemed colossal. And so he organized a company to hold the land thereabouts, with dams and sluices, the origin today of the vilest swillhole in christendom, the Passaic River; impossible to remove the nuisance so tight had he, Hamilton, sewed up his privileges unto kingdomcome, through his holding company, in the State legislature. *His* company. *His* United States: Hamiltonia—the land of the company.

You violate your own concept of what history should be when you speak so violently.

The pendulum must swing. Is it not time that it swung *back?*

But was Burr really better who founded Tammany?

Child's play.

So you have raised the point that once the Revolution over the New World instead of being freed slipped into a tyranny as bad as or worse than the one it left behind; that, of this tyranny, Hamilton was the agent; and that—perhaps —in Burr reposed the true element, liberty, which a party in power tried to smother. What basis, other than the one adopted under the Constitution, could the new Government have taken firmer? Burr proposed none. This is the charge against him: that he proposed nothing yet refused to abide loyally by the established order.

In that man there burned a springtime of the soul, a mounting desire that makes him seem, beside the harness animals of that dawning period like a bird in flight. But they, the others, wanting to escape their load, each puts his harness on a lesser nag,—the government on top, after the text, perhaps—

> *Set thy servant to work, and thou shalt find rest:*
> *Leave his hands idle, and he will seek liberty.*
> *And for an evil servant* (that's Burr) *there are*
> *racks and tortures.*

The Colonial Government was not perfect, but can the oyster live without his shell? They did what they were able. What did Burr propose?

I say that what Burr stood for—and that this is typical of us—is lost sight of in the calumny that surrounds his name, through which the truth is not so easily to be discovered. Let us dig and we shall see what is turned up—and name it if we can.

Go on.

A new world, that's what we were. It was a springtime that the colonists, at their most impassioned, were attempting. But as it is a winter we are now in, and the more ordered the more wintry—dulled values, stereotyped effects of bygone adventures—so it began to be after the Revolution; a sense of life killed, systematically, as with school children—

> *Under a cruel eye outworn.*

But some one must rule, even children know that and accept it with pleasure and relief.

What matter who rule? to rule is without sense. There

can be no rule. Burr saw America in his imagination, free. His spirit leaped to it—and his body followed out of a sick bed. But his spark was not preserved. He saw America, or he had seen America, as a promise of delight and it struck fine earth, that fancy. Now he saw a sombre Washington— with shrewd dog Hamilton at his side—locking the doors, closing the windows, building fences and providing walls. He dreaded this. He saw that they would only lock up themselves, and he rebelled.

Inspired by devil or angel, Burr was a frightful danger to the young state and needed to be curbed.

So much the worse for the young state then. But it's the malice I decry. Burr's account in history is a distortion. The good which history should have preserved, it tortures. A country is not free, is not what it pretends to be, unless it leave a vantage open (in tradition) for that which Burr possessed in such remarkable degree. This is my theme.

But has he not that place? He's there in history just as you design him.

He's in myself and so I dig through lies to resurrect him. We are deceived by history. America had a great spirit given to freedom but it was a mean, narrow, provincial place; it was NOT the great liberty-loving country, not at all. Its choice spirits died.

Ah, my friend, you are an enthusiast, rash guesses and the same loose talk of which you complain.

The Federal Government was slipping in its fangs. The banks were being organized.

A central power is strength.

"Morals and happiness will always be nearest to perfection in small communities." In big ones men are theorists and outlaws. Make it big enough and it becomes a wood where thieves protect each other from the more general evil—

Oh balderdash, anarchy, exploded theory—

One thing was sure, he used to say, no one would steal his hat, it would fit no one else he had so big a head.

All very well, but let me hear you tell the story now, how his life, in its detail, supports your roseate view of him. I doubt if you can do it.

He had a good beginning. He was a brilliant student while at Princeton—howbeit there were stories of a wild life there. Jonathan Edwards was his grandfather on the mother's side and his father was President of the University. He was wealthy and of a pleasing personal appearance,— though short. After the university an interest in theology took him to Connecticut for private study—

Now the mill begins.

To the consternation of his friends he did a rightabout-face, threw the whole mass of religious dogma from him and declared himself a disbeliever.

He was twenty at that time, if I remember.

If his world believed in freedom he came out with it. This fits in with my design. Unlike a schemer, he stood from the first in the open. Then, rising from a sickbed, he rushed off with Arnold to Quebec. The thing that offers to the eye is his enthusiasm; headlong he goes. On that campaign, through direst hardships he returned a brilliant record; he led, he supported, he adventured by himself. When there was difficult work he did it. He carried his commander from the field through snow kneedeep before the British guns. Fearless, he offered himself without stint. He was frail; it weakened him. He paid no heed. When he returned, still nothing but a boy, Washington claimed him for his staff.

It was a startling opportunity for him.

Burr stayed six weeks.

They say that to the personal dislike between the boy and Washington that followed, much of Burr's later unsuccess is to be traced.

In fairness to them both, if there was ever an antithesis between two men, both good in essence, it was here, both fine but one the earth itself, the other—air. Somehow they should have joined.

It is a fascinating moment, many chapters could be written just upon this meeting.

No need of that. There was a plain reason for what took place. Burr could not stomach the restraint and the perfunctory nature of his work. Hamilton, himself, had not been able to do it. The General's aides were merely clerks to him; he himself did all the planning. This was no place for a high-spirited young man demanding action. Washington fell from high hopes into disappointment, and, reading Burr's impatience in his looks, distrusted him. A fixed dislike sprang up between them.

I do believe you sometimes when you speak of a natural malice of events; here truly there was no need for such an outcome.

At least the break was clean; there was no flattery, no carping.

Burr no doubt found the General slow-witted. He could not see the power in Washington or else resented it. He chaffed at his superior's dignity and deliberation. It made him restless.

But, transferred to Putnam's staff, he had brilliant service till through ill health he had to quit.

A humbler devotion, such as the time required, he could not stomach. He was self-willed, rash in judgment and unbridled in both speech and deed.

Yet how clearly in everything he does his virtues and his faults stand out. Admit that he was rash: Mrs. Washington, he said, knit well; Mrs. Putnam was a wondrous spinner! Well enough; he looked at that, rejected it as passing and looked for more. The simpler manners of the time did not encircle him. He wanted other things of women. But, right or wrong, he must have known such preferences could not bring him popularity. It is evidence of the man's sincerity

and open disregard for the opinion of the world. He was no
schemer. Washington, he said, should have retired after the
war,—he would have made a picturesque figure as a country gentleman. As President, Burr did not fancy him.

A very shallow judgment.

At least it followed his logic candidly. What cause had he
to praise the everlasting prudence of the President that
negated so much of value in order to conserve that which
he, Burr, thought nothing? Three times the committee
unanimously recommended him for the post in Paris and
each time Washington vetoed the choice.

Three times right then.

Well, maybe; but—here's still a young man, dashing, rich
—a proven soldier. The Clintons, the Livingstons, the Van
Rensselaers all had eligible daughters. Let young Burr
marry one of them. Did he? It would have been a shrewd
move if one were the man avid for political ascendency. He
married whom? A nobody, a widow of Paramus, New Jersey, older than himself and with two sons; unbeautiful, a
scar on her face—but the most refined, courteous, gracious
creature he had ever laid his eyes upon. He loved these
things, as in all he does, openly—in the teeth of the world.
He found her an inspiration, one who opened his eyes to
the blessed pages of literature, to the deeper values that he
sought—and she gave him his Theodosia. This constant evidence of the man's clarity and disrespect for the applause of
the world is in everything he does.

Immoral virtues—

He loved and straight he went to the mark. It was an
impossible plane in that world. That sort of independence
was bound to bring him into disrepute with the rulers of
the colonies. Never though with the people, whom he
knew, lovers of the senses, as was he. Men believed in him.
He tied for the presidency in spite of nearly all the upper
ten against him. Jefferson succeeded. He hated Burr. Over-
bearing toward the Vice President he told him—to
look in the papers for the news. The Vice Presidency was

never better served, however. And when he ran for Governor of New York, with every daily paper hounding him, is that like a clever schemer, not to have support?—the lowest gossip was not too low for the New York Post. They poured their venom on him from every side. He was defeated, thanks to this, not a single paper backed him, a very awkward schemer that, and yet he nearly got it. That's why they hated him: they feared his power. It was the dread and the love of his free spirit.

And then the duel—

Hamilton had hounded him for years. At length he openly called Burr "politically dangerous." What did he mean? Burr wrote demanding an explanation. To the party in power, yes, dangerous he may have been, but to the country—How? Hamilton refused to answer. Then let it be pinned down. Either it must be one or the other. Burr was not angry. If any one feared it was not he. His head was clear, he slept well, he was refreshed and went to the place of the duel.

Hamilton was fifty-seven. Burr somewhat younger.

Hamilton fired first, the bullet clipping a twig above Burr's head. His hand was trembling. Did he fire wild, as his seconds say he did, on purpose? Burr's seconds said no, and stuck to it; the bullet came too close to their man's head to have been anything but a plain miss due to a shaking hand. Then Burr fired. He shot coolly, seriously and with conviction. He killed his man, logically and as he meant to do and knew he must. For a moment, as he saw his adversary fall, he was overcome with compassion, then he turned away. Hamilton, before he died, dictated his astonishing testament, in which he says—imagine the flimsy nature of his lifelong enmity toward the man—that, regarding Burr, he "might have been misinformed of his intentions." Good God, what an answer! Work till you are fifty-seven to ruin a man, insult him, malign him and then say, dying: I may have been misinformed.

May it not have been so?

It may, but that's a poor excuse for Hamilton. No, Burr was not tractable; but, the villain they imagine him, he was not either. It was his hatred of the Virginia Junto and their success against him that undid him.

Did he intend an empire in the west?

Sam Houston was later to be called a hero for that, if he did. Perhaps he did dream: a man whose schemes, if they were so, were so poor they never once succeeded. He was a bad scholar of his betters—whose schemes succeeded. His expedition into the west was, in effect, his hatred of the Junto. It was his protest against the major fault of tyranny with which he accused the Federalist Party. If his wild scheme, whatever it may have been, was traitorous, it was no more so than theirs was subtly sinister. He hated them. They knew it. He sought new worlds.

The trial—

A farce. No one believed in it. It's most noteworthy incident was John Marshall's graciousness in permitting the defense to subpoena Jefferson, the real accuser, though he was President. Tea was served in the afternoons. Nothing was proved. But now, yes, all hope of power was ended. For twenty-five years he fought that party; in the end, he broke them backing Andrew Jackson whom he ardently admired. But he, himself, was ended.

How then did he deport himself?

They exiled him to Europe where his journal shows him never much depressed—a lover of his brilliant daughter. After four years he returned to meet the bitterest tragedy experience could deal him, the death of his small grandson whom he loved tenderly; then, on top of that, the death at sea of Theodosia herself. He felt at last "cut off from humanity."

His Theodosia—

He had taught her everything he knew, hoping in his last years to enjoy with her a rare companionship. Now even that hope was lost.

Did he intend his gross journal for her eyes as it is said?

Every word of it. He had told her everything; he had created her into his free world where he lived in unconstraint. She was as far above the women of her time as he would have had himself above the men.

They say he paid to keep ten women.

And there were, perhaps, an hundred bastard children—for the legend's sake. But what I would drag out to the light is this: If they were wrong, those who judged him in his time, the intent was deliberate and malicious—and that this is typical of us.

I can see how you would wish to prove that so but not how you will prove it.

Knowing in the marrow what they must lose, the self-styled "free and independent," to become a nation—

That is, what they must give up of personal liberty for the general good—

What they must sacrifice of hard-won freedom, whittling themselves down—it was dispiriting—they realized with a nostalgic tremor that Burr had KEPT. An unbecoming jealousy sprang up instanter, as with pioneers in a bad country who know that one of them is hoarding up his sugar. Burr would not give in. Let others shift and scheme and draw away, he would not.

He proved himself, by that measure, wanting in good feeling for his fellows.

Nothing of the sort. By any measure that you choose, what we find good our virtue is to cling to it. The common good he found common—and did not hesitate to show it. The common good he found lacking, in no matter what—but lacking. He would not stand for its tyrannical assertions. The rare thing—liberty—he saw disappearing in the dreadful leveling, the machinations of a Junto, no matter how well intentioned, were seeking to negate for themselves by seizing power.

Was he so great a rock of liberty?

They knew they must give up much, he refused—and demanded still a place for himself, whole. They yielding to the crowd, yet felt regret to take its dust. The degradation which they suffered and he refused to suffer brought their hatred down on him with double force. It was all in that feeling. He gave it vent. The loss to Jefferson of a glass candlestick, and more later, which he imagined he could sacrifice; Washington retiring disheartened to his farm to breathe the air; Burr *carried into politics.*

At last we have it!

A humanity, his own, free and independent, unyielding to the herd, practical, direct. That was his violent party that, based on the rock, could not be moved.

Did he present it in that light?

What light? Who shall name that thing? It is the hidden flame, but like all that's universal it cannot be packed into three common words.

They called him frivolous.

Because he was serious, because he gave himself wholly where they played and ducked and hedged and took their sorrow off into the parlor or among the cattle. He stood up and was arrogant, unyielding. They strutted pompously—shyly, great liberals; he struck straight for liberty and did not kid himself that he had it, he who believed in himself and his teaching and his blood, when he was smothering it in pretty fancies and high-sounding phrases and dung. Either they had what they were fighting for or they did not have it. England or the mob, it made small difference to him. He WAS serious, *they* were the triflers—their own dupes.

They said he was immoral.

He was, safely so, by the flesh. He found safety in that flesh and among its sturdy guardians—women. Were they too idle in recognizing him? They loved him. Frivolous? He was perhaps the only one of the time who saw women, in the flesh, as serious, and they hailed and welcomed with deep gratitude and profound joy his serious knowledge and regard and liberating force—for them. Freedom? Then for women also—but such a freedom that the one defense must be—immoral. He laughed at that and dug in the deeper.

He treated them lightly.

Never. He kept their secrets; no man has a better record. Asked his opinion he could say of women: all seriousness, yet you must speak light nothings to them. The rest were frivolous with women. The rest denied them, condoned the female flesh, found them helpmates at the best and at the worst, horses, cattle, provincial accessories, useful workers to make coffee and doughnuts—and to be left to go crazy on the farms for five generations after—that's New England, or they'd hide the bull behind the barn, so that the women would not think it knew the cows were—Bah, feudal dolls gone wrong, that's Virginia. Women? necessary but not noble, not the highest, not deliciously a free thing, apart, *feminine*, a heaven;—afraid to delve in it save like so much dough. Burr found the spirit living there, free and equal, independent, springing with life. Or did he? I say if he did he was before his time. Surely they drank of him like water.

Of children he was passionately fond, and they of him.

Those little images of freedom, children, fascinated him. They, loving seriousness and openness and all things with light in them—loved him. He adored them, his stepsons among the first, and after them, that little grandson, Theodosia's baby who died—and broke the old man's heart.

He was immoral as a satyr.

It is a cry of fear and disappointment—and perverse pleasure. The acute delight Americans have always got from denying themselves joy and maiming others that they might be "saved" from some obliquity of moral carriage is only lately understood. One step further and it leads to persecutions. The world is made to eat, not leave, that the spirit may be full, not empty.

It is every licentious man's excuse for his excesses. Freedom is not so easy. There is no tyranny save ignorance and no escape from it save clear and persistent moral achievement, deeply followed. Doubtful of an advance the mere sensualist flaps and flounders.

Burr knew what a democracy must liberate.

What then?

Men intact—with all their senses waking. He had, raised to a different level, the directness of "common people" which reformers, that is to say, schemers, commonly neglect, misname, misapprehend as if it were anything but to touch, to hear, to see, to smell, to taste.

Transcendental theory, my dear countryman.

What is; the delicious sincerity of pioneer people? In Burr this aristocratic strain, straight out of the ground, was *seeing* its own ground belied. To maintain the truth up through the scale is the hard thing. A while ago, just here, I heard a Polish woman saying to her daughter: "You bust your coat with your fifty sweaters."

What's that: You bust your coat with your fifty sweaters?

Its immediacy, its sensual quality, a pure observation, its lack of irritation, its lack of pretense, its playful exaggeration, its repose, its sense of design, its openness, its gayety, its unconstraint. It frees, it creates relief. In the great it is the same, or would be if ever it existed, a delicious sincerity (in greater things of course) not a scheme, nor a system of procedure—but careless truth.

A second China you would have.

Burr's life was of that stuff. It is *this* that is trying to escape in a democracy.

Traitors have it, maybe; also the incapable.

Yes, they have (maybe); it saves them. And if it has not appeared in the great rulers of the world it is because they lack power of the spirit and *it is yet to appear*. It is difficult but it is IT.

Not too enlightening, that.

What does it matter on this earth about scientists, philosophers or saints? Snake charmers. An amusement. Their schemes amount to nothing. But to the men themselves every moment, every detail, the devotion, the clarities are vital—and so we value them, in short, by their style. They must ponder deeply, pass hours of suspense, give themselves wholly, seriously that they may have the authenticity of a shepherd—or a clown, without which their lives are so much paper.

Well, yes. But how is Burr concerned in this?

If politics could be the science of humanity, I think his place was there. He was the essence of the schemes the others made.

Granted that the value of all things—and men—is purely spiritual, a devotion in themselves to painstaking truthfulness, with no interfering, yet how will Burr—?

Such things have an aspect, on the world's side, that bewilders us. That obscene flesh in which we dig for all our good, man and woman alike, Burr knew and trusted. Here he lived, giving and receiving to the full of his instinctive nature.

But passion will obscure our sense so that we eat sad stuff and call it nectar. Burr was heavily censured by his time, immoral, traitorous and irregular. What they say of him, I still believe.

Believe it if you will but listen to this story: Near the end of his life a lady said to him: "Colonel, I wonder if you were ever the gay Lothario they say you were." The old man turned his eyes, the lustre still undiminished, toward the lady—and lifting his trembling finger said in his quiet, impressive whisper: "They say, they say, they say. Ah, my child, how long are you going to continue to use those dreadful words? Those two little words have done more harm than all others. Never use them, my dear, never use them."

Advent of the Slaves

THE COLORED MEN and women whom I know intimately add a quality, that is delightful, to the life about me.

There is little use, after all—save in a title—of speaking of the advent of the slaves; these were just men of a certain mettle who came to America in ships, like the rest. The minor differences of condition were of no importance—the mere condition of their coming is of no importance—

The colored men and women whom I have known intimately have a racial character which has impressed me. I have not much bothered to know why, exactly, this has been so—

The one thing that never seems to occur to anybody is that the negroes have a quality which they have brought to America. It is not important that it is available or not to us for any special use—

Poised against the *Mayflower* is the slave ship—manned by Yankees and Englishmen—bringing another race to try upon the New World, that will prove its tenacity and ability to thrive by seizing upon the Christian religion—a thing to replace their own elephant-, snake- and gorilla-filled jungles—on which to fasten for stability, blowing into it the soul of their own darkness, where, as were the Aztecs in their bloody chapels, they are founded—

They helped to build "a society that was rich and in some ways sumptuous and curiously oriental." "Puritan Massachusetts unable to rid itself of the idea of man's essential wickedness, could not envision this earthly paradise, Georgia—" "In many families every child had his individual slave; great gentlemen almost openly kept their concubines;

208

great ladies half dozed through the long summer afternoons on their shaded piazzas mollified by the slow fanning of their black attendants, and by the laving of their feet in water periodically fetched anew from the spring house"—it is a sunken quality, or it is a living quality—it is no matter which.

All the rest is to keep from having to say anything more —like a nigger: it is their beauty. When they try to make their race an issue—it is nothing. In a chorus singing *Trovatore*, they are nothing. But saying *nothing*, dancing *nothing*, "*NOBODY*," it is a quality—

Bert Williams, author of a Russian ballet, *The Kiss;* that's worse than nothin'. But "Somewhere the sun am shinin'— for ME . . ." That's SOMETHIN'. Taking his shoes off; that's SOMETHIN'.

. . . dancing, singing with the wild abandon of being close, closer, closest together; waggin', wavin', weavin', shakin'; or alone, in a cabin, at night, in the stillness, in the moonlight —bein' nothin'—with gravity, with tenderness—they arrive and "walk all over God's heaven—"

There is a solidity, a racial irreducible minimum, which gives them poise in a world where they have no authority—

Or a ramshackle "castle," peaked with doll's house gables, all awry, by the railroad; where the boys came with their "brides" in those good old days JUST before the war; old shoes and a shambling independence: a tigerish life, lived in defiance over a worthless son, by virtue of fierce courage, a heavy fearless voice and a desperate determination to be let alone—with two reminiscent, shrewd, remembering eyes stamping authenticity upon her words—and long gorilla arms to deal a heavy blow upon man or woman who may threaten her, with a shouted threat of knife-thrust or hatchet stroke if that fails. She was knocked down, bellowing like a buffalo, maltreated—by whom? You wouldn't get it out of her. But she announced to whoever has ears, in this place or the next, that it wouldn't happen another time, —and it hasn't. On a Saturday night shuffling along absorbed, with slow, swinging gait, or staring into odd corners, or settling back on her heels with a belligerent scowl if greeted—ready to talk: "Why how are ya?"—anywhere. "Go ahead, kill me, I ain't afraid of ya."

I remember with thrilling pleasure and deep satisfaction E. K. Means' tale, *Diada Daughter of Discord*, an outstanding story of a wild nigger wench, billeted upon a friend's family by her owner while he went for a short boat trip without her. Read *Diada*—cutting cane stalks, sharpening them with lightning speed and driving them through the attacking hounds.

> "faces like
> old Florentine oak.
>
> Also
>
> the set pieces
> of your faces stir me—
> leading citizens—
> but not
> in the same way."

Nothin' makes much difference—to Otie: Butcher knife, butcher knife, Mr. Gould wants you.

It's a quality, the same as "Sweet everlasting voices be still."

Of the colored men and women whom I have known intimately, the most loquacious is M.—who can't eat eggs because it gives him the hives. Language grows in the original from his laughing lips, "You know that bloom of youth stuff," his shy crooked smile, weary, slow, topping his svelt figure, his straight, slim six feet of willowy grace, drooping from the shoulders, smiling sleepy eyes. "White blood and colored blood don't mix," said he nursing his injury, "Doc, I got a hemorrhage of the FLUTE," he said. "Cocaine for horses, cocaine for mules, IN THE *TRENCHES*!" he yelled as I removed the bandage. "I'm going to feed this to the ducks," he said. The relief is never ending, never failing. It is water from a spring to talk with him—it is a quality. I wish I might write a book of his improvisations in slang. I wish I might write a play in collaboration with him.

His old man is a different sort: I once made several pages of notes upon his conversation—but I lost them; he was an able fisherman along the North Atlantic shore, resistant as an eel. In the hold of the vessel when they were packing porgies, ice and fish filling the hold of the schooner in heavy layers, it was he who could stay down there at work longest—

For sheer sordidness we never touch them, the desperate drunkenness, upon foul stuff, in which they nearly die in a heap of rags under the eaves in the attic of some revolting, disease-ridden female's dump—fly-covered, dazed—

For purity of religious devotion, in the simplicity of their manoeuvres, they exceed our greatest application. Personal cleanliness becomes them with an oriental grace before which our ablutions pale to insignificance.

They wear the BEST fabrics that money can buy, man and woman alike.

It is nothing, nothing.

There was Georgie Anderson whom I remember as some female who walked upon air and light—in her wild girl-hood.

And there was "Dudu," gentle as the dew or rain in April,—but I knew she had a temper for those who offended her—

And there are many others.

Put them on a ship, under any circumstances you may fancy and you have them coming, coming. Why for?

Nothin'—

As old man Hemby said to me at the door: "I'm here. I come after you yesterday but I couldn't find you. Doctor, I'm in a bad fix; I want you to do something for me."

Descent

AT FIFTEEN YEARS of age Samuel Houston, born 1793, Scotch-Irish, ran away from his brothers of whom he was a charge and joined the Cherokee Indians of Western Tennessee. He lived with them until eighteen, then reascended to the settlements for school. . . . The primitive destiny of the land is obscure, but it has been obscured further by a field of unrelated culture stuccoed upon it that has made that destiny more difficult than ever to determine. To this latter nearly all the aesthetic adhesions of the present day occur. Through that stratum of obscurity the acute but frail genius of the place must penetrate. The seed is tough but the chances are entirely against a growth. It is possible for every vestige of virtue from the New World to be lost, like the wood pigeon.

Houston was one of the few men of his time suited mentally, morally, physically for dominant achievement. Governor of Tennessee, 1829, he married Eliza Allen of a prominent family of Sumner County, of that state. After three months she left him. None knows the reason, both remained silent. He wrote, "Eliza stands acquitted by me." The brief duration of the marriage, the violence and permanence of the separation, the prominence of Houston and the lack of all information forthcoming concerning the incident give it an arresting character. Surmise will suit the fancy: he accused her of a romantic attachment; she accused him of worse; or there was, more likely, a disproportion between them; a man of primitive vigors loosed upon her in private, she was overborne by him in some manner, or she refused to be overborne.

He, swept off his feet by the emotional recoil from the misfortune, first pleaded with her father to intercede for him that his wife might return; failing in this, he resigned the governorship of Tennessee, left everything behind him and took the descent once more, to the ground. He rejoined the Cherokees, now removed to Arkansas. The state was in an uproar, people spoke badly of him; there was nothing too bad for them to say. His wife divorced him and remarried. For a while he took to drink. . . . He turned back to the Indians, it is the saving gesture—but a gesture of despair. Poe can be understood only in a knowledge of his deep roots. The quality of the flower will then be seen to be normal, in all its tortured spirituosity and paleness, a desert flower with roots under the sand of his day.

Whitman had to come from under. All have to come from under and through a dead layer.

But his primitive ordeal, created by a peculiar condition of destiny (the implantation of an already partly cultured race on a wild continent) has a plant in its purpose, in its lusts' eye, as gorgeous as Montezuma's gardens of birds, wild beasts and albino natives in wooden cages.

But he who will grow from that basis must sink first.

If he goes to France, it is not to learn a *do re mi fa sol*. He goes to see a strange New World.

If not definitely a culture new in every part, at least a satisfaction. He wants to have the feet of his understanding on the ground, his ground, *the* ground, the only ground that he knows, that which *is* under his feet. I speak of aesthetic satisfaction. This want, in America, can only be filled by knowledge, a poetic knowledge, of that ground. Since this is difficult, due to the hardships which beset the emergence of a poet: A poet is one related to a basis of material, aesthetic, spiritual, hypothetical, abnormal—satisfaction, . . . since this is so, the want goes for the most part unsatisfied in America or is satisfied by a fillgap. The predominant picture of America is a land aesthetically satisfied by temporary fillgaps. But the danger remains: Taste is so debauched in the end that everything of new will be forgotten and—

In spite of size its genius is shy and wild and frail, the loveliest, to be cherished only by the most keen, courageous and sensitive. It may die.

Meanwhile, taste is pandered to somehow. . . . Among the Indians Houston lived, from the time of his separation from his wife, eleven years. He was adopted into the tribe; he, maintaining silence upon the calamity which had overtaken him, preferred to be among those who accepted him for what he was and let no rumor of his past affect them. It was a courtesy he knew how to find as they to proffer. It came from the ground like water. He took an Indian woman for his wife.

The instigation to invasion is apparent: ready profit. The excuse also is apparent: progress. The refusal of these things is like feathered darts on armor. We are tyros in what we are glad to believe are the fundamentals of artistic understanding. We crave filling and eagerly grab for what there is. The next step is, floating upon cash, we wish to be *like* the others. Now come into the Universities, the conformists of all colors from the arch-English to the Italian peasant and his goats.

It is imperative that we *sink*. But from a low position it is impossible to answer those who know all the Latin and some of the Sanskrit names, much French and perhaps one or two other literatures. Their riposte is: Knownothingism. But we cannot climb every tree in that world of birds. But where foreign values are held to be a desideratum, he who is buried and speaks thickly—is lost.

There is nothing for a man but genius or despair. We cannot answer in the smart language, certainly it would be a bastardization of our own talents to waste time to learn the language they use. I would rather sneak off and die like a sick dog then be a well known literary person in America—and no doubt I'll do it in the end. Our betters we may bitterly advise: Know nothing (i.e., the man on the street), make no attempt to know. With a foreign congeries of literary claptrap, come without courtesy to a strange country and make for yourself a smooth track to the pockets of the mob by catering to a "refined" taste and soiling that which you do not know how to estimate. Courtesy would at least bid him be informed or keep still. . . .

Those who come up from under will have a mark on them that invites scorn, like a farmer's filthy clodhoppers. They will be recognized only from *abroad*, being so like the mass out of which they come as to be scorned from anear, etc., etc., etc. . . . After the many years with the Cherokees, having settled down thoroughly, this time, Houston rose again: defeated Santa Ana at San Jacinto and received the soubriquet "Sam Jacinto," Governor of Texas, U. S. Senator during a long term, several times mentioned for the presidency, married again, several children, when in deep thought whittled pine sticks, tigerskin vest, blanket, sombrero, joined Baptist Church, opposed secession of southern states, lived to have Lincoln recognize him by offer of a Major-Generalship, which he refused.

However hopeless it may seem, we have no other choice: we must go back to the beginning; it must all be done over; everything that is must be destroyed.

Edgar Allan Poe

POE was not "a fault of nature," "a find for French eyes," ripe but unaccountable, as through our woollyheadedness we've sought to designate him, but a genius intimately shaped by his locality and time. It is to save our faces that we've given him a crazy reputation, a writer from whose classic accuracies we have not known how else to escape.

The false emphasis was helped by his Parisian vogue and tonal influence on Baudelaire, but the French mind was deeper hit than that. Poe's work strikes by its scrupulous originality, *not* "originality" in the bastard sense, but in its legitimate sense of solidity which goes back to the ground, a conviction that he *can* judge within himself. These things the French were *ready* to perceive and quick to use to their advantage: a new point from which to readjust the trigonometric measurements of literary form.

It is the New World, or to leave that for the better term, it is a *new locality* that is in Poe assertive; it is America, the first great burst through to expression of a re-awakened genius of *place*.

Poe gives the sense for the first time in America, that literature is *serious*, not a matter of courtesy but of truth.

The aspect of his critical statements as a whole, from their hundred American titles to the inmost structure of his sentences, is that of a single gesture, not avoiding the trivial, to sweep all worthless chaff aside. It is a movement, first and last to clear the GROUND.

There is a flavor of provincialism that IS provincialism in the plainness of his reasoning upon elementary grammatical, syntactical and prosodic grounds which awakened

Lowell's derision. But insistence upon primary distinctions, that seems coldly academic, was in this case no more than evidence of a strong impulse to begin at the beginning. Poe was unsophisticated, when contrasted with the puerile sophistications of a Lowell. It is a *beginning* he has in mind, a juvenescent *local* literature. By this he avoids the clownish turn of trying to join, contrary to every reasonable impulsion, a literature (the English) with which he had no actual connection and which might be presumed, long since, to have passed that beginning which to the *new* condition was requisite.

But Mr. Lowell's comment had to be answered:

"Here comes Poe with his Raven, like Barnaby Rudge—
Three fifths of him genius, and two fifths sheer fudge;
Who talks like a book of iambs and pentameters
In a way to make all men of common sense damn meters
Who has written some things far the best of their kind;
But somehow the heart seems squeezed out by the mind."

It brings a technical retort from Poe upon the grounds that, "We may observe here that *profound* ignorance on any particular topic is always sure to manifest itself by some allusion to 'common sense' as an all-sufficient instructor." Then he tears L.'s versification to pieces, adding, "Mr. L. should not have meddled with the anapestic rhythm: it is exceedingly awkward in the hands of one who knows nothing about it and who *will* persist in fancying that he can write it by ear." But, previously, he had nailed the matter in a different vein. Lowell "could not do a better thing than to take the advice of those who mean him well, and leave prose, with satiric verse, to those who are better able to manage them; while he contents himself with that class of poetry for which, and for which alone, he seems to have an especial vocation—the poetry of *sentiment*." But Poe might have added finally, in his own defense, what he says elsewhere, concerning the accusation in L.'s last two lines: "The *highest* order of the imaginative intellect is always preeminently mathematical—" . . .

The whole passage is noteworthy not only for the brilliance of such a statement as that, but also because of its use of the provincial "we" (*Mr. Griswold and the Poets*): "That we are not a poetical people has been asserted so often and so roundly, both at home and abroad that the slander, through mere dint of repetition, has come to be received as truth. Yet nothing can be farther removed from it. The mistake is but a portion, or corollary, of the old dogma, that the calculating faculties are at war with the ideal; while, in fact, it may be demonstrated that the two divisions of mental power are never to be found in perfection apart. The highest order of the imaginative intellect is always preëminently mathematical; and the converse."

"The idiosyncrasy of our political position has stimulated into early action whatever practical talent we possessed. Even in our national infancy we evinced a degree of utilitarian ability which put to shame the mature skill of our forefathers. While yet in leading strings we proved ourselves adepts in all the arts and sciences which promoted the *comfort* of the animal man. But the arena of exertion, and of consequent distinction, into which our first and most obvious wants impelled us, has been regarded as the field of our deliberate choice. Our necessities have been taken for our propensities. Having been forced to make railroads, it has been deemed impossible that we should make verse. Because it suited us to construct an engine in the first instance, it has been denied that we could compose an epic in the second. Because we are not all Homers in the beginning, it has been somewhat rashly taken for granted that we shall be all Jeremy Benthams to the end."

"But this is purest insanity . . ."

In the critical note upon *Francis Marryat*, the distinction between "nationality in letters," which Poe carefully slights, and the preëminent importance, in letters as in all other branches of imaginative creation, of the *local*, which is his constant focus of attention, is to be noted.

Poe was NOT, it must be repeated, a Macabre genius, *essentially* lost upon the grotesque and the arabesque. If we have appraised him a morass of "lolling lilies," *that* is surface only.

The local causes shaping Poe's genius were two in character: the necessity for a fresh beginning, backed by a native vigor of extraordinary proportions,—with the corollary, that all "colonial imitation" must be swept aside. This was the conscious force which rose in Poe as innumerable timeless insights resulting, by his genius, in firm statements on the character of form, profusely illustrated by his practices; and, *second* the immediate effect of the locality upon the first, upon his nascent impulses, upon his original thrusts; tormenting the depths into a surface of bizarre designs by which he's known and which are *not at all* the major point in question.

Yet BOTH influences were determined by the locality, which, in the usual fashion, finds its mind swayed by the results of its stupidity rather than by a self-interest bred of greater wisdom. As with all else in America, the value of Poe's genius TO OURSELVES must be *uncovered* from our droppings, or at least uncovered from the "protection" which it must have raised about itself to have survived in any form among us—where everything is quickly trampled.

Poe "saw the end"; unhappily he saw his own despair at the same time, yet he continued to attack, with amazing genius seeking to discover, and discovering, points of firmness by which to STAND and grasp, against the slipping way they had of holding on in his locality. Either the New World must be mine as I will have it, or it is a worthless bog. There can be no concession. His attack was *from the center out.* Either I exist or I do not exist and no amount of pap which I happen to be lapping can dull me to the loss. It was a doctrine, anti-American. Here everything was makeshift, everything was colossal, in profusion. The frightened hogs or scared birds feeding on the corn— It left, in 1840, the same mood as ever dominant among us. Take what you can get. What you lack, copy. It was a population puffed with braggadocio, whom Poe so beautifully summarizes in many of his prose tales. To such men, all of them, the most terrible experience in the world is to be shown up. This Poe did, in his criticisms, with venomous accuracy. It was a gesture to BE CLEAN. It was a wish to HAVE the world or leave it. It was the truest instinct in America demanding to be satisfied, and an end to makeshifts, self-deceptions and grotesque excuses. And yet the grotesque inappropriateness of the life about him forced itself in among his words.

One is forced on the conception of the New World as a woman. Poe was a new De Soto. The rest might be content with little things, not he.

"Rather the ice than their way."

His attack upon the difficulty which faced him was brilliantly conceived, faultlessly maintained and successful. The best term is perhaps: immaculate.

What he wanted was connected with no particular place; therefore it *must* be where he *was*.

"We have at length arrived at that epoch when our literature may and must stand on its own merits, or fall through its own defects. We have snapped asunder the leading-strings of our British Grandmama, and, better still, we have survived the first hours of our novel freedom,—the first licentious hours of hobbledehoy braggadocio and swagger. *At last,* then, we are in a condition to be criticized—even more, to be neglected;..."

What Poe says gains power by his not diminishing his force for the slightness of the object; it is a sense of an inevitable, impartial tide. "We have *no* design to be bitter. We notice this book at all, only because it is an unusually large one of its kind, because it is lying here upon our table, and because, whether justly or unjustly, whether for good reason or for none, it has attracted some portion of the attention of the public." There is no softening for the department of names, old or new, but a sense of the evidence examined, as it lies on the page, by a faultless mechanism which he brings from the rear of his head for the trial.

Lowell, Bryant, etc., concerned poetry with literature, Poe concerned it with the soul; hence their differing conceptions of the use of language. With Poe, words were not hung by usage with associations, the pleasing wraiths of former masteries, this is the sentimental trap-door to beginnings. With Poe words were figures; an old language truly, but one from which he carried over only the most elemental qualities to his new purpose; which was, to find a way to tell his soul. Sometimes he used words so playfully his sentences seem to fly away from sense, the destructive! with the conserving abandon, foreshadowed, of a Gertrude Stein. The particles of language must be clear as sand. (See *Diddling.*)

This was an impossible conception for the gluey imagination of his day. Constantly he labored to detach SOMETHING from the inchoate mass—That's it:

His concern, the apex of his immaculate attack, was to detach a "method" from the smear of common usage—it is the work of nine tenths of his criticism. He struck to lay low the "*niaiseries*" of form and content with which his world abounded. It was a machine-gun fire; even in the slaughter of banality he rises to a merciless distinction. (See *Rufus Dawes.*) He sought by stress upon construction to hold the loose-strung mass off even at the cost of an icy coldness of appearance; it was the first need of his time, an escape from the formless mass he hated. It is the very sense of a beginning, as *it is the impulse which drove him to the character of all his tales;* to get from sentiment to form, a backstroke from the swarming "population."

He has a habit, borrowed perhaps from algebra, of balancing his sentences in the middle, or of reversing them in the later clauses, a sense of play, as with objects, or numerals which he *has* in the original, disassociated, that is, from other literary habit; separate words which he feels and turns about as if he fitted them to his design with *some* sense of their individual quality: "those who belong properly to books, and to whom books, perhaps, do not quite so properly belong."

The strong sense of a beginning in Poe is in *no one* else before him. What he says, being thoroughly local in origin, has some chance of being universal in application, a thing they never dared conceive. Made to fit a *place* it will have that actual quality of *things* anti-metaphysical——

About Poe there is—

No supernatural mystery—

No extraordinary eccentricity of fate——

He is American, understandable by a simple exercise of reason; a light in the morass—which *must* appear eerie, even to himself, by force of terrific contrast, an isolation that would naturally lead to drunkenness and death, logically and simply—by despair, as the very final evidence of a too fine seriousness and devotion.

It is natural that the French (foreigners, unacquainted with American conditions) should be attracted by the SURFACE of his genius and copy the wrong thing, (but the expressive thing), the strange, the bizarre (the recoil) without sensing the actuality, of which that is the complement—and we get for Poe a REPUTATION for eccentric genius maimed, the curious, the sick—at least the unexplainable crop-up, unrelated to his ground—which has become his inheritance.

* * *

"The fiery serpent that bit the children of Israel when they wandered through the wilderness was possibly the guinea worm, which enters the body as a water flea, develops, and ultimately, lies coiled under the skin, from one to six feet in length. It formerly was coaxed out by winding it on a stick little by little each day. Then the zoologist found that it seeks water in which to lay its eggs, and will naively crawl out if the affected leg or arm is simply submerged in water for a few hours.

"The mysterious is so simple when revealed by science!"

*   *   *

On him is FOUNDED A LITERATURE—typical; an anger to sweep out the unoriginal, that became ill-tempered, a mono-maniacal driving to destroy, to annihilate the copied, the slavish, the FALSE literature about him: this is the major impulse in his notes—darkening as he goes, losing the battle, as he feels himself going under—he emerges as the ghoulish, the driven back. It is the crudeness with which he was attacked in his own person, scoffed at—

He declares, maintains himself, presupposes himself and IS first rate. FIRST!—madly, valiantly battling for the right to BE first—to hold up his ORIGINALITY—

"If a man—if an Orphicist—or SEER—or whatever else he may choose to call himself, while the rest of the world calls him an ass—if this gentleman have an idea which he does not understand himself, the best thing he can do is to say nothing about it; . . . but if he have any idea which is actu-ally intelligible to himself, and if he sincerely wishes to render it intelligible to others, we then hold it as indis-putable that he should employ those forms of speech which are the best adapted to further his object. He should speak to the people in that people's ordinary tongue. He should arrange words such as are habitually employed for the preliminary and introductory ideas to be conveyed—he should arrange them in collocations such as those in which we are accustomed to see those words arranged." "Mean-time we earnestly ask if *bread-and-butter* be the vast IDEA in question—if *bread-and-butter* be any portion of this vast IDEA? for we have often observed that when a SEER has to speak of even so usual a thing as bread-and-butter, he can never be induced to mention it outright..."

The language of his essays is a remarkable HISTORY of the locality he springs from. There is no aroma to his words, rather a luminosity, that comes of a disassociation from anything else than thought and ideals; a coldly nebulous, side to side juxtaposition of the words as the ideas—It seems to fall back continuously to a bare surface exhausted by having reached no perch in tradition. Seldom a long or sensuous sentence, but with frequent reduplication upon itself as if holding itself up by itself.

Thought, thought, mass—and the sense of SOMETHING over the heads of the composite particles of the logic, the insignificance of the details, WHICH HE DID ACTUALLY achieve. A "childlike," simple, deductive reasoning IS his criticism—a sense of BEGINNING—of originality that presupposes an intrinsic WORTH in the reasoner—a sense of *stripped*, being clothed, nevertheless.

Unwilling to concede the necessity for any prop to his logical constructions, save the locality upon which originality is rested, he is the diametric opposite of Longfellow—to say the least. But Longfellow was the apotheosis of all that had preceded him in America, to this extent, that he brought over the *most* from "the other side." In "*Longfellow and Other Plagiarists*," Poe looses himself to the full upon them. But what had they done? No more surely than five hundred architects are constantly practicing. Longfellow did it without genius, perhaps, but he did no more and no less than to bring the tower of the Seville Cathedral to Madison Square.

This is the expression of a "good" spirit. It is the desire to have "culture" for America by "finding" it, full blown—somewhere. But we had wandered too far, suffered too many losses for that. Such a conception could be no more than a pathetic reminiscence. It had NOTHING of the New World in it. Yet, it was bred of the wish to bring to the locality what it lacked.

What it lacked, really, was to be cultivated. So they build an unrelated copy upon it; this, as a sign of intelligence, vigor. That is, to bring out its qualities, they cover them. Culture is still the effect of cultivation, to work with thing until it be rare; as a golden dome among the mustard fields. It implies a solidity capable of cultivation. Its effects are marble blocks that lie perfectly fitted and aligned to express by isolate distinction the rising lusts which threw them off, regulated, in moving through the mass of impedimenta which is the world.

This is culture; in mastering them, to burst through the peculiarities of an environment. It is NOT culture to *oppress* a novel environment with the stale, if symmetrical, castoffs of another battle. They are nearly right when they say: Destroy the museums! But that is only the reflection, after all, of minds that fear to be slavish. Poe could look at France, Spain, Greece, and NOT be impelled to copy. He could do this BECAUSE he had the sense within him of a locality of his own, capable of cultivation.

Poe's use of the tags of other cultures than his own manages to be novel, interesting, useful, *unaffected*, since it succeeds in giving the impression of being not in the least dragged in by rule or pretence but of a fresh purpose such as I have indicated. There is nothing offensively "learned" there, nothing contemptuous, even in the witty tricks with bogus Latin which he plays on his illiterate public, which by *its* power, in turn, *permits* him an originality, *allows him*, even when he is satiric, an authenticity—since he is not seeking to destroy but to assert, candidly, and to defend *his own*.

He was the first to realize that the hard, sardonic, truculent mass of the New World, hot, angry—was, in fact, not a thing to paint over, to smear, to destroy—for it WOULD not be destroyed, it was too powerful,—it smiled! That it is NOT a thing to be slighted by men. Difficult, its very difficulty was their strength. It was in the generous bulk of its animal crudity that their every fineness would be found safely imbedded.

Poe conceived the possibility, the sullen, volcanic inevitability of the *place*. He was willing to go down and wrestle with its conditions, using every tool France, England,

Greece could give him,—but to use them to original purpose.

This is his anger against Longfellow.

The difficulty is in holding the mind down to the point of seeing the *beginning* difference between Poe and the rest. One cannot expect to see as wide a gap between him and the others as exists between the Greek and the Chinese. It is only in the conception of a *possibility* that he is most distinguished. His greatness is in that he turned his back and faced inland, to originality, with the identical gesture of a Boone.

And for *that* reason he is unrecognized. Americans have never recognized themselves. How can they? It is impossible until someone invent the ORIGINAL terms. As long as we are content to be called by somebody's else terms, we are incapable of being anything but our own dupes.

Thus Poe must suffer by his originality. Invent that which is new, even if it be made of pine from your own yard, and there's none to know what you have done. It is because there's no *name*. This is the cause of Poe's lack of recognition. He was American. He was the astounding, inconceivable growth of his locality. Gape at him they did, and he at them in amazement. Afterward with mutual hatred; he in disgust, they in mistrust. It is only that which is under your nose which seems inexplicable.

Here Poe emerges—in no sense the bizarre, isolate writer, the curious literary figure. On the contrary, in him American literature is anchored, in him alone, on solid ground.

In all he says there is a sense of him *surrounded* by his time, tearing at it, ever with more rancor, but always at battle, taking hold.

But Poe—differing from pioneers in other literatures, the great beginners—due to the nature of the people, *had first to lift his head through* a successful banality. This was a double impost. But he did it, NOT by despising, ignoring, slighting the work that preceded him but in attacking it.

"Among all the pioneers of American literature, whether prose or poetical, there is *not one* (Note: In his own estimate even, he begins.) whose productions have not been much overrated by his countrymen."

"But originality, as it is one of the highest, is also one of the rarest of merits. In America it is especially, and very remarkably, rare—this through causes sufficiently well understood."

He abhorred the "excessively opportune."—Of course, he says, to write of the Indians, the forests, the great natural beauty of the New World will be attractive and make a hit —so he counsels writers to AVOID it, for reasons crystal clear and well chosen. (See *Fenimore Cooper*.) His whole insistence has been upon method, in opposition to a nameless rapture over nature. He admired Claude Lorraine. Instead of to hog-fill the copied style with a gross rural sap, he wanted a lean style, rapid as a hunter and with an aim as sure. One way, in the New World, men must go. Bust gut or acute wit. Find the ground, on your feet or on your belly. It is a fight. He counsels writers to *borrow nothing* from the scene, but to put all the weight of effort into the WRITING. Put aside the GRAND scene and get to work to express yourself. Method, punctuation, grammar—

The local condition of literature FORCED Poe's hand. It is necessary to understand this if his names are to be grasped. By avoiding, of necessity, the fat country itself for its expression; to originate a style that does spring from the local conditions, not of trees and mountains, but of the "soul"—here starved, stricken by loss of liberty, ready to die—he is *forced in certain directions for his subjects.*

But this left him in difficulties. When he had narrowed himself down to a choice of method and subject, when all the meaningless lump of the lush landscape and all that that implies had been swept away, THEN, and only then will he begin to search for a subject. A voluntary lopping off of a NATURAL landscape, forced him into a field which he must have *searched* for, a field of cold logic, of invention, to which his work must still present a natural *appearance:* into his imaginative prose.

His criticism paves the way for what *must* be his prose— illustrating his favorite theory that the theory *includes the practice.*

No better means of transit from the criticism to the tales could be imagined than his discussion of the merits and demerits of Hawthorne as a proseist. He expresses his delight and surprise at finding Hawthorne's work of such excellence, but then he finds a fault:

"He has the purest style, the finest taste, the most available scholarship, the most delicate humor, the most touching pathos, the most radiant imagination, the most consummate ingenuity, and with these varied good qualities he has done well as a mystic. But is there any one of those qualities which would prevent his doing doubly as well in a career of honest, upright, sensible, prehensible, and comprehensible things? Let him mend his pen, get a bottle of visible ink, come out from the Old Manse, cut Mr. Alcott, hang (if possible) the Editor of *The Dial,* and throw out of the window to the pigs all his odd numbers of *The North American Review.*"

Hawthorne has no repugnance for handling what Poe purposely avoids, the contamination of the UNFORMED LUMP, the "*monstrum, horrendum, informe, ingens, cui lumen ademptum.*" And it is precisely here that lies Hawthorne's lack of importance to our literature when he is compared with Poe; what Hawthorne *loses* by his willing closeness to the life of his locality in its vague humors; his lifelike copying of the New England melancholy; his reposeful closeness to the town pump—Poe *gains* by abhorring; flying to the ends of the earth for "original" material—

By such a simple, logical twist does Poe succeed in being the more American, heeding more the local necessities, the harder structural imperatives—by standing off to SEE instead of forcing himself too close. Whereas Hawthorne, in his tales, by doing what everyone else in France, England, Germany was doing *for his own milieu*, is no more than copying their *method* with another setting; does not ORIGINATE; has not a *beginning* literature at heart that must establish its own rules, own framework,—Poe has realized by adopting a more elevated mien.

This feeling in Poe's tales, that is, the hidden, under, unapparent part, gives him the firmness of INSIGHT into the conditions upon which our literature must rest, always the same, a local one, surely, but not of sentiment or mood, as not of trees and Indians, but of original fibre, the normal toughness which fragility of mood presupposes, if it will be expressive of anything— It is the expression of Poe's clearness of insight into the true difficulty, and his soundness of judgment.

* * *

To understand what Poe is driving at in his tales, one should read first NOT the popular, perfect—*Gold Bug, Murders in the Rue Morgue*, etc., which by their brilliancy detract from the observation of his deeper intent, but the less striking tales—in fact all, but especially those where his humor is less certain, his mood lighter, less tightly bound by the incident, where numerous illuminating faults are allowed to become expressive, *The Business Man, The Man That Was Used Up, Loss of Breath, BonBon, Diddling, The Angel of the Odd*—and others of his lesser Tales.

It should be noted how often certain things take place—how often there is death but not that only; it is the body broken apart, dismembered, as in *Loss of Breath*—

Then, as in *Hop Frog, The System of Dr. Tarr and Professor Fether* and the *Murders in the Rue Morgue*—the recurrent image of the ape. Is it his disgust with his immediate associates and his own fears, which cause this frequent use of the figure to create the emotion of extreme terror?—

"Your majesty cannot conceive of the *effect* produced, at a masquerade, by eight chained orang-outangs, imagined to be real ones by the most of the company; the rushing in with savage cries, among the crowd of delicately and gorgeously habited men and women. The contrast is inimitable."

Note, in *Silence—a Fable:* "sorrow and weariness and disgust with mankind and a longing for solitude."

Many colloquial words could be detached from Poe's usage if it were worth while, to show how the language he practices varies from English, but such an exercise would be of little value—*hipped, crack,* etc.—it does not touch bottom.

The Tales continue the theories of the criticism, carrying out what they propose:

1. In choice of material, abstract. 2. In method, a logical construction that clips away, in great part, the "scenery" near at hand in order to let the real business of composition *show.* 3. A primitive awkwardness of diction, lack of polish, colloquialism that is, unexpectedly, especially in the dialogues, much in the vein of Mark Twain.

One feels that in the actual composition of his tales there must have been for him, as they embody it in fact, a fascination other than the topical one. The impulse that made him write them, that made him enjoy writing them—cannot have been the puerile one of amazement, but a deeper, logical enjoyment, in keeping with his own seriousness: it is that of PROVING even the most preposterous of his inventions plausible—that BY HIS METHOD he makes them WORK. They go: they *prove* him potent, they confirm his thought. And by the very extreme of their play, by so much the more do they hold up the actuality of that which he conceives.

If there ever had been another American to use his Greek, Sanscrit, Hebrew, Latin, French, German, Italian and Spanish—in the text—with anything like the unspoiled mastery of Poe, we should have known, long since, what it meant to have a literature of our own.

It is to have a *basis*, a local stanchion, by which to *bridge over* the gap between present learning and the classical; that asserts the continuity of the common virtues of style; that asserts their aristocratic origin, or their democratic origin, the same, as it has been pointed out recently, since an aristocracy is the flower of a locality and so the *full* expression of a democracy.

Of this method in the Tales, the significance and the secret is: authentic particles, a thousand of which spring to the mind for quotation, taken apart and reknit with a view to emphasize, enforce and make evident, the *method*. Their quality of skill in observation, their heat, local verity, being *overshadowed* only by the detached, the abstract, the cold philosophy of their joining together; a method springing so freshly from the local conditions which determine it, by their emphasis of firm crudity and lack of coordinated structure, as to be worthy of most painstaking study— The whole period, America 1840, could be rebuilt, psychologically (phrenologically) from Poe's "method."

* * *

It is especially in the poetry where "death looked gigantically down" that the horror of the formless resistance which opposed, maddened, destroyed him has forced its character into the air, the wind, the blessed galleries of paradise, above a morose, dead world, peopled by shadows and silence, and despair— it is the compelling force of his isolation.

The one earthly island he found where he might live in something akin to the state he imagined, the love of his wife, had to be single and inviolate. Failing of a more comprehensive passion, which might have possessed him had the place been of favorable omen, only in this narrow cell could he exist at all. Of this the poems are the full effect. He is known as a poet, yet there are but five poems, possibly three.

When she died, there was nothing left. In his despair he had nowhere to turn. It is the very apotheosis of the place and the time.

He died imploring from those about him a love he could not possess, since his own love, as his poems, had been so mingled in character with the iron revenge which completely surrounded him that it could not be repeated once its single object had been lost.

But here, in his poetry least of all, is there a mystery. It is but the accumulation of all that he has expressed, in the criticism, in the prose tales, but made as if so shaken with desire, that it has come off as a flame, destroying the very vial that contained it—and become, against his will almost it would seem,—himself.

It is not by a change in character but by its quickened motion that it has turned from mere heat into light—by its power of penetration that it has been brought to dwell upon love. By its acid power to break down truth that it has been *forced* upon love—

I meant that though in this his "method" has escaped him, yet his poems remain of the single stuff of his great "theory": to grasp the meaning, to understand, to reduce all things to method, to control, lifting himself to power—

And failing, truth turning to love, as if metamorphosed in his hands as he was about to grasp it—now the full horror of his isolation comes down—

In his prose he could still keep a firm hold, he still held the "arrangement" fast and stood above it, but in the poetry he was at the edge—there was nothing—

Here in poetry, where it is said "we approach the gods," Poe was caught, instead, in his time.

Now, defenseless, the place itself attacked him. Now the thinness of his coat, the terror of his isolation took hold.

Had he lived in a world where love throve, his poems might have grown differently. But living where he did, surrounded as he was by that world of unreality, a formless "population"—drifting and feeding—a huge terror possessed him.

His passion for the refrain is like an echo from a hollow. It is his own voice returning—

His imagery is of the desperate situation of his mind, thin as a flame to mount unsupported, successful for a moment in the love of—not so much his wife—but in the escape she filled for him with her frail person, herself afflicted as by "ghouls."

Disarmed, in his poetry the place itself comes through. This is the New World. It is this that it does, as if——

It is in this wraithlike quality of his poems, of his five poems, that Poe is most of the very ground, hard to find, as if we walked upon a cushion of light pressed thin beneath our feet, that insulates, satirises—while we lash ourselves up and down in a fury of impotence.

Poe stayed against the thin edge, driven to be heard by the battering racket about him to a distant screaming—the pure essence of his locality.

The best poem is *To One in Paradise*.

Abraham Lincoln

THE GREAT Railsplitter's, "All I am or ever hope to be I owe to my angel mother"; the walking up and down in Springfield on the narrow walk between the two houses, day after day, with a neighbor's baby, borrowed for the occasion, sleeping inside his cape upon his shoulder to give him stability while thinking and composing his coming speeches; and apart from its cowardice, the blinding stupidity of his murderer's *sic semper tyrannis*, after he had shot him in the back—in his trinity is reflected the brutalizing desolation of life in America up to that time; yet perversely flowering.

Mengelberg, a great broad hipped one, conducts an orchestra in the same vein. It is a woman. He babies them. He leans over and floods them with his insistences. It is a woman drawing to herself with insatiable passion the myriad points of sound, conferring upon each the dignity of a successful approach, relieving each of his swelling burden (but particularly, by himself), in the overtowering symphony—It is the balm of command. The violins, surrounded, yet feel that they have come alone, in silence and in secret, singly to be heard.

It is Lincoln pardoning the fellow who slept on sentry duty. It is the grace of the Bixby letter. The least private would find a woman to caress him, a woman in an old shawl—with a great bearded face and a towering black hat above it, to give unearthly reality.

Brancusi should make his statue—of wood—after the manner of his Socrates, with the big hole in the enormous mass of the head, save that this would be a woman—

The age-old torture reached a disastrous climax in Lincoln. Failing of relief or expression, the place tormented itself into a convulsion of bewilderment and pain—with a woman, born somehow, aching over it, holding all fearfully together. It was the end of THAT period.

Some New Directions Paperbooks

Complete descriptive catalog available free on request from
New Directions, 80 Eighth Avenue, New York 10011   † Bilingual